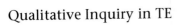

Qualitative Inquiry in TE

Qualitative Inquiry in TESOL

Keith Richards

Director, Language Studies Unit
Aston University, Birmingham

First published 2003 by
PALGRAVE MACMILLAN
Houndmills, Basingstoke, Hampshire RG21 6XS and
175 Fifth Avenue, New York, N.Y. 10010
Companies and representatives throughout the world

PALGRAVE MACMILLAN is the global academic imprint of the Palgrave Macmillan division of St. Martin's Press, LLC and of Palgrave Macmillan Ltd. Macmillan® is a registered trademark in the United States, United Kingdom and other countries. Palgrave is a registered trademark in the European Union and other countries.

ISBN 1–4039–0134–1 hardback
ISBN 1–4039–0135–X paperback

This book is printed on paper suitable for recycling and made from fully managed and sustained forest sources.

A catalogue record for this book is available from the British Library.

Library of Congress Cataloging in Publication Data
Richards, Keith, 1952–
    Qualitative inquiry in TESOL/Keith Richards.
        p.   cm.
    Includes bibliographical references (p.) and index.
    ISBN 1–4039–0134–1 — ISBN 1–4039–0135–X (pbk.)
    1. English language—Study and teaching—Foreign speakers.   I. Title.
PE1128.A2R487 2003
428′.0071—dc21

                                              2003040548

Printed and bound in Great Britain by
Antony Rowe Ltd, Chippenham and Eastbourne

For Marie
with love

Contents

List of Boxes, Extracts, Figures and Tables

Boxes

Extracts

Figures

Tables

List of Tasks and Study Strategies

Tasks

Study strategies

Acknowledgements

This book arose from my work with postgraduate students on Aston University's MSc in TESOL/TESP and PhD programmes and I should like to extend my thanks to them for all their enthusiasm, encouragement and insights. Over the years I have enjoyed rediscovering through their work the wonders that qualitative inquiry can reveal. I should also like to express a particular thank you to the British Council team in Mexico and to teachers and teacher trainers in universities there. Their enthusiasm for research and their positive response to my talks and workshops over the years contributed significantly to my decision to write this book. My particular gratitude extends to those novice researchers in all of the above groups who have kindly allowed me to include examples from their work in the text, where they are acknowledged by name.

It would be impossible to summarise here the many ways in which my colleagues in the Language Studies Unit have helped me over the years, but I would like to thank them here for all their help, support and encouragement. They are a wonderful team. Particular thanks must go to Heather Phillips for bailing me out on numerous occasions and to Sue Garton for her helpful comments on Chapter 2. Outside the Unit, I'd like to thank my boss, Anne Stevens, for her unstinting support and Lourdes Ortega for valuable comments on my original ideas for the book.

More than anything else, though, I am grateful to my friends and colleagues Julian Edge and Steve Mann, who read the manuscript and made detailed and illuminating comments on every section. After a hard spell of writing, it was hugely refreshing to take advantage of their generosity in order to share time with them and see my work in new ways. Any remaining errors are, of course, my own, but the book has benefited immensely from their wisdom and insight – as have I, in so many ways.

Finally, my thanks and love to Francesca and Louisa for reminding me every single day why it is worth trying to understand.

KEITH RICHARDS
Stratford upon Avon

Introduction

Research and Teachers of English to Speakers of Other Languages (TESOL)

I have been accused – unfairly I think – of being a researcher. It was a Saturday afternoon at the end of the second conference in the Teachers Develop Teachers Research series and participants had gathered to reflect on the events of the previous couple of days in the context of the relationship between teaching, research and professional development. I forget what I said now, or even if I was the person who sparked the response, but one of the participants laid down a very blunt challenge to the legitimacy of any claims made by those of us who worked in universities. 'You', she said, 'are not teachers, you're researchers'. At the time I think I embarked – in fact, all the 'researchers' embarked – on a huge salvage operation based on administering massive and repeated doses of Understanding. But since then I've had time to think.

My instinctive response was that the accusation was unfair, partly because I thought of myself as primarily a teacher, albeit no longer of ESOL, and partly because I could think of plenty of people who were much more deserving of the charge, people who had spent the best part of their days researching and writing. At a deeper level, though, it seemed to me that the accusation arose from an assumption that teaching and research are mutually exclusive, when for me they seem naturally to go together. That's what I tried to articulate at the time. From where I stand now, though, the relationship seems more complicated.

The complications have arisen from a tension that seems to have developed between the perceived value of research in TESOL and the ways in which this is used. The integration of research into teacher education programmes at all levels is an encouraging endorsement of the extent to which teaching is an exploratory activity, drawing strength from an understanding of the educational and social world it inhabits. The growing recognition that qualitative inquiry (QI) has an important part to play in deepening that understanding as part of a broader research agenda is also very encouraging. However, the ways in which QI has been embraced give cause for concern in at least two respects.

The first of these, and the one addressed directly by this book, is the quality of the research that is produced. There is a common misconception that QI is soft, that it can make do with a few interviews and perhaps a dash of transcribed talk, which can then be worked up into an attractively speculative piece nodding vaguely in the direction of 'ethnography'. I exaggerate – but only slightly. It would be easy enough to trace the sources of this misconception in TESOL, but it's much more important to respond to it. This book, which represents my contribution to that response, is based on the belief that QI is essentially a craft and that fundamental to it is the development of appropriate skills, something that appears to have been badly, though not universally, neglected in TESOL to date. The next section describes how the structure of the book is designed to develop these important skills at all levels.

The second problem is not one that this book can address directly, though it might have a small contribution to make. There seems to be a growing feeling among some teachers that they're expected to be researchers *as well as* teachers – as if TESOL wasn't demanding enough. Comfortable assumptions about the value of teacher research and reflective practice translate for them into unreasonable demands on their already pressurised time. To respond by pointing out that research is rarely obligatory is to miss the point: explicit coercion may be rare, but the luxury of refusal is expensive if career development depends on evidence of research activity.

The only evidence we have of where such demands might lead in terms of career satisfaction are disturbing:

> Teachers who steered clear of reforms or other multiple-classroom innovations, but who invested consistently in classroom-level experiments – what they called 'tinkering' with new materials, different pupil grouping, small changes in grading systems – were more likely to be satisfied later on in their career than most others, and far more likely to be satisfied than their peers who had been heavily involved in school-wide or district-wide projects. (Huberman 1992:131)

This suggests that as a profession we need to work towards a proper sense of perspective, something that lies beyond the scope of this book. But it also indicates that small-scale research can be career-enhancing, which is where the book can help because it is founded on the assumption that, provided it is done well, small-scale individual research is every bit as respectable as large funded projects and that therefore all levels of research must be treated equally seriously. If you are a novice researcher and decide to limit yourself to the Level 1 elements in this book, you will develop skills that will enable you to better understand your professional world and to 'tinker' more effectively in your classrooms. You will also come to see how this can be naturally integrated into your development as a teacher. TESOL attracts all sorts of people for all sorts of reasons, but as initial motivations fall away the sustaining force for most who remain is the desire to make a difference. This is where QI finds itself able to make its most natural and important contribution.

Structure

What is unusual about this book is its focus on the development of research skills at three different levels. These correspond roughly to novice, intermediate and advanced levels and might be *very roughly* mapped onto a typical suite of teacher education and research programmes as follows:

- Level 1: Introductory to Intermediate: Certificate and Diploma;
- Level 2: Intermediate to Advanced: Masters and Doctoral;
- Level 3: Advanced: Doctoral and Post-Doctoral.

However, because the subject of the book is research skills, such mapping is fairly arbitrary; for example, someone beginning an introductory teacher preparation programme may already have research experience gained from their undergraduate or postgraduate studies, but it may be that this experience relates to only one method of data collection. The book is therefore designed so that each element at each level will stand alone while also linking naturally to each other level. This means, for example, that one reader might decide to work through the book at the introductory level, returning to it later to tackle more advanced levels; another might decide to concentrate on one method at a time, working through the levels; while a third might design an individual route through the book based on personal needs.

However, these decisions are best made after reading through the book as a whole because what counts as difficult will be determined by our natural strengths and weaknesses as much as by our experience and familiarity. In addition, some research techniques are much more demanding than their simple description might suggest, while others call for rather detailed elaboration but are straightforward once mastered. My decisions as a writer, therefore, have not always been straightforward. For example, I originally placed structured observation at Level 2 but decided to move it to the highest level because of the technical nature of its content, though some researchers might argue that this mistakenly gives the impression that it is more demanding than other forms of observation.

To facilitate ease of access, the book is structured on the basis of three parts:

- Part I: orients the reader to the subject of the book;
- Part II: focuses on data collection;
- Part III: deals with the practicalities of the research project.

In addition, each chapter begins with a preview and ends with a reading guide to facilitate further study and development. In Part II, all levels include a case study and each chapter also has a skills development section. An outline of parts, chapters and levels can be found at the end of this introduction.

To my knowledge, all introductions to qualitative research address issues of design at an early stage and certainly before they deal with the practicalities of data collection. This is understandable and perfectly defensible in terms of the chronology of a research project, but in pedagogic terms I think it gets things the wrong way round. If you start by planning a project before you've developed appropriate data collection skills, it's hard to get a proper perspective on just what's involved, and the drive to complete the project encourages a utilitarian standpoint that can all too easily lead to an unbalanced and insufficiently rigorous approach to skills development. Working on skills does not preclude an element of project planning, but settling down to serious planning needs to be informed by experience. For this reason, having shown what research involves in Part I, the book then moves on to data collection skills, returning to project planning and execution only at the end.

Approach

The approach in this book arises from my own experience of doing and teaching QI, and my belief that QI is a craft that has to be learned through guided practice and exposure to good models. This position can be represented in three core statements: skills matter, understanding research takes time, and exposure to research is essential.

Skills matter

Craft skills can be developed only through practice and the book is designed with this in mind. However, such skills are not reducible to a collection of recipes or developed through the completion of tasks without a necessary understanding of what lies behind them, so the approach needs to reflect this. My aim has therefore been to rely on explanation supported by integrated tasks where necessary. It is perfectly possible to read the text without responding to the (relatively few) invitations embedded within it, but this would assume understanding without testing it.

The heart of the book, where these tasks are particularly important, is to be found in the three central chapters which cover the core data collection methods: observation, interviews, and the analysis of spoken interaction. The 'application' chapters in Part III are approached slightly differently, being advisory in nature and based around a collection of key resources that can be drawn on for the purposes of planning and exploitation.

Understanding takes time

In my experience, the most dangerous trap lying in wait for novice researchers is baited with categories. The temptation to assign categories and count them seems to be almost irresistible to some, but superficial description is no substitute for hard-won understanding. I have therefore held categorisation back until the benefits of immersion in the data and attention to detail have been demonstrated. This means that all work at Level 1 in Part II is based on learning to look hard and look deep, so that when categories are introduced the value of these in the broader context of QI will be appreciated and they will be used properly and appropriately. And because the most demanding aspect of QI is learning to live with the richness of its possibilities, higher levels aim to develop greater sensitivity to the options available.

Exposure to research is essential

As someone who is trying to pass on skills they have learnt, I feel that it is essential to use my own work for the purposes of illustration. I have therefore deliberately included, with very few exceptions, original and previously unpublished data in order to expose more clearly the process of analysis, so that the reader can orient to me as a fellow researcher and compare my efforts with their own (all extracts are from my own data unless otherwise specified). In keeping with the pedagogic orientation appropriate to the passing on of craft skills, the book is therefore a (research) product in creation. This is certainly not to say that the small extracts here should stand as models: for these the reader must follow my directions to research and researchers whose outstanding contribution to the field repays close study.

Three points of orientation

Rather than attempt to articulate a personal philosophy of qualitative inquiry, I offer three quotations that triangulate my standpoint in the field of QI:

> There is no part of the social world that will remain boring after the application of a little curiosity. (Rock 2001:32)

> Research is in large part a craft skill, learned through personal experience of doing research and from an appreciation of what is good in other people's research studies. (Seale 1999:31)

> Serious reflection on the nature and purpose of interpretive inquiry raises questions of our being; it requires each of us to come to terms with a union of moral and cognitive concerns in our own and others' lived experience. (Schwandt 1996:84)

What follows should enable you to assess this stance from a position of your own choosing.

A note on personal pronouns and terminology used

Qualitative inquirers must learn to live with the unresolved, so although I have strong feelings on the need to avoid gendered pronouns, I find the continuing debate on alternative forms fascinating rather than irritating. I've opted here to use 'they', 'their' and 'themself' in preference to 'he or she', 'his or her' and 'himself or herself' and hope that not too many readers will choke over their cornflakes or add exclamation marks in the margin. I've also decided to restrict the use of *sic* to cases where it is necessary to confirm accuracy in quotation, which means that where gendered pronouns appear in quotations they remain unmarked.

In line with the book's title, I use (T)ESOL throughout but take this to embrace a whole range of alternative acronyms (for example, TEFL, ESL, ELT, ESP), not all of them coterminous. In research terms, I see no problem with this, or with extending what I have to say here to the field of education generally. Much of what I have to say applies to this wider field and often to QI in general, but TESOL has been my guiding reference throughout.

An outline of topics, chapters and levels

Parts	Chapters	Level 1	Level 2	Level 3
I Orientation	1 The nature of qualitative inquiry	The inquiring mind	Working within a tradition	Paradigmatic choices
II Investigation	2 Interviewing	Learning how to listen	Issues of structure	Aspects of analysis
	3 Observation	Learning to see	Participant observation	Structured observation
	4 Collecting and analysing spoken interaction	Getting started	Developing an analysis	Different approaches to analysis
III Application	5 Planning a project	The personal project	Resources for project planning	Wider engagement
	6 Analysis and representation	Discovery	Analysis	Interpretation
Epilogue	Qualitative inquiry and teaching			

1
The Nature of Qualitative Inquiry

Preview

Two days ago I was in a meeting held to discuss a submission for the award of a PhD by published work when one of my fellow committee members referred to the qualitative nature of the work under consideration as 'soft' research. We exchanged friendly words, but I don't think either of us left the meeting with any greater respect for the other's position.

The accusation that qualitative inquiry (QI) doesn't measure up to the more demanding standards of 'hard' or 'scientific' research is a common one, drawing strength from a fund of prejudices that arise from our everyday exposure to the word 'research'. This chapter sets out to examine the roots of those prejudices and to identify the distinctive contribution that QI can make to our understanding of the social world. It introduces research traditions particularly associated with QI and examines the intellectual foundations of a qualitative stance.

Level 1 identifies essential characteristics of any research and shows how uninformed assumptions about its nature can lead to a distorted perception of QI. The level ends by showing what is distinctive about QI and highlighting where its contribution lies.

The best way of getting to grips with the issues that matter in QI is to become thoroughly acquainted with a particular tradition and *Level 2* is designed to facilitate this. It comprises descriptions of seven key traditions, and to facilitate ease of comparison each description follows the same pattern, beginning with the tradition's basic position, moving to methods used, typical outcomes, key concepts, potential relevance to TESOL and challenges to be overcome.

Level 3 probes more deeply into the philosophical foundations of QI, something that has more than mere abstract relevance. The discussion shows how a misunderstanding of the thinking behind this sort of inquiry can lead to serious distortions in approach and methodology and illustrates how everyday decisions reflect ontological and epistemological orientations. The level also includes a brief summary of three core paradigmatic positions.

Level 1: the inquiring mind

What is research?

Research has shown that most people live their whole lives without ever having to provide a definition of it. Research has shown no such thing, of course, but we're all familiar with that formulation and the effect it can have on our lives: fear of the possible consequences of past mistakes, hope of improvement in the future, uncertainty about where new discoveries are leading. We are constantly in receipt of advice on the basis of what 'research has shown', but we also know that yesterday's advice is tomorrow's warning in the light of what 'new research has shown' and it's easy to sympathise with the naïve response that research simply can't make its mind up.

Something so deeply embedded in the discourse of our everyday lives is not susceptible to easy reconfiguration; the associations, assumptions and prejudices that come with it will inevitably colour our view of what counts as 'proper' research. Because QI challenges many of our ordinary beliefs about research, it is intellectually less disturbing to dismiss it than to make an effort to understand the important contribution it can make to the ways in which we understand our social world. But the effort is worth making, and a useful first step is to identify the essential characteristics of any research, whatever its conceptual stripe.

We could simply say that research boils down to finding out about something, and in the broadest sense this is true: this is how my daughters describe using books and the Internet in order to find out about something for themselves. However, there is a slightly narrower sense of the term that refers to setting out to discover something directly about the world, and this provides a better starting point because it helps to distinguish research from the ordinary claims we make on the basis of our everyday experience. Consider the following everyday claim, made by my brother's partner upon returning from a brief visit to my local supermarket:

I've never seen so many people in Tesco's on a Friday night. And the trolleys are piled up to the hilt. All that panic buying just because it's going to be closed tomorrow morning – you'd think they were closing for a week.

In the event, my response was along the lines of, 'Dear oh dear, would you credit it?' This was designed as a suitable expression of solidarity in response to the frustration that she clearly felt: a deliberate probing of the evidence upon which her claim was based would have been pedantic and inappropriate. Although there is a conclusion here, reached on the basis of an analysis of the evidence, it would be very odd indeed to describe this as research and it's instructive to consider why.

Purpose

One of the essential characteristics of research, not evident here, is that it is purposeful. The researcher sets out deliberately to discover something about the world with the intention of eventually making claims on the basis of the evidence gathered. Suppose, then, that the claim about panic buying is the outcome of a personal project to identify the effects of closing on a Saturday morning and that the speaker has spent Friday evening observing behaviour in my local store. What response might it prompt?

Design

I certainly wouldn't wish to accept the claim at face value and I might wish to make the following points:

1. This is just one Friday evening in one store that the speaker may not have visited before, so we have no way of knowing whether the behaviour is typical or exceptional.
2. It's possible that the trolleys are piled high because the weekend shop is a big one, perhaps representing almost a week's worth of shopping. I'd like to know whether this was checked out and whether shoppers were consulted. I might also ask how the counting was done.
3. Even if the number of customers is greater than normal, this is not really surprising because, assuming they still want to do the weekend shopping, the people who normally shop on a Saturday morning will have to choose between: (a) skipping the shopping; and (b) shopping on Friday night or Saturday afternoon. If we therefore

assume that 50 per cent of the Saturday morning shoppers have transferred to Friday night, things are going to be abnormally busy.

Given these considerations, I would be reluctant to accept the claim that this was 'panic' buying at its face value. The first two reservations (and there could be more) are addressed to the design of the research, and they reflect the fact that research is more than simply finding out: it has to be carefully and thoughtfully designed in order to produce the information we need in order to make reasonable inferences about the way things are.

Procedure

This takes us deeper into the research process itself. Even if the purpose and design of the project are acceptable, we still need to be reassured that the procedures adopted are appropriate. For example, if the supermarket researcher has used interviews as a source of data, I will want to be reassured they provide a realistic picture of the shoppers involved. For example, I might not be satisfied with the question, 'Is this your local Tesco supermarket?' unless it is backed up by further questions about shopping habits, or I might feel that some of the questions are loaded in a way that encourages a particular response.

Questions like this can provoke quite heated debate because different researchers have different ideas about the advantages and limitations of different procedures. Even if there are no fundamental flaws in the procedures adopted, there are always alternative approaches and sometimes these need to be aired. What matters is that a defensible case can be made, not that it should necessarily convince everyone.

Analysis

Once the data are collected, they will need to be analysed, and here again appropriate and robust methods will be called for. Adequate analysis is the link that allows the researcher to respond confidently to the question, 'How did you come up with that claim on the basis of that data?' I've included it here as a separate item because of its importance, but it could be subsumed under 'procedure'.

Claim

The desire to make the strongest claims we can is a perfectly natural one, but our success will depend on whether we can establish a link between evidence and assertion. My brother's partner, for example, didn't want to say simply that this was the biggest crowd she'd seen in any Tesco supermarket on a Friday night; she wanted to make a much more general claim about people's response to closing a store for a single morning, and hence about human behaviour in general. Unfortunately, as the third of my reservations showed, lots of trolleys piled high with shopping are not in themselves evidence of panic buying.

Relevance and worth

But there's more at stake than just the acceptability of the claims. How would the researcher respond to the question, 'So what?' It's a simple one but potentially devastating, and it takes us right back to the issue of purpose. When I suggested at the start of this section that research is distinguished by its purposeful nature, I side-stepped issues of value and relevance: the extent to which research represents a worthwhile contribution to our knowledge and/or understanding.

I might, for example, discover something that is already known and although this may be very valuable to me as a developing researcher, its benefits are likely to be entirely personal; it will have little if any relevance to the wider world. That is why researchers who publish their work take such care to establish very clearly how it relates to other work in the field and highlight the contribution it is making, relating their work to other findings and the theories on which these draw. But this is still no guarantee that the research will in itself be valuable – we also have a right to expect that it will make a contribution that is *worthwhile*. Researchers who were able to provide an explanation of why buttered bread, when dropped, nearly always falls butter-side down were recently featured on a local news programme. Nobody disputed the validity of their claims, their entertainment value, or even their topical relevance, but the researchers were asked to justify the time and money spent in the pursuit of their unusual goal. They were able to explain that their research was worthwhile for all sorts of reasons related to our understanding of aerodynamics, irrelevant to the layperson picking hairs from their sandwich but really quite exciting and valuable to an expert in the field.

How, then, might QI be said to be worthwhile? Where does its distinctive contribution lie? Before reading on you might like to think about your reactions to the following statements:

- Research has to be scientific to be of any value.
- Research has to be objective.
- Research has to involve some quantification.
- Research has to be generalisable: a description of a single case has no practical value.

Qualitative research

I chose the statements at the end of the last section because they represent a fairly typical view of what research involves and are associated with two fundamental misconceptions about QI: that because QI can be based on a single case that involves no quantification and is neither 'scientific' nor 'objective', it is (a) not research at all; and (b) at best a soft option. In fact, QI is anything but a soft option – it demands rigour, precision, systematicity and careful attention to detail. In order to account for this misguided perspective, we need to reflect on the view of research that pervades our everyday experience, a view that treats 'experiment' and research as almost synonymous and that treats 'scientific' as a term of praise for almost anything, as this comment on Pepys' diary by a leading writer illustrates: 'The shamelessness of his self-observation deserves to be called scientific.' (Claire Tomalin in *The Guardian* 'Review', 21.09.02, p. 4.) How do we explain this?

'100 per cent of experiments have shown . . .'

It's not really surprising that people associate experiments with research. Here are a few influential factors that spring immediately to mind as I write:

- Ever since the Enlightenment, the whole thrust of research has been towards finding out about the natural world in an effort to understand its laws, and experimentation plays an important part in this.
- Most people's first exposure to research is through experiment. When in the school physics lesson the ball bearing rolls down the inclined plane faster than the wooden cube, it confirms our beliefs not only about the laws of nature but also about the ways in which these can be established.
- The expression 'experiments have shown' is part of our everyday vocabulary, and where we find 'experiment' the word 'proof' is rarely far away, usually accompanied by its quantitative minders.

The power of such factors to influence our assumptions about science and discovery is forcefully illustrated by one respected qualitative researcher's *volte face*:

For example, as late as 1995, Morse and Field wrote: 'If qualitative research is to fulfill one of its main functions, these theories should be significant enough and polished enough for subsequent quantitative testing' (p. 10). Now, with the enlightenment of this volume, please correct your copy: TEAR OUT THE PAGE!!!! (Morse 1997:3)

Although it would be perverse to deny the immense contribution that science and experimentation have made to our happiness and well-being, we should nevertheless not underestimate the effects of this on our assumptions about research. For an example of the seductive appeal of quantification, consider the following extracts (Extracts 1.1 and 1.2) from an otherwise very sound small-scale qualitative research project that was designed to find out more about certain features of telephone talk (written up, it has to be said, in examination conditions fairly early on in a Masters programme):

Extract 1.1 'Experiment' (1)

Due to the context of my experiment and the time limits, I only analysed one example of telephone conversation and thus I can in no way make any serious claims. Any conclusions will be purely speculative. My approach was thus very much qualitative as opposed to quantitative – I was looking into the presence or absence of data.

Extract 1.2 'Experiment' (2)

I wanted however to try to transcribe as many features as possible ... and this was an opportunity to experiment with that.

The use of the word 'experiment' is interesting. In the second extract the word is employed in its everyday sense and seems to be perfectly acceptable: the writer tried out (experimented with) an approach to transcription which involved transcribing as many features as possible. In the first extract, however, we have the collection and analysis of telephone conversation described as an 'experiment', although there is no sense in which it could be so described. On the basis of other examples I've come across, it seems to me that this is a case of an everyday assumption about 'research' breaking the surface. There are other assumptions here, too, as in the statement that a study of a single case precludes any 'serious' claims and commits one to mere 'speculation'. The outcome is that the approach is labelled as 'qualitative' rather than 'quantitative'. I detect a distinctly apologetic tone in this formulation, as if the unfortunate absence of quantification is the result of inadequate opportunity. The desire for quantification is a perfectly natural one: we find ourselves better equipped in argument when we have the figures at our fingertips.

Finally, there is the decidedly odd reference to looking for the presence or absence of data. Given the exam conditions, we can treat this as no more than a slip (for 'data', read 'specific features'), but it does fit in with the general tenor of the extract: qualitative research is soft, speculative, and concerned with 'data'; quantitative research is scientific (experimental), serious, and concerned with facts. It's almost as if the statement about panic buying in Tesco might pass muster as a 'qualitative' conclusion but wouldn't last long in the more demanding world of 'quantitative' research. Unfortunately, such prejudices have not been helped by the dismissive attitude adopted by some researchers in our own field. For example, when van Lier (1994) introduced qualitative perspectives in a 'complementary' way into a discussion of second language acquisition research in the journal *Applied Linguistics*, the editors of the special issue involved (Beretta *et al.* 1994:347) judged, from their 'rationalist' perspective, that this was 'not a piece that can be replied to, even if we thought it worth our while'. What, then, is the case for QI?

Why bother with qualitative research?

There are at least three compelling reasons for rejecting the claim that we ought simply to build on the success of quantitative approaches by putting all our efforts into refining their procedures. The first of these arises from the fact that experiments or surveys will only take us so far. They can explain many things and can provide us with valuable information and insights, but they are not designed to explore the complexities and conundrums of the immensely complicated social world that we inhabit. Even in more narrowly defined circumstances, there are situations where a qualitative approach offers the best source of illumination. For example, I can conduct experiments until I'm blue in the face in order to identify 'effective' procedures for designing language learning tasks, but if I want to know how successful task designers think and work, then I need to find other ways of exploring this (e.g. Johnson 2002). At least one leading researcher has identified this need to get close to practice as one of the main reasons for the recent growth of qualitative research:

> One reason for change is that scholars have become attracted to the idea of getting close to practice, to getting a first hand-sense of what actually goes on in classrooms, schools, hospitals and communities. That kind of knowledge takes time. The one-shot commando raid as a way to get the data and get out no longer seems attractive. You need to be there. A clean research design with tight experimental

controls might be right for some kinds of research, but not for all kinds. (Eisner 2001:137)

A second reason for adopting a qualitative approach is that it is above all else a person-centred enterprise and therefore particularly appropriate to our work in the field of language teaching. This is dangerous territory for the experimental researcher for, as Peshkin (1993:27) notes, 'most of what we study is truly complex, relating to people, events, and situations characterized by more variables than anyone can manage to identify, see in a relationship, or operationalize'. Human beings are wonderfully adept at confounding the sort of predictions that operate in the natural world, which is why a different sort of investigative approach is needed in the human sciences, one that will seek to understand the patterns and purpose in our behaviour and provide insights that will enrich our understanding. As practising teachers, we operate in a professional context which is at best only loosely predictable but where we can draw strength from our shared understandings and experiences.

The third profound strength of qualitative inquiry is its transformative potential for the researcher. The claim to objectivity implicit in the representation of quantitative outcomes and explicit in experimental research allows the researcher to stand aside from the findings, but this is not an option in qualitative inquiry. Investigation depends on engagement with the lived world, and the place of the researcher in the research process itself is something that needs to be addressed. The investigation impacts on the person doing the research and may have profound effects upon them, and it is in order to reflect this broader picture that from now on I shall where possible use the term 'inquiry' rather than 'research'. The latter, it seems to me, tends to be associated with specific projects while the former sits more comfortably with the broader notion of personal inquiry and discovery. To illustrate this personal dimension, consider two novice researchers – one female, one male, one in the dominant ethnic group, one in a minority group in their respective academic contexts – who find that the process of inquiry in their separate studies of particular ethnic groups in educational settings has transformed their understanding. Petty (1997:83) realises that '[t]he experience has altered my perspectives about policies related to racial issues', while what emerges from González's work (2001:560) is a framework that 'is liberating for me as it shifts my self-reflection as oppressed object to culturally working actor'. These are not merely matters of belief but of behaviour.

The nature of qualitative inquiry

The broad aim of qualitative inquiry is to understand better some aspect(s) of the lived world. This has a number of implications for the nature of the research itself, summed up in Box 1.1.

Box 1.1   Characteristics of qualitative inquiry

It will:	*It will not:*
• study human actors in natural settings, in the context of their ordinary, everday world;	• set up artificial situations for the purposes of study or try to control the conditions under which participants act;
• seek to understand the meanings and significance of these actions from the perspective of those involved;	• attempt to describe human behaviour in terms of a limited set of pre-determined categories;
• usually focus on a small number of (possibly just one) individuals, groups or settings;	• attempt to study a large population identified on the basis of particular characteristics;
• employ a range of methods in order to establish different perspectives on the relevant issues;	• base its findings on a single perspective or feature;
• base its analysis on a wide range of features;	• base its analysis on a single feature;
• only use quantification where this is appropriate for specific purposes and as part of a broader approach.	• represent its findings in primarily quantitative terms.

It might be said that the power of qualitative research derives from its ability to represent the particular and that this distinguishes it from those sorts of research which depend on generalisability (an issue taken up in Chapter 6), but it would be going too far to claim this as a defining characteristic. In fact, characterisations of qualitative inquiry range from short sentences to whole chapters, though Denzin and Lincoln's representation, below, is widely recognised. Their formulation reflects the richness and complexity of the qualitative field, a far cry from the hard-edged certainties of 'science':

> Qualitative research is multimethod in focus, involving an interpretive, naturalistic approach to its subject matter. This means that qualitative researchers study things in their natural settings, attempting to make sense of, or interpret, phenomena in terms of the meanings people bring to them. Qualitative research involves the studied use and collection of a variety of empirical materials – case study, personal experience, introspective, life story, interview, observational, historical, interactional, and visual texts – that describe routine and problematic moments and meanings in individuals' lives. Accordingly, qualitative researchers deploy a wide range of unconnected methods, hoping always to get a better fix on the subject matter at hand. (Denzin and Lincoln 1994b:2)

Because the term *qualitative* inquiry draws attention to one item in a contrasting pair, it might be thought that there should be nothing *quantitative* about it, but this is far from being the case. In pursuing qualitative inquiry, we are, as Eisner (2001:138) puts it, 'trying to develop some insights we can work with'. And we can often do this without worrying too much about precise figures, although more general representations in terms of 'many' or 'the majority' might well feature in our descriptions. If occasionally more precise quantification has a contribution to make, it would be foolish to deny ourselves this resource on ideological grounds. But this is a very different position from one that says the only significant claims are those expressible in quantitative terms. It recognises that decisions about degrees of precision are matters to be determined in the course of our inquiry rather than as a prelude to it. Hammersley puts his finger on the real issue:

> We are not faced, then, with a stark choice between words and numbers, or even between precise and imprecise data; but rather with a range from more to less precise data. Furthermore, our decisions about what level of precision is appropriate in relation to any particular claim should depend on the nature of what we are trying to describe, on the likely accuracy of our descriptions, on our purposes, and on the resources available to us; not on ideological commitment to one methodological paradigm or another. (Hammersley 1992:163)

The contexts in which such 'commitments' might arise will become clearer as this chapter unfolds.

Level 2: working within a tradition

One of the biggest challenges facing anyone new to qualitative research is coming to terms with the plethora of definitions, traditions and approaches that characterise the field. Here's flavour of the problem, first in terms of the range of what's available:

> The quest for a useful organizational map of qualitative methods is not unlike the quest for the holy grail. The methods derive from multiple disciplines and from 20 or more diverse traditions, each with its own particular language. (Miller and Crabtree 1992:13)

... and then from the point of view of trying to make sense of this:

> But as comprehensive and clarifying as these catalogs and taxonomies may be, they turn out to be basically incommensurate, both in the way the different qualitative strands are defined and in the criteria used to distinguish them. The mind boggles in trying to get from one to another. (Miles and Huberman 1994:5)

There is no easy way to negotiate this complex territory, but an essential first step is to clarify basic terminology. The terms in Box 1.2 will be used consistently throughout this book. They correspond to what most researchers would recognise, and although not everybody would use them in exactly the same way, exposure to the literature will quickly familiarise you with the relevant variations.

Box 1.2   Research terms used in this book

Paradigm   At the highest level, representative of a set of basic beliefs.
Example: Constructivism

Tradition   A historically situated approach to research covering generally recognised territory and employing a generally accepted set of research methods.
Example: Ethnography

Method   A means of gathering, analysing and interpreting data using generally recognised procedures. (A *methodology* is

	a theoretically grounded position that the researcher takes up with regard to the research methods that will be used.) Example: Interviewing
Technique	A specific procedure for obtaining information informed by the research methodology employed. Example: Asking open-ended questions

Seven core traditions

Based on an approach used by Cresswell (1998), this section will provide you with a brief general introduction to seven core traditions in qualitative research that are relevant to our work in TESOL (Box 1.3.) It is supported by the recommendations in the Guided Reading section, which will enable you to deepen your understanding across the range. The traditions described are ethnography, grounded theory, phenomenology, case study, life history, action research and conversation analysis.

Box 1.3 Some qualitative research traditions

Focus (outcome)	*Tradition*	*Primary means of data collection*
The social world (Description and interpretation of group)	**Ethnography**	Observation, interview, recording, documents
The social world (Development of theory)	**Grounded theory**	Observation, interview, recording, documents
Lived experience (Understanding nature of experience of phenomenon)	**Phenomenology**	Interview
Particular cases (Detailed description of individual cases)	**Case study**	Interview, documents, observation, recording
The person (Picture of individual life experience)	**Life history**	Interview

Box 1.3   (Continued)

Professional action (Improvement of professional practice)	**Action research**	Journal, interviews, documents, recording
Social interaction (Explication of how shared understandings are constructed)	**Conversation analysis**	Recording

The descriptions that follow are not designed as substitutes for a proper understanding of the traditions covered and they make no claims to completeness, but taken together they form a useful overview of the field, a means of orientation for those who wish to chart their own path through it. I have written them so that they can be comfortably read as a whole, following a standard pattern of headings to facilitate comparison across traditions: (1) basic position; (2) methods used; (3) what outcomes of research might look like; (4) some key concepts; (5) potential relevance to TESOL; and (6) challenges to be overcome. For the purposes of comparison, I have taken 'Teacher meets class' as a very rough focus for the discussion under 'possible outcomes of research'.

Ethnography

Basic position

Ethnography fits comfortably into the description of qualitative research that we have so far developed. It seeks to describe and understand the behaviour of a particular social or cultural group. In order to do this, researchers try to see things from the perspective of members of the group and this requires extended exposure to the field.

Methods used

Fieldwork is central to all ethnography, which means that the researcher has to negotiate entry into the research site, often as a *participant observer*, a role in which the researcher undertakes work in the setting (for example, as a part-time teacher) but at the same time gathers data. Adopting this perspective enables the researcher to move from outsider to insider status, although the aim is not to become a complete insider because this would mean taking for granted the sorts of beliefs, attitudes and routines that the researcher needs to remain detached from in order to observe and describe. The main sources of data are fieldnotes and interviews, though documents may also be used and it may also be possible to tape interaction. The analysis of data will depend on the identification and categorisation of key themes, perspectives and events, working towards an account that embraces adequate description and interpretation, which may include amongst other things extracts from fieldnotes, narrative vignettes and samples of talk. The form of presentation is traditionally textual, but newer ethnographies embrace a variety of other forms including the dramatic, poetic and visual.

Possible outcomes of research

A typical ethnography might be a study of a group of teachers in their institutional setting over a term or year, focusing particularly on their relationships with students as these are exemplified in staffroom and classroom behaviour. The researcher might join the staff as a temporary teacher, taking fieldnotes, observing lessons, interviewing teachers (and perhaps students), even taping some staff meetings, focusing particularly on the ways in which teachers deal with new students in their classes and how these students are represented in staffroom talk. There might be big differences in the ways that students are represented in the staffroom and the way they actually behave, and it may be that there are implicit (or even explicit) behavioural categories into which all students are fitted. Hammersley, a well-known writer on ethnography began his own research with a PhD on a topic very similar to this (Hammersley 1980; see also 1981, 1984a).

Some key concepts

The terms *emic* and *etic*, derived from anthropology, are sometimes used to refer – rather crudely – to an insider's perspective on events (emic) as opposed to an outsider's (etic). The terms are sometimes illegitimately used with evaluative force, implying that an insider's view is somehow 'better' than an outsider's, when in fact both are potentially important. Ethnographers try to establish different perspectives on the situation they are studying and will use different theories, methods, techniques, and so on in order to avoid a one-sided view. The idea of getting a fix on things in this way is often described as *triangulation*, though there is no implication that only three sources need be used. You may also occasionally hear people referring to *thick description*, an expression coined by Clifford Geertz to refer to an account that is rich in detail, embracing different perspectives. The idea behind this is that it is possible to learn a great deal from narrowly focused observation, provided that the observation is sufficiently penetrating and comprehensive.

Potential relevance to TESOL

Ethnography has a lot to offer in the field of TESOL, especially as a means of understanding our own professional world or, for ESP (English for Specific Purposes) practitioners, the professional world of our students. Perhaps the most interesting line of thinking is the one that sees students as potential ethnographers (see Roberts *et al.* 2001), integrating ethnographic investigation with the process of language learning itself.

Challenges

The main drawback of this tradition as far as TESOL is concerned is that it requires extended exposure to the field, which makes it very difficult for the researcher to stay in work during the period of investigation. It is methodologically unacceptable to settle for quick forays into the field in order to scoop up data and retreat (an approach known by the pejorative term 'blitzkrieg ethnography'), so while it may be legitimate to use methods characteristic of ethnography, these do not in themselves mean that you are working within this tradition. Unfortunately this has not been widely recognised within TESOL and the term 'ethnographic' is much abused, being invoked for any work that might be described as broadly 'qualitative'. In ethnography there is no substitute for extended immersion in the field, and where this is not possible researchers should consider traditions where participant observation is not essential, the two most obvious being grounded theory and the case study.

Grounded theory

Basic position

Novice researchers in TESOL might be forgiven for assuming, as they often do, that any approach 'grounded' in the data necessarily falls within this tradition. However, this is only half the picture because while the tradition does insist that the research process works from data to theory rather than vice versa, it also insists that the aim of the process is to generate a theory – a possibility open to every researcher and not limited to a tiny group of influential thinkers who develop 'grand' theory. The theory is derived from or discovered through analysis of the data.

Methods used

Data collection in grounded theory is similar to that of ethnography, although observation and interviews are not necessarily privileged and if necessary the researcher can draw on a wide range of sources (for example photographs, documents). Central to the methodology of grounded theory is the interrelationship between theory and data collection. The researcher does not begin with a particular theory in mind but adopts an inductive approach that allows theory to develop from the data. Using coding procedures that allow categories in the data to be identified, the researcher writes theoretical memos on the emergent theorising and as this thinking develops the researcher uses it to inform further data gathering that is the basis for further coding, theorising and data collection. Eventually memos, data sets and procedures (including operational diagrams) are integrated and used, through a process of refinement, as the basis for the articulation of a core explanatory theory.

Possible outcomes of research

A typical grounded theory project might involve a study of the experience of the first few weeks at a new language school from the learner's point of view. Learners might be asked open-ended questions about their views of language learning, the experience of arriving at a new institution and the approaches to language learning that they encountered; they might be asked to keep learner diaries; the researcher might observe lessons and interview teachers, collect a variety of documents (administrative and academic) and read accounts of other initial language-learning experiences. What might emerge is a theory about the ways in which a dominant view of what language learning involves comes to be shared by the students.

Some key concepts

The process of using emerging theory to inform data collection is known as *theoretical sampling*, a procedure central to grounded theory that involves three sorts of coding: *open*, *axial* and *selective* (all described in detail in Chapter 6). Categories are either identified by the actors themselves, in which case they are described as *in vivo*, or constructed by the researcher as part of the process of analysis, in which case they are referred to as *in vitro*. Once a category has been identified, examples are gathered to enrich the description of it, but eventually a point will be reached where new examples are adding nothing to the picture that has developed, in which case the category is said to be *saturated*.

Potential relevance to TESOL

Because grounded theory does not demand the extended exposure necessary for a full ethnography but still offers a means of developing an understanding of educational contexts, it is a tradition that is likely to have strong practical appeal to TESOL practitioners. Perhaps the greatest attraction of grounded theory is that it offers a systematic way of analysing and interpreting the data, normally a messy and frustrating process that is traditionally seen as something of a mystery, causing even the best researchers to feel 'at sea' (Hammersley 1984b:60–2). 'Establishing categories from qualitative data', laments one group of ethnographic researchers, 'seems rather like a simultaneous left-brain right-brain exercise' (Ely *et al.* 1991:87), so the practical guidelines offered in this tradition are reassuring.

Challenges

However, the process of analysis is still very time-consuming and the need to produce a theory can put considerable pressure on the researcher. Critics have reacted negatively to the strong focus on method, the place of the researcher and the status of the 'theories' produced, but the growing popularity of this tradition cannot be ignored.

Phenomenology

Basic position

The name of this tradition reflects its essentially philosophical orientation. Originating in the work of Husserl, its aim is to penetrate to the essential meaning of human experience, to focus on the phenomenon or 'thing' in order to generate understanding from within. Its approach was further developed from a descriptive to a more interpretive (*hermeneutic*) orientation through the work of Heidegger and Gadamer, later researchers such as Ricoeur combining the two (*hermeneutic phenomenology*) and focusing on our self-understanding as active, meaning-making participants in the human world.

Methods used

Research methods are designed to move from exploring the experience of experience (what it's like) to penetrating the meaning of experience itself, which means that researchers must set aside their own memories, knowledge, speculation and so on concerning the phenomenon itself so that the data can reveal themselves naturally as meant by the actor:

> [T]he starting point of the phenomenological approach is to consider *every* phenomenon, including known ones, as if they are presenting themselves for the very first time to consciousness. In this way we

can (again) become aware of the fullness and richness of these phenomena. (Mason 2001:138)

Crotty (1998) identifies the steps in this process, beginning with a very general question (for example, What is it like to be a new and inexperienced teacher in a school full of very experienced staff?) and then working towards detailed description of the experience via phenomenological reduction. This is a complex and demanding process in which the questioner tries to free themself of all possible influences (theoretical constructs, preconceived ideas, and so on) in order to accept the respondent's views in a completely open and passive way. The description is then examined to ensure that it too is free of contamination from sources outside the experience itself, and in this way the researcher tries to capture the essence of the experience. This requires 'a sensitive attunement to opening up the meaning of experience both as discourse and as text' (Ray 1994:129) and will produce a thematically ordered descriptive account, though approaches and outcomes do vary according to which branch of the tradition the researcher follows.

Possible outcomes of research

A TESOL research project in this tradition might seek to understand the experience of being forced to learn a new language when the learner has strong negative feelings about this. The first step would be to identify a group of perhaps 10 to 20 students who have had this experience and to set up a series of in-depth interviews, perhaps beginning with the general question, 'What is it like having to start learning a language when you feel a strong antipathy to this?' The aim would then be to follow the procedures outlined above in order to understand the essence of this particular language-learning experience.

Some key concepts

There are two terms of fundamental importance in phenomenology, both related to the avoidance of contamination by outside prejudices and presuppositions. The process of removing these from the research process, or setting them aside, in order to penetrate to the essence of the phenomenon, is known as *bracketing*. The resulting suspension of such elements and uncontaminated access to the essence of the phenomenon is known as *epoche*. A related concept sometimes referred to is *ideation*, where 'we try to go from the particular to the general: starting from what appears to consciousness . . . we try to acquire an understanding of the idea that determines its meaningfulness' (Mason 2001:140).

Potential relevance to TESOL

If we want to understand more about the *experience* of teaching or learning a language, this tradition offers a potentially interesting way forward. In addition, because we are teachers investigating our own field, we inevitably bring with us all sorts of assumptions and presuppositions, so techniques that could enable us to set these aside are to be welcomed.

Challenges

As will already be clear from the brief description above, this tradition is demanding. To begin with, anyone wishing to work within it must take on the serious study of its philosophical foundations and subsequent development. In addition, there can probably be no more demanding ambition than to understand the very essence of an experience, so the research experience will require considerable effort and application if the outcome is to be more than merely superficial. There must also be a suspicion that the challenging complexities of the discourses involved in this tradition and the difficulty of penetrating these may serve to obscure the extent to which bracketing is actually possible in practice.

Case study

Basic position

'Case study', as its practitioners readily admit, means different things to different people. While some would use the term as almost synonymous with qualitative research, others allow that case studies can be quantitative; and while some researchers claim that case study is nothing more than a method, there are those who would elevate it to the level of paradigm. This means that if you are new to the field and read more than one introduction you should be prepared for a certain amount of apparent contradiction, although this is not something to be unduly concerned about. All that really matters is that the focus of the research should be on a particular unit or set of units – institutions, programmes, events and so on – and the aim should be to provide a detailed description of the unit(s).

Methods used

Given the range of application, more or less any qualitative methods are appropriate provided that there are multiple sources of information generating a sufficiently rich description. Interviews are a common method of collecting data and documents might well feature, perhaps supported by observation and recording. There seems to be a growing willingness among case study researchers to resist the call for generalisation and to insist instead on the importance of the particular case, though the area is a contentious one.

Possible outcomes of research

A case study in TESOL might focus on a single teacher and perhaps a small group of students in order to explore how the relationship develops as the latter settle into a new language school. The institutional setting would need to be carefully delineated and we would need to know a lot about the background of the individuals involved, so a number of in-depth interviews would be necessary and these might be linked to lesson observation and perhaps also to critical incidents. Documentary evidence might also be sought out where relevant and the researcher would aim to develop a rich picture of the experiences of those involved within this particular setting, perhaps including narrative accounts as well as descriptive vignettes. In discussing the case, attention will be drawn to features of particular interest, relating these to broader issues and developing explanations where appropriate.

Some key concepts

When so much attention is lavished on a particular case, selection is something that demands careful attention. In most cases *sampling* is likely to be *purposeful*, though there are other options and these are discussed in Level 2 of Chapter 5. The eventual decision will be influenced to some extent by whether the case is chosen for its own worth (*intrinsic*) or in order to focus on a broader issue (*instrumental*).

Potential relevance to TESOL

In a field as broad geographically, socially and intellectually as TESOL, where generalisations are likely to be blandly true, suffocatingly narrow or irresponsibly cavalier, the power of the particular case to resonate across cultures should not be underestimated. High quality, detailed cases can contribute to what Stenhouse, referring to schools, has described as the archaeology of the future:

> It is an exciting possibility that current interest in the careful study of cases might produce a national archive of such case records. If we had such an archive now, we could understand in much greater intimacy and depth the recent history of our schools. (Stenhouse 1980:5)

Challenges

As with most other things that seem superficially easy, there is a danger that the inexperienced researcher will be deceived into thinking that case study is merely a matter of description and detail alone is enough. But this research demands at least as much rigour as other approaches and the problematic nature of the relationship between case and theory building requires careful negotiation.

Life history

Basic position

This is another tradition that represents something of a terminological challenge, and a distinction should perhaps be drawn between a biography, where the focus is on the individual life as an unfolding story, and life history, where the context plays an important part. In fact, the two approaches are very close and could be included under the broader umbrella of case study. Most of the points made there apply equally well here, especially in the case of life history, as a leading practitioner makes clear:

> The distinction between the life story and the life history is therefore absolutely basic. The life story is the 'story we tell about our life'; the life history is a collaborative venture, reviewing a wider range of evidence. The life story teller and another (or others) collaborate in developing this wider account by interviews and discussions and by scrutiny of texts and contexts. (Goodson 1992:6)

Methods used

At the heart of any life history research is the prolonged interview, which usually consists of a series of interviews (Sikes *et al.* 1985:13). The length of such interviews can vary from between a couple of hours to totals well into double figures. Woods (1985), for example, mentions between two and fifteen hours, while Huberman (1989) settles for a consistent five hours over two sessions. Woods also argues (1985:16) that triangulation is important in order to overcome two important challenges to authenticity in such interviews: that the informant may not be telling the truth and that the truth as perceived by the informant does not represent what they truly believed or felt at the time. The first problem can be tackled by ensuring the reliability of the informant, considering the plausibility of the account, checking, and so on, but the second is more difficult to overcome. Woods suggests that attention to other accounts, other evidence, internal inconsistencies, and so on, can be valuable.

Possible outcomes of research

A possible TESOL project might be a life history of the teacher in our encounter, using this as a way of deepening our understanding of the encounter between teacher and new students that we are taking as our theme. Over a period of time and through a number of in-depth interviews, supported perhaps by lesson observation (to prompt questions and deepen the researcher's understanding) and documentary evidence (photographs, reports, influential texts, etc.), the researcher would develop an account of the individual, their beliefs and experiences. This can then be used, as with any good case study, to deepen our understanding of teachers and the world that they inhabit.

Some key concepts

Woods (1985) suggests an approach to interviewing based on *progressive focusing* over a number of interviews, since this allows the interviewer to identify missing details, points needing correction (inconsistencies, *non sequiturs*, and so on) and issues that are worth following up, so that subsequent interviews can be effectively focused. As the life history is analysed, certain key events, or *epiphanies*, will emerge that will have particular significance in an unfolding story that can in turn be checked through *respondent validation*. Measor and Sikes (1992:219) suggest that this checking also acts as an important ethical safeguard.

Potential relevance to TESOL

The argument for life histories in TESOL is the same as that for the case study, with the added consideration that from the point of view of the profession there are good reasons for understanding the lives and beliefs of those at its core.

Challenges

However, data collection based so heavily on interviews carries with it particular dangers. Huberman's anecdote concerning the background of researchers is illuminating in this context. He tells (1993:25) how the backgrounds of interviewers were reflected in the analyses they produced, so that while someone with a clinical background produced an account rich in psycho-dynamic detail, a sociologist colleague accentuated data which reflected institutional aspects of school life. As we shall see in the chapter on interviewing, there are even deeper and more subtle challenges to be overcome.

Action research

Basic position

Although this research tradition is also firmly case-based, it represents a move from a descriptive/interpretive stance to an interventionist position, where a key aim of the research is to understand better some aspect of professional practice as a means of bringing about improvement. This may involve institution-wide investigation, producing recommendations that are implemented by relevant groups, the new practices being assessed by the researchers, who report back and, if necessary, recommend further changes or refinements. Alternatively, an individual may engage in action research with a view to improving their own practice. Participatory or emancipatory action research involves groups of concerned practitioners who work together to improve not only their own practice but also the situation in which they work. As two leading proponents of this approach note, its aims are not merely instrumental:

> There are two essential aims of action research: to *improve* and to *involve*. Action research aims at improvement in three areas: firstly, the improvement of a *practice*; secondly, the improvement of the *understanding* of the practice by its practitioners; and thirdly, the improvement of the *situation* in which the practice takes place. The aim of *involvement* stands shoulder to shoulder with the aim of *improvement*. (Carr and Kemmis 1986:165, original italics)

The element of personal and professional investment in the research itself and in its outcomes is another aspect that marks this research as different from the other traditions described here.

Methods used

The characteristic approach associated with this tradition is the action research spiral of planning→acting and observing→reflecting→planning, and so on. (The following description follows a tradition familiar in TESOL and focuses on the practitioner–researcher, though it is possible for the researcher not to be involved in the practice.) The process begins with reflection on some aspect of the practitioner-researcher's work that leads to possible lines of intervention, then once the nature of the intervention has been decided a plan is developed and implemented within the context of professional practice. The implementation is monitored by the practitioner–researcher(s) (and possibly others, in the case of a team project or complementary projects) and when analysis of this leads to a better understanding of relevant processes, this is used as the basis for further reflection, which in turn may indicate the need to plan further intervention. The description suggests an eternal cycle spiralling through a professional life, but in practice there will be limits to what is possible or desirable, and a project may concentrate on a single cycle. The data sources we have seen in the first three traditions (interviews, recordings, documents, observation) may be used here to inform the planning and to provide a picture of the implementation, though journal keeping by the practitioner–researcher is perhaps more prominent than in other traditions.

Possible outcomes of research

The language teacher in our hypothetical TESOL situation might reflect on their treatment of new students and decide that intervention would be appropriate. The nature of appropriate intervention might be apparent to the teacher, or it may be necessary to wait for a new intake, keep a journal and record lessons in order to build up a picture of the ways in which induction is handled in class. Analysis of this might reveal very prescriptive teacher-centred approaches that are not conducive to building a classroom community, so the teacher might develop a set of more appropriate strategies for achieving this end. These strategies could then be implemented with the next intake and their success evaluated on the basis of journals, recordings and perhaps interviews.

Some key concepts

Action research is typically associated with a *cycle* of activities and the term *empowerment* is often associated with its outcomes. Where this is used, it embeds the research within a professional context where the practitioner seeks, through deeper understanding and intervention, to bring about changes in their working practices and to explore the *emancipatory* potential of their activities.

Potential relevance to TESOL

In the light of its popularity, the case for action research in TESOL perhaps does not need to be made (for an eloquent expression of its value, see Edge 2001b), but its legitimacy as a serious research tradition needs to be underlined. Provided that appropriate methods of data collection and analysis are used, it offers a potentially rich source of professional understanding (and incentive to action) derivable from the fully articulated particular case.

Challenges

Unfortunately, the status of action research has not been accepted in all quarters because its popularity with practitioner–researchers and with others involved in professional development has led to the term being applied to a wide range of practices, some of them falling far short of the minimum criteria for acceptable QI. Its instrumental orientation will always bring with it this risk, but that should not be allowed to undermine its appeal to the serious researcher.

Conversation analysis

Basic position

This tradition originated in a series of lectures delivered by Harvey Sacks in the 1960s in which he used the careful analysis of conversation to highlight significant aspects of social organisation. For him, ordinary conversation provides a unique insight into the ways in which people understand and represent their social world. The analytic emphasis falls on how speakers jointly construct conversation and their shared understanding of what is happening in it, or 'the means by which individuals participating in the same interaction can reach a shared interpretation of its constituent activities and of the rules to which they are designed to conform' (Taylor and Cameron 1987:103).

Methods used

Conversational analysis (CA) focuses on the sequential development of the conversation: how each turn relates to what has gone before and looks forward to what will follow. Nothing is considered in isolation and everything is interpreted in terms of the participants' own understanding of it as revealed in their talk; there are no appeals to wider social rules or to extraneous contextual factors. Utterances, like actions, are *context shaped* and *context renewing* (Drew and Heritage 1992:18). When Sacks said 'do not let your notion of what could conceivably happen decide for you what must have happened' (1985:15), he was drawing attention to an analytical stance that finds expression in four fundamental methodological rules:

1. *Use naturally occurring data.* This is the most basic condition of research: invented data is *never* used, even for the purposes of illustration. Sacks emphasises the point repeatedly: 'the kind of

phenomena I deal with are always transcriptions of actual occurrences in their actual sequence' (1984:25).

2. *Move from observation to hypothesis.* Conversation analysis is not hypothesis testing. The analyst's aim is to treat the talk as something fresh, something to be approached on its own terms.

3. *Rule nothing out.* This derives directly from the first two points and might therefore be subsumed under them. Atkinson and Heritage (1984a:4) make the point well: 'nothing that occurs in interaction can be ruled out, *a priori*, as random, insignificant, or irrelevant'.

4. *Focus on sequences.* Because conversation is jointly constructed, we must treat each utterance in the context of its response to what has gone before and its relevance to what follows; isolated turns or utterances do not represent legitimate units of analysis.

Possible outcomes of research

A CA project might focus on an aspect of classroom interaction such as the way in which certain talk is oriented to by the class. Perhaps a new overseas teacher has recently begun to teach an intermediate class and there seems to be something unusual about the ways in which certain teacher turns are received, even though it is not immediately clear what is distinctive about them. By collecting lots of examples of classroom talk, transcribing extended sequences in which this phenomenon occurs as well as others where the response is different, and analysing these carefully, the researcher might discover that the teacher's turn in these cases has particular features to which the students are demonstrably orienting, so that the exchanges develop in quite a distinctive way. This might then provide valuable information about the nature of interaction in this classroom and perhaps open up possibilities that might otherwise have remained unnoticed.

Some key concepts

Much of the vocabulary in CA relates to the sequential evidence of jointly constructed talk, where *participant design* and *procedural relevance* (or consequence) are important. Specific features of this include *turn-taking*, *repair* of talk, *preference organisation* and *pre-sequences*, terms that will feature in analyses in Chapter 4.

Potential relevance to TESOL

In a profession with language at its heart, an analytical tradition such as CA will always have a contribution to make, and particular areas of interest are likely to be those of classroom interaction and cross-cultural encounters. These and other potential topics are discussed in Schegloff *et al.* (2002).

Challenges

Although the influence of CA is growing, it is methodologically very demanding and requires a ferocious attention to detail that not all researchers can muster. Some critics have also argued that its insistence on looking only at what can be discovered in the talk means that its contribution to our understanding, however valuable in itself, must necessarily remain very limited. However, in Chapter 4 I adopt an analytic approach that draws heavily on this tradition precisely because of its rigorous approach and its refusal to be distracted by aspects extraneous to the talk itself.

Conclusion

The summary above has provided a brief overview of different research traditions and, along with the guided reading, it will enable you to develop a good picture of the territory. If you choose to pursue the recommended reading on particular traditions, you should also be able to get to grips with the fundamental concepts, methods and procedures. However, this general approach is not the approach that suits everybody, especially those who have found their way into qualitative research via interest in a particular topic. In this case, general reading may be distracting and the more focused approach, described in Level 2 of Chapter 5, might be more appropriate. If you can support this by joining relevant email lists, reading key journals and attending conferences where key researchers are speaking, so much the better. In the end, though, the real journey of discovery only properly gets under way when the research itself begins.

Level 3: paradigmatic choices

Epistemology and *ontology* aren't words that trip lightly off the tongue, and in some quarters they are best left tucked safely away in the mental lexicon – which is the best explanation I can offer of why some researchers give them a wide berth. In fact, it is possible to work within a particular tradition without thinking too hard about its intellectual foundations, but this can lead to serious confusion and not a little wasted effort. In Level 2 I introduced key traditions in the field of QI, traditions that represent a continually growing and developing body of work within which researchers are able to position their own contribution.

Such traditions are based on fundamental beliefs about the world and a grasp of the relationships among these different basic viewpoints promotes a deeper understanding of the nature of the inquiry itself. This is what makes the consideration of paradigms a practical as well as a philosophical enterprise.

I begin this level with an illustration of how a failure to understand the fundamental beliefs upon which a tradition is based can have serious repercussions at the level of method. I then introduce the concept of paradigm before moving on to a consideration of the two orientations that underlie all paradigmatic positions. Finally, I offer an overview of paradigmatic options.

Getting below the surface

If you've read the descriptions of the different traditions in the previous level and are already familiar with the tradition in which you will be working, any further probing into its philosophical foundations might seem redundant, so I offer the following as a fairly typical illustration of the need for at least a basic familiarity with the beliefs that underlie these traditions (see Box 1.4). If you're not familiar with conversation analysis, you may find it difficult to spot the flaws, but the potential fault lines in the research design will nevertheless emerge clearly.

Box 1.4   A misconceived project

Stewart has decided to investigate the ways in which teachers give feedback to students and, having read about the concept of repair in conversation analysis, decides that he will work within this tradition. He reads as many accounts as he can on the subject of repair and is soon familiar with the different sorts of repair trajectory. He also discovers that the preferred form for the classroom is different from that of conversation, so he decides to investigate why this might be. He tapes classes of six different teachers, sub-categorises the different types of repair, then presents a breakdown of these in terms of the different language activities taking place. Having identified a correlation between certain categories of repair and language activity, he suggests reasons why this might be so, and when he interviews the teachers concerned they confirm his interpretation. On the basis of this, he develops a full description that he hopes will be useful to teacher trainers.

I have invented this description but it's typical of many proposed 'conversation analysis' projects that I've encountered. Its weaknesses might be put down to a fairly superficial reading of research within the CA tradition, or it might equally arise from reading introductions to this tradition within the TESOL discourse analysis literature that focus on findings rather than fundamentals. It is a fact that conversation analysis has made very important contributions to our understanding of some important features of talk, such as turn-taking and repair, but the descriptive appeal of this has led to serious misunderstandings about its approach. If we examine the above project from a methodological perspective, it should be possible to identify some procedures that are not found in the CA literature, but in order to understand why this is so and – more importantly – to avoid similar mistakes in the future, we need to dig deeper into the roots of the tradition.

Some methodological flaws

Procedures that would not be found in mainstream CA literature and are not part of its methodology are:

1. a process of categorisation based on items that are (a) pre-determined and (b) separated from the surrounding talk;
2. the establishment of a 'correlation' between features of talk derived in this way and categories of activity similarly determined;
3. speculation (presumably based on assumptions about the linguistic and/or educational context, human relationships, or individual motivations) as to the reasons for this link;
4. the use of actors as informants in order to identify their motivations.

Taken together, this is a pretty damning collection and a novice researcher faced with it might be prompted to ask either, 'So what do I need to do if it *is* to be counted as CA?' or, 'Well what tradition *am* I working in then?' A response to this based on a different list of methods might, with hefty slice of luck and a following wind, get the researcher back on track, but it would be a shallow basis for future success and would hardly encourage the sort of thoughtful orientation that is the mark of a good researcher. A far better approach would be to expose the intellectual roots of this tradition, relating these to its methodological stance. I will not repeat the details already provided in Level 2 but will briefly sketch the conceptual background to these.

The ethnomethodological roots of conversation analysis

Although the development of conversation analysis as a distinct discipline is associated with the work of Harvey Sacks in the 1960s, its roots lie in ethnomethodology, a term invented by its founder, Harold Garfinkel. Garfinkel's overriding interest was in the pervasiveness of common-sense knowledge, and the ways in which this is utilised to maintain a shared understanding of the world around us and the activities in which we are involved. Fundamental to this position was a rejection of the tradition in sociology that made claims to objectivity despite relying heavily on the construction and imposition of categories created by the analyst. Garfinkel's position, crudely put, is that such categories are developed by the actors in social situations as part of a dynamic process of situated knowledge and shared understandings (see Heritage 1984a for a discussion and Garfinkel 1984 for illustrations).

The emphasis in ethnomethodology is on 'practical reasoning', and although there is an interest in the orderliness that certain activities display, of particular concern are the methods or procedures needed to produce such orderliness. The methods of reasoning used are procedural, unceasing and socially shared, so that our social world is jointly constructed. It depends, if you like, on our shared understanding of it, and this emphasis is reflected in CA's insistence on paying close attention to how the sequential construction of talk reveals aspects of social organisation. In a nutshell, the belief that social reality is interactively constructed leads to an interest in how this is achieved and a methodology which refuses to admit explanations from outside the direct evidence of that interaction. As we shall now see, this is a far cry from what is on offer in the project we are considering.

How the plot was lost

The most fundamental mismatch between the project and conversation analysis lies in the two differing views of reality they represent. For CA social reality is jointly constructed and the only legitimate categories are those evidenced in the talk itself, while Stewart begins with an assumption of an objective reality that is susceptible to categorisation and quantification quite independently of the participants' own constructions – a view that ethnomethodology explicitly rejects. From this basic misunderstanding of CA, everything else follows. Although Stewart uses naturally occurring data, he does not examine sequences of talk to discover how it is interactively constructed, but instead imposes a set of categories that he himself determines. This means that all sorts of things must be ruled out, for once a category is determined anything that it does not cover can safely be ignored as irrelevant to the analysis. Finally, instead of using the evidence of the talk itself, he hypothesises about the reasons it takes the shape it does and seeks to confirm this by checking with the speakers involved, an analytical resource explicitly rejected as speculative by CA, which relies entirely on the recorded evidence.

What needs to be emphasised here is that the problem lies not so much in the project itself but in Stewart's characterisation of it as CA. If he had realised that two incompatible paradigms were at issue here, he would have been in a much better position to identify an appropriate tradition and assess his methodological options. It is with this in mind that the rest of this level is developed. At the end of it I return briefly to Stewart's project, seeing how he might have approached it in three very different ways, but we begin with a clarification of the nature of paradigms.

Paradigms

Although an interest in paradigms does not commit us to studying Kuhn's hugely influential work on the subject, *The Structure of Scientific Revolutions* (1962), it is as well to be familiar with the general position he develops there. Kuhn's interest in the ways in which scientific knowledge develops led him to challenge naïve assumptions about steady progress through the disinterested accumulation of theories and findings and to offer instead a context-dependent, historically situated picture in which change takes place through the breakdown of theories, methods and techniques in the face of challenges arising from problems or anomalies that they are unable to resolve. When this happens, new paradigms emerge as theories and methods cohere to form a new body of principles, ideas and practices that will inform approaches to research. There will be competing paradigms, each with its own ways of interpreting reality, each subject to growth and decay over time, and those working within the same paradigm will share the same beliefs and commitments, distinct from those characterising other paradigms – they will see and interpret the world in different ways.

The situation is complicated by the fact that Kuhn uses the term paradigm in over 20 different ways. Masterman (1970), who first noticed this, groups these under three broad headings: metaphysical (a world view), sociological (a concrete set of habits, models or universally accepted scientific achievement), and construct (instruments, tools, procedures, techniques for producing and collecting data). Fortunately, the term is predominantly used in the first sense, as in the following definition:

A paradigm may be viewed as a set of basic beliefs (or metaphysics) that deals with ultimates or first principles. It represents a world view that defines, for its holder, the nature of the 'world', the individual's place in it, and the range of possible relationships to that world and its parts, as, for example, cosmologies and theologies do. The beliefs are basic in the sense that they must be accepted simply on faith (however well argued); there is no way to establish their ultimate truthfulness. (Guba and Lincoln 1994:107)

The comparison with cosmologies and theologies is worth bearing in mind. Although it may be human nature to regard one's own position as the right one and everyone else's as misguided, it's possible to waste an awful lot of valuable energy on fruitless attempts to convert the unconvertible. We should certainly invest some effort in understanding our own belief system, but not in order to forge arguments that will swell the ranks of the faithful; the best way of convincing others of the value of our position is to produce research that demonstrates its worth, and this is where our efforts should lie. In fact, a leading writer on research methodology prefers to avoid introducing paradigmatic issues to new researchers, arguing that courses based on them 'actually provide a learned incapacity to go out and do research' (Silverman 2000a:85).

The focus in what follows, then, will be on the sorts of questions that we might ask about our research position and what the implications of these might be. Only when the issues here have been adequately aired will I move on to summarise three dominant research paradigms in the human sciences.

Ontology and epistemology

Any paradigmatic position can be represented in terms of these two intimately related aspects, which have to do with the nature of our beliefs about reality (ontology) and about knowledge (epistemology), beliefs that impinge not only on our research but on other aspects of our lives. Inevitably, when so much is at stake, debates tend to be vigorous and often involve quite fundamental questions about how the territory should be represented, so that any attempt to convey the situation impartially must somehow find a position between the safe ground of crude generalisation and a morass of subtle detail. My compromise is based on a sketch rooted in classroom experience, highlighting how beliefs and behaviour are related. It involves two very different teachers.

Two teachers, Kylie and Cecily

Kylie

Cecily

Kylie believes that there are laws governing language learning, many of which we have already understood, and she further contends that there are clear rules of behaviour that should be applied for the good of those involved. Her language classes are formal affairs, following established procedures and patterns, and with sufficient variety and good humour to make them popular with her students, though some find them a bit too regimented. They tend to be teacher-centred affairs, orchestrated by Kylie, who makes sure that she covers all the pedagogic points in her plan and provides plenty of teacher feedback and correction.

Cecily believes that we are making progress in our understanding of language learning, but that what matters most is the classroom context and relationships between the learner and the environment. She thinks it's a mistake to settle for straightforward answers and explanations; we have to work together towards understanding and need always to be aware of the importance of context. Her lessons are more informal and student-centred than those of Kylie, exploiting learning opportunities as they arise and sometimes taking risks in terms of what is explored. Students find them entertaining but some would prefer a clearer structure and more teacher input.

Teachers like Kylie and Cecily may never have given much thought to the philosophical roots of their ideas about teaching, but underlying their beliefs are two very different ontological positions. Ontology, literally the science or study of being, is concerned with the nature of reality and their stances might be expressed as follows:

Kylie believes that the world 'out there' is a very real one that can be studied and understood in order to identify the laws and rules that govern behaviour. Hers is a *realist* position.

Cecily's view is *relativist*, denying that there is any single reality independent of our ways of understanding it, and preferring instead to think in terms of various realities created by different individuals and groups at different times in different circumstances.

These contrasting views imply incompatible epistemological viewpoints. Epistemology, the science or study of knowledge, refers to the views we have about the nature of knowledge and the relationship between knower and known. Again, the two teachers take up very different positions:

From Kylie's *objectivist* perspective negotiated positions are unacceptable: because she believes that the truth is accessible, she would be remiss in her duty if she did not pass on her knowledge to her students.

Cecily adopts a *subjectivist* stance that sees knowledge as something created through interaction between the world and the individual, so we find her less willing than Kylie to take up dogmatic positions, preferring instead to build on local understandings.

So while it would be acceptable to say that Kylie has a transmission view of knowledge and teaching, while Cecily adopts a more exploratory approach, it is nevertheless true that underlying these are more fundamental beliefs about being and knowing. Such differences also underlie research positions.

Some extreme formulations

The descriptions above have drawn some very crude connections between belief and behaviour, when in fact the relationship is both subtle and complex. At the epistemological level there are broadly two extremes between which all positions are to be found: *objectivism* and *subjectivism*. Neither of these should be swallowed in their undiluted forms, which might facetiously be summed up as 'The Truth is out there' and 'The Truth is in here'. An extreme representation of objectivism would hold that all objects in the world exist apart from any consciousness and that they are essentially just as they are: the tree outside my window is the physical essence of treeness, the fact of which exists independently of any mind to apprehend it (and therefore in the absence of any concept of fact). A similar formulation for subjectivism would claim that no object exists apart from consciousness, that the so called 'external world' is not external at all but a mental construct: this table is no more than an idea (without a head to be in). These representations, like my cheap rebuttals, do not do justice to the complex and important philosophical issues associated with them, but I include them in this form because it is essential to recognise that these are extremes and not beliefs that we should unthinkingly attribute to positions we happen to disagree with – a mistake that is all too common. With this reservation firmly in mind, I offer Box 1.5 as a useful but very crude summary of the two positions I have outlined, including a third perspective that is also relevant to research: the *axiological,* that which is concerned with truth or worth.

Box 1.5 Two positions

	Position A	*Position B*
From an ontological perspective	It is possible to build up a coherent picture of the structure of an external world and the relationship between events within it.	The concept of reality is essentially a construction based on the interaction of the individual with the environment.
From an epistemological perspective	On the basis of such observation/ investigation it is possible to establish general truths and laws that are accessible to all and can inform action.	The exploration of this relationship enables us to understand the ways in which the world is interpreted and common understandings are constructed.
From an axiological perspective	These truths and the processes by which they are established are essentially value-free.	All truths, like all investigations and understandings, are value-laden.

Qualitative paradigms

The two basic positions we have so far established provide a relatively stable perspective on the tortuously complicated world of qualitative research paradigms. In what follows I adopt an approach that begins with the two main paradigms based on these positions, then shifts to a third position that rejects both:

- Position A: *(post-) positivism*
- Position B: *constructivism* (aka constructionism, interpretivism, or naturalism)
- Position C: *the critical perspective*

To give you an idea of how the overall arrangement fits in with others that have been offered and to provide you with a general sense of a terminologically fluid field, Box 1.6 summarises four other categorisations (equivalences across the table are approximate).

Box 1.6 Examples of paradigm divisions

Schubert 1989	Guba and Lincoln 1994	Rossman and Rallis 1998	Travers 2001
–	Positivism	Positivism	Positivism
Empirical/ Analytical	Post-positivism	–	–
Hermeneutic	Constructivism	Interpretivism	Interpretivism
Critical	Critical Theory	Radical objectivism	Realism
–	–	Radical subjectivism	Poststructualism

(Post-)positivism

In the previous section I made no distinction between the natural and the human/social sciences, but it is clearly the case that an approach that works in the natural world may be less successful in the social world. This explains why the only serious attempt ever to bring the two together, that of Auguste Comte in the early nineteenth century, proved ultimately unsuccessful. *Positivism* is based on the fairly naïve objectivist assumption that just as there is an objective world which is governed by laws discoverable by science alone, so there are social laws governing the relationships among individuals, institutions and society as a whole, as well as laws of historical development, and that these laws, once discovered, will not only explain the past and the present but enable us to predict future developments. 'Positivism', as Byrne (1998:37) pithily observed, 'is dead. By now it has gone off and is beginning to smell.' Unsurprisingly, it 'has become little more than a term of abuse' (Hammersley and Atkinson 1995:3), but despite this, and the fact that it has been replaced by post-positivism, some writers still feel the need to attack it.

Post-positivism is built on a recognition of the limitations of positivism and represents an attempt to come to terms with these. For example, while it assumes the existence of reality, it accepts that this can be only imperfectly understood, recognising that the researcher's background knowledge, theories and values will influence what is observed. Accepting that objectivity is a problematic concept, it aims for a probabilistic account of findings that will be acceptable to a critical community of researchers but always open to falsification. Those who defend the scientific case for post-positivism (see, for example, Phillips 1987, or, for a shorter account, Phillips 1990) have been concerned to point out what they regard as elementary misunderstandings of the position, though it is fair to say that this debate has now moved on. Some writers (for example, Guba and Lincoln 1994:10) have emphasised the importance of the 'critical community' from an epistemological perspective and 'critical multiplism' as a methodological position, which explains why critical realism is seen as fitting within this paradigm, though its own proponents see things differently:

> Post-positivist researchers can be viewed as recognizing, sometimes reluctantly, that the battle for positivism has been lost, but as still hankering after the mantle of respectability and authority that it conferred. It is argued below that they can find their salvation in critical realist approaches. (Robson 2002:27)

Constructivism

The fundamental tenet of this position is that reality is socially constructed, so the focus of research should be on an understanding of this construction and the multiple perspectives it implies. Actors are individuals with biographies, acting in particular circumstances at particular times and constructing meanings from events and interactions. An understanding of this develops interpretively as research proceeds, so the relationship between the researcher and the object of investigation is of fundamental importance:

> [Constructivists] share the goal of understanding the complex world of lived experience from the point of view of those who live it. This goal is variously spoken of as an abiding concern for the life world, for the emic point of view, for understanding meaning, for grasping the actor's definition of a situation, for *Verstehen*. The world of lived reality and situation-specific meanings that constitute the general object of investigation is thought to be constructed by social actors. That is, particular actors, in particular places, at particular times, fashion meaning out of events and phenomena through prolonged,

complex processes of social interaction involving history, language, and action. (Schwandt 1994a:118)

This is a view holding firmly to the position that knowledge and truth are created rather than discovered and that reality is pluralistic. Constructivists seek to understand not the essence of a real world but the richness of a world that is socially determined. Within this very broad compass there are numerous shades of thought and application, and some wish to draw distinctions between the terms constructivism, constructionism and interpretivism (for example, Crotty 1998), but the most interesting issues centre on what have been described as the crises of legitimation, authority and representation (for a discussion of these and an interesting discussion of different forms of representation, see Denzin 1997).

Meanings, postmodernists have argued, are equivocal, unstable moments in the ongoing process of interpretation, reflecting linguistically constituted subjectivities – the assumption of a self is problematic. They, like facts or theories, are constructs reflecting an ongoing power struggle centred on the definition of what counts as reality, and the representations of researchers are not neutral windows on the social world. 'Writing,' as Denzin (2000:256) points out, 'is not an innocent practice'. For the most part, these debates are part of the texture of constructivism itself, though some writers do recognise separate poststructuralist or radical subjectivist positions within the domain of qualitative inquiry. However, the rejection of constructivism and postpositivism has normally been realised through the adoption of an explicitly critical perspective, to which we will now turn.

Critical perspectives

This, again, embraces a range of positions, but all are united in rejecting the assumption that a social construction of reality is essentially unproblematic and that it is possible to adopt a neutral position with regard to its representation (Kincheloe and McLaren 2000). Researchers in this tradition are realists, but not in the sense that postpositivists would use the term. For the former, reality is a product of social and historical forces, an apprehendable construct that is taken for granted as though it were independent of and uninfluenced by the very factors that give it shape. For this very reason, actors will be unaware of their false consciousness and the researcher who reflects their understandings is simply reproducing the oppressive structures that have given rise to them.

The task of the critical analyst is therefore to lay bare such false understandings in order to open up the possibility of change. This demands the interrogation of precisely those things that constructivism takes for granted, penetrating underlying assumptions and value orientations in order to expose the power relationships that permeate social structures and interactions. Reality, from this perspective, might be described as essentially coercive, and the process of research must therefore be seen as transformative and emancipatory: the researcher and the researched stand in a dialogic relationship in which the former seeks to bring about a change in the consciousness of the latter that will facilitate action designed to redress the unequal and oppressive structures that have now been exposed. This is not a value-free enterprise, for facts themselves are value-laden and recognition of the injustice of current power relationships entails a commitment to intervene.

Those working within the critical paradigm seek not merely understanding but change, and research is part of a wider struggle for a just society free from oppression and inequality. Researchers must adopt a standpoint from which to critique current power structures, Marxism and feminism being two particularly prominent orientations, and the focus in research is often on marginalised groups. The global success of TESOL, arising as it does from the hegemony of the English language, offers rich grounds for the critical researcher (see, for example, Canagarajah 1993). However, of the three paradigms considered here, this is certainly the most dogmatic and probably the least well established. Its critics (for example, Widdowson 1995, 1996, 2000) argue that its arguments are shored up by selective representation motivated by an explicitly ideological stance, though there are signs that some researchers are seeking to broaden its scope (see, for example, Robson 2002; Porter 2002).

Different plots

This level closes with a brief consideration of the opening project, an ill-conceived foray into the supposed world of CA. It should be obvious now that the researcher had approached his project with positivist assumptions and failed to recognise that CA is located firmly within a constructivist paradigm. Had he seen this, he might have sought to develop a slightly different project, making use of the terminology of CA in respect of repair but not positioning his research within this tradition. He might instead have recast it as a case study, adopting a 'subtle realist' position (Hammersley 1992) and using triangulation (see Seale 1999a for a discussion of this technique from a paradigmatic perspective) to get a better fix on the way repair is handled in these teachers' classes. The recordings would have remained, though the teacher interviews would need to have been more carefully thought out, designed not for the purposes of checking his analysis but as a means of developing a better understanding of the classroom world and the participants' place in it. Observation and perhaps even teacher journals could also have contributed to the same end.

The constructivist and post-positivist paradigms are not the only ones in which the project might have been located. Classrooms offer a pre-eminent example of the unequal distribution of power and raise wider institutional and societal issues. Although the debate between conversation analysis and critical discourse analysis is a lively one (Schegloff 1997, 1998; Wetherell 1998; Billig and Schegloff 1999), the two approaches may in fact be complementary (van Dijk 1999) and there is an interesting study of classroom repair that brings the analytical precision of the former together with the broader concerns of the latter (Reynolds 1990).

The most important lesson to take from this brief discussion of options is that it began with the project and not with paradigmatic alignment. No researcher begins a project by deciding on a paradigm and working things out from this at increasing levels of detail. In this level I have argued the case for paradigmatic awareness, but this must be interpreted as an intellectual responsibility, not a procedural step. The extent to which we choose to engage in debate at the level of paradigm will depend on the sorts of issues raised by our research and perhaps also on our personal disposition.

Reading Guide

Although there are no general books covering the same territory as this chapter, anyone seriously interested in qualitative research in TESOL should try to track down the issue of *TESOL Quarterly* dedicated to this topic (1995:29/3). Papers by Davis (1995), Lazaraton (1995) and Peirce (1995) are particularly relevant. The relevance of ethnography to our work is also covered in a useful introduction by Watson-Gegeo (1988).

Level 1

For an excellent brief overview of different views of qualitative research, see Silverman 1993:23–9. If you don't think my brief introduction has allowed you to get a fix on the territory, these additional perspectives should do the trick.

Chapter 1 of Rossman and Rallis 1998 provides a slightly different perspective on the process from the one I've adopted. Included in their chapter is a discussion of different uses of research and an interesting section on 'habits of mind and heart'.

If you'd like to read a short example of a qualitative research written by someone with extensive experience in the field, Wolcott 1994:261–86 ('The teacher as an enemy') offers a very enjoyable and accessible account. The example itself includes a useful preface that highlights some of the issues raised by the paper. Wolcott's very readable style makes the whole process seems deceptively easy, but it's good to finish a paper thinking that this sort of research is within reach.

Level 2

Overviews

If you're the sort of person who likes to get to grips with a meaty diagram, Miles and Huberman (1994:6–7) offer a couple of excellent examples. The book itself, though, is relatively heavy going.

Cresswell (1998) offers an excellent introduction to five important traditions (biography, phenomenology, grounded theory, ethnography and case study), providing clear descriptions, examples, summaries and recommendations for further reading. If you want to develop a solid understanding of the range of approaches involved, there is probably no better starting point (see Study strategy 1.1).

Another approach would be to start from a particular perspective and explore the relationship between this and related traditions. If this appeals to you, the papers on symbolic interactionism, ethnomethodology, phenomenology, grounded theory, the ethnography of communication and life stories in Atkinson *et al.*'s (2001) handbook of ethnography provide a heavy but rewarding set.

Study strategy 1.1   Compare and contrast

Read Cresswell's book with a view to identifying how these different approaches relate. Then study the diagrams in Miles and Huberman and try to make sense of the thinking underlying them. How do they differ and why? Where do Cresswell's five traditions fit in and what does the surrounding territory look like? Which approach to classification appeals most strongly to you? If you have a project in mind, does this help you form a better understanding of the contribution it might make? Would any of the other traditions offer a reasonable alternative?

> (If your tradition is not in Cresswell, include one of the texts below in your preliminary reading, then follow the same procedure for the diagrams.)

Particular traditions

The following list, which includes interaction-centred traditions omitted from my general overview, is based on the assumption that most people would wish to begin with a book providing a sound practical introduction to the tradition and one which is enjoyable to read. Where possible, I've limited my choice to one, but in many cases it has been necessary to add others. (For those who would prefer briefer introductions, one or two key papers or chapters are included in brackets at the end of the recommendation.)

Life history: Goodson (1992) provides a entertaining collection of papers prefaced by an enthusiastic case for this sort of research. (For a brief introduction, try Huberman 1989, or any of the papers in the 1989 (13/4) special issue of the *International Journal of Educational Research* on 'Research on Teachers' Professional Lives'.)

Phenomenology: there's no shortage of books on the philosophical roots of this tradition, but van Manen's (1990) is a researcher's account and the more readable for that.

Ethnography: Hammersley and Atkinson (1995) is still probably the best general introduction, and if you want a very different perspective and a sense of just how wide the tradition is, you could also try Denzin (1997). (Travers 2001, Chapter 2, provides a useful historical summary of symbolic interactionism.)

Grounded theory: this has become a very contentious area, but Dey (1999) offers a detailed and balanced account with plenty of practical advice. An update jointly written by one of the original founders of the approach also offers plenty of guidance on procedures (Strauss and Corbin 1998). Glaser (1993) is a collection of brief research projects within this tradition, but the absence of anything relating to our field limits its appeal.

Case study: for practical issues, both Yin (1994) and Stake (1995) are useful, though Bassey (1999) has a more educational orientation, with examples. If you want to dig into the research issues, though, the collection by Gomm *et al.* (2000a) offers both breadth and depth, and the annotated bibliography at the end is very valuable.

Action research: for a sample of cases in TESOL, you can do no better than Edge (2001a), which also benefits from an excellent opening paper by the editor. Reason and Bradbury (2001) is a substantial collection, while a recent paper by Christenson *et al.* (2001) describes a particular project in the context of a useful discussion of action research (and excellent references).

Conversation analysis: Ten Have's introduction (1999) to *Conversation Analysis* provides an excellent starting point for anyone wishing to get to grips with the basic conceptual and practical issues. For a discussion of some of the historical context and main themes with some good practical examples, you could also try Hutchby and Wooffitt (1998), while Silverman's study of the work of Harvey Sacks (1998) provides a very clear introduction to the roots of the tradition. This also includes a useful discussion of Membership Categorisation Analysis, which can be followed up in Hester and Eglin (1997).

Interaction-centred approaches: for a general introduction that takes account of the social dimension, Cameron (2001) offers a serious but accessible entry to the field, while Schiffrin's *Approaches to Discourse* (1994) is rich in examples.

The best single introduction to the ethnography of communication is still Saville-Troike (1989), which contains some useful examples of the analysis of speech events. (Her briefer introduction (1996) has the advantage of appearing in the context of a collection of papers with a TESOL/TESL orientation, but it lacks the examples.)

A related but non-comparative approach is *Ethnographic Microanalysis*, developed by Frederick Erickson (1992, 1996) and relying primarily on audio and video recordings as data sources. This offers an alternative approach for anyone with a particular interest in social situations and 'the immediate ecology of relations among participants as they interact in communicative situations' (Erickson 1996:284).

Level 3

There is no single overview that does justice to this complex field (see Study strategy 1.2), though Guba (1990) offers at least a genuine flavour of the debate for those who are interested (although some of the positions are now a little dated). A list of the key texts follows.

Study strategy 1.2 Reading around a subject

One way of getting a sense of the ways different writers approach this territory is to read different accounts from those who are attempting to summarise the various positions involved. As well as firming up your grasp at the conceptual level and introducing you to many different ways of cutting an extremely rich cake, this should also give you a sense of how writers establish their own perspective on the decision-making in the research process, usually implicitly but sometimes overtly. The list below selects succinct summaries (together amounting to just under 100 pages) that offer an interesting range of positions.

Schubert 1989:27–32	A bit dated, but it's written from an educational perspective, offers a couple of new angles and covers a lot of territory in a short space.
Guba and Lincoln 1994:105–17	A key position paper, comparatively summarising the four central paradigms across different dimensions.
Crotty 1998:2–17	A different perspective, moving from epistemology, through theoretical perspectives, to methodology and methods. Also gets to grips with key issues.
Rossman and Rallis 1998:26–43	Based on an earlier typology (Burrell and Morgan 1979), this offers a description in terms of different continua. Distinctively different.
May 2001:8–17	Brief, mainstream summaries of a range of positions, drawing on one or two unusual sources.
Travers 2001:6–12	A very succinct summary of the main bones of contention with some useful references to illustrative studies.

Robson 2002:16–44   Useful because it develops the case for critical realism, though at times it nails its colours pretty aggressively to the mast.

For a different perspective eschewing paradigms, try Silverman (either 1993:20–9, or 2000:75–87), and for a very readable collection of personal intellectual journeys towards the interpretivist perspective see Heshusius and Ballard (1996) (see also Study strategy 1.3).

Study strategy 1.3   A hierarchical approach to reading

An alternative approach to the field would be to select the paradigm that most closely reflects your own beliefs and read an authoritative summary of it. Having done this, you should do the same for the remaining three paradigms in order to orient yourself in terms of alternative views. If this is your preferred option, the following will provide starting points: Phillips 1990 (post-positivism), Schwandt 1994a (constructivism), Kincheloe and McLaren 2000 (Critical Theory).

2
Interviewing

Preview

> Interviewing is rather like marriage: everybody knows what it is, an awful lot of people do it, and yet behind each closed door there is a world of secrets.
>
> Oakley 1981:41

Since Oakley drew this slightly provocative comparison, interviews have become something of a public spectacle. We live in a world where Warhol's fifteen minutes of fame has become almost a fact of life, where interviewers' sights have extended beyond politicians and celebrities and into the private lives of those in the next street. It is a world where reputations are ruined by a phrase taken out of context and where private motivations are made the subject of explicit attention and public critique. Hardly surprising, then, that Oakley's world of secrets is now also a world of dark suspicions.

Despite these changes in the public perception of interviews, there is no sign that the research interview is falling out of favour, as the following pair of widely separated claims make clear:

> Modern sociology is 'the science of the interview'. (Benney and Hughes 1956)

> In-depth interviewing is the hallmark of qualitative research. (Rossman and Rallis, 1998:124)

Silverman's suspicion that 'the choice of the open-ended interview as the gold-standard of qualitative research is pretty widely spread'

47

(2000a:291) is therefore probably not far wide of the mark. However, the challenges facing the interviewer now, in terms of both data collection and data analysis, are probably greater than ever before. This chapter introduces you to different sorts of interviews and to the practicalities of using these in order to collect data. It will involve some discussion of transcription and analysis, although the former is dealt with in more depth in the Chapter 4, while Chapter 6 describes procedures for analysis. It will also crudely divide interviews into unstructured and semi-structured, ignoring the sort of tightly structured interview that has at best a rare place in qualitative research.

Level 1   will focus on the basic skills of open interviewing. It introduces different sorts of questions and summarises basic rules for effective interviewer responses. It also suggests ways in which you can structure your questioning in order to allow interviews to develop naturally, and it concludes by identifying a straightforward approach to evaluating your performance as an interviewer.

Level 2   introduces more formal and more tightly structured approaches to interviewing. It explains how to prepare for and set up a formal interview, and how to develop an interview guide, including how to link research questions to interview questions. It also looks briefly at elicitation techniques, building on the foundations established at Level 1.

Level 3   addresses more problematic aspects of qualitative interviewing and shows you how to deal with some of the thornier problems of analysis, developing a four-level model that serves as a basis for improving interview technique as well as informing analysis. It also pays particular attention to the ways in which interviews are constructed by both the participants and proposes an approach to analysis that takes account of this.

Level 1: learning how to listen

Introduction

I started this chapter by describing the outcomes of interviews in fairly unflattering terms, but I have no cause to regret the part they have played in my life. For example, I have audiotapes of my children when they were young that still delight me, though in coaxing them to talk I was unashamedly putting into practice some of the techniques I'd developed through interviewing. On a more professional level, there are ways of understanding and of sharing with our colleagues that the skills of interviewing will open up to us.

At this level I'll be mainly concerned with passing on some of these skills, because interviewing isn't just a matter of finding the right people to talk to and asking them the right questions. We also need to be aware that, in the words of Atkinson and Silverman (1997), we live in an 'interview society', where techniques of self-presentation are becoming second nature. Interviews are part of our lives and the research interview is just one among many types. Consider, for example, some of those you may have encountered in your profession so far: job interview, appraisal interview, lesson observation feedback interview, student placement interview and so on.

To get a sense of the subtleties of interactional negotiation in interviews, consider Extract 2.1. What does this tiny exchange tell us about relationship of the participants and the activity in which they are engaged?

Extract 2.1   Careful where you breathe

Shortly before the UK general election in 1997, I listened to a radio interview between the then prime minister and James Naughtie, an experienced political interviewer, in which the following exchange occurred as the PM was speaking:

JN: (Audible intake of breath.)
PM: Please don't interrupt me.
JN: I didn't interrupt you.
PM: No, but you were going to.

On a very basic level we can note our sensitivity in talk to the implications of even the most minor contribution, and we can also say that the speaker here considers that his turn (in response to an earlier question) is not yet complete when the intake of breath is heard. We all know that it's rude to interrupt, and this is the social rule that the PM explicitly invokes. But this is no politely cooperative engagement: when the interviewer denies the validity of the request, the speaker draws attention to the intake of breath that indicates someone is about to speak. These interviews are sophisticated affairs which politicians are trained to handle, and one of the most basic techniques involves keeping the floor by replacing falling intonation (a sign that a turn is at an end) with continuing contours. Sooner or later the interviewer will have to try to ask a question, but this will now seem like an interruption. Here the interviewee scores his point even before the interruption happens!

The point of this game is not a trivial one: these interviews are directed to a listening audience, and if you can portray the other person as rude *and* keep to the line you want to deliver, you'll emerge smelling of roses. It's all very competitive, there's a lot at stake and the arena is often bloody.

Of course, qualitative interviews aren't like this, but we live in a world where broadcast interviews of this kind are common, where people's ordinary lives are laid bare for public dissection and where they are damned on the basis of a single careless utterance 'taken out of context.' Researchers have become more aware of this wider context and of the extent to which the interview is no mere question and answer routine – it is an interactional event.

The qualitative interview

In TESOL we live in the professional world of interactional events, so this should come as no shock to our system, but if we are interviewing teachers we are also dealing with linguistically sophisticated people. In order to understand the implications of this for our research, we do need to clear away once and for all the natural assumption that the interview is simply a matter of gathering facts. Of course it can be used for that, but in qualitative inquiry we need to go deeper, to pursue understanding in all its complex, elusive and shifting forms; and to achieve this we need to establish a relationship with people that enables us to share in their perception of the world.

A popular way of capturing the essence of the qualitative interview is to describe it in terms of everyday interaction, as 'conversation with a purpose' (Burgess 1984b:102) or 'professional conversation' (Kvale 1996:5), and that's how I'll approach it here. But it is a very special sort of conversation, as we can see if we compare the way that we use listening in ordinary conversation and in interviews. In the former we listen in order to participate, in order to find the right thing to say so as to either encourage the speaker to continue or find ways of bringing our own points into the talk. In interviews we are concerned only with encouraging the speaker, not with putting our own point across, so the skills we need are still collaborative but they are focused on drawing from the speaker the richest and fullest account possible.

Silverman has drawn a very useful distinction between the 'interview-as-technique' and the 'interview-as-local-accomplishment' (1993:104). In this level I will concentrate largely on technique, leaving the analytical implications of the interview-as-local-accomplishment until Level 3. However, your own development as an interviewer will be affected by the extent to which you are prepared to listen carefully to your own interviews and develop a sensitivity to the interactional and relational dimension illustrated in the short exchange in Extract 2.1, above. The key to this is open-minded listening and a willingness to be self-critical, so that your ear for what is happening develops along with your awareness of the part you can play in the interview event. Kvale captures the relationship well when he insists that interviewing is a craft, but one that rests in the researcher's judgement rather than following 'content- and context-free rules of method' (1996:105).

Interview types

It is as well at the start to dispense with the notion that we can simply package up interviews as either directive or non-directive. There is a difference between those following a specific agenda, where the interviewer controls the development of the interview, and those which are allowed to develop more naturally, but in both cases the interviewer is aiming to elicit information and must design responses with this in mind. In fact, there is no such thing as a completely 'non-directive' interview:

> 'Non-directive' interviews are anything but non-directive. What one person will say to another depends on what he or she assumes the other is 'up to' in the situation. If the respondents have no clear idea of what the researchers' interests and intentions are, they are less likely to feel unconstrained than constrained by the need to put energy into guessing what these are. (Jones 1985a:47–8)

There is, however, a useful distinction between formal and informal interviews. Some interviews are formally arranged in advance and all parties understand what is taking place, but others arise in the context of the sort of observation described in the next chapter. When we observe, and listen, we don't shut ourselves off from what is happening around us, and in the course of our work there will be plenty of opportunities to talk with the people we encounter. Whether or not such talk could be described as interviews really doesn't matter too much because it's all part of data gathering and susceptible to the sort of skills we'll explore in this section. If a distinction has to be drawn, we could say that talk becomes an interview when the researcher designs their contribution to elicit responses focused on a particular topic, but experienced researchers recognise that such things are rarely cut and dried:

> As a participant observer, most of your interviewing will be done informally, simply listening to what people are saying and sometimes

asking them to explain how they feel about the situation they are describing. (Whyte 1997:25)

I believe that this relatively grey area offers exceptional opportunities in terms of skill development and I've designed this level on the assumption that it's best not to set up a formal interview before you've developed basic interview skills through more informal interaction. If you disagree with this, it might be better to study the section on The Formal Interview in Level 2 before reading about techniques; otherwise I recommend the approach outlined in Box 2.1.

Box 2.1 Developing interviewing skills

1. Decide on a fairly general topic that interests you and for which those around you (e.g. friends, colleagues, family members) can provide information. Obvious examples would be career trajectories, biographical details, views of their work.
2. Decide who you would like to 'interview' and what the likely settings would be.
3. Find ways of introducing this topic into conversations and try to elicit as much information as you can. Reflect on the strategies you use to do this.
4. Don't worry if you find this too difficult or too awkward, or you're unable to find the right opportunities – it's much more challenging than it seems. In this case you can either broaden your range of interests (which will make your efforts socially less obvious), or announce an interest in the topic that will explain your willingness to pursue it.
5. Study the section on interview skills and gradually introduce these into your talk, reflecting after each interaction on the nature of your contributions and the effects of these.

Important note
Because this is the sort of thing people do anyway, it does not raise any specific ethical research issues *provided you do not treat it as research.* This means that you should approach it as a matter of seizing opportunities where they arise and treating what emerges from them as you would any ordinary conversation, i.e. you should not take notes or make any other recordings of the event.

Interview techniques

Fortunately, interviewing is one of the methods of data collection where it is possible to develop specific skills that will improve your performance and where practice adds polish, provided it is followed by proper reflection. The advice offered here applies to any interviewing whether highly structured or not, but it is particularly valuable in a fairly open approach. If you feel that some of it is best reserved for formal interviews, set this aside until you are ready to arrange these – let your development here be as natural and comfortable as you can make it. There is, in fact, a golden rule for all interviewing: *Always seek the particular.*

In ordinary conversation we don't expect too much precision – if I ask you when you last saw Ted I'm expecting something along the lines of 'a few weeks back' and not 'at two-thirty on Friday 3rd May' – but a good interview is rich in detail and this means we have to encourage the interviewee to provide responses that are slightly different from the norm. This means, for example, that we may have to focus specifically on events, letting attitudes and beliefs emerge from this context (Whyte 1984:102).

Listening: a good interviewer is a good listener; if you don't get this right you may as well take your best questions and shout them into the wind. Sustained listening is not easy, and at least one experienced researcher (Wengraf 2001) has underlined how challenging it can be. For one thing, there are natural distractions arising from the task in hand (How does this fit in? What's the next move? and so on), but there's also the effort involved in focusing attentively on extended accounts while also monitoring the fact that you are visibly doing this.

An exercise suggested by Edge (2002:44–5) illustrates the power of attention. Two people think of an experience that really matters to them (Edge suggests a teacher they remember well) and prepare to talk about it for a few minutes. A describes this while B shows complete indifference, making no response at all. They change roles, but this time when B tells the story A will show full attention, responding as though it's one of the most interesting things they've ever heard. Finally, the participants compare what emerged in the two cases and how the speakers felt.

Box 2.2 provides you with a list of things to bear in mind when responding in the interview, but the best way of making progress is to reflect on where your particular areas of weakness are and work on eliminating these. If you're interested in working on your skills as a listener, the best treatment I know is Edge (2002), which also provides an original and very powerful framework for shared professional development. Otherwise, simply take advantage of the fact that you can practice the skills of good listening more or less anywhere, at any time.

Box 2.2 Interview respones: some do's and don't's

Do:	*Don't*:
Listen carefully (e.g. non-verbally say, 'I'm listening')	Close off interviewee space
Offer supportive feedback (e.g. 'hmm', 'yes')	Interpret for the interviewee
Respond to emotion (give interviewee chance to talk about it)	Judge (e.g. offer moral comment, advice or consolation)
Let the interview take its own shape – let interviewee discover things as well	Stick rigidly to the topics you think are important
Monitor your responses to give interviewee proper space	Interrupt unthinkingly

---

Prompting: There are no hard and fast rules about what sort of questions you should ask because so much depends on the purpose of the interview and the way the interviewee is responding, but it is possible to refine your questioning technique. As you may have predicted, open questions are generally much more effective than closed ones, though the latter may sometimes be necessary (e.g. for checking). A good interview will negotiate the territory between the Scylla of unfocused rambling produced by too many general or abstract questions, and the Charybdis of mere accumulated detail arising from an excess of Wh-questions requiring specific detail.

As a means of charting a safe passage through these deceptive waters, I offer a synthesis of two partly overlapping approaches, one based on question types and the other on degrees of directiveness. First, though, decide how you would categorise the question types in this edited extract from an interview with a secretary from one of my research sites (Extract 2.2), where I am particularly interested in finding out about interaction routines.

Extract 2.2 What's your morning routine?

```
01  IR:  I wonder if you could just talk me through what you
02       do when you go into the office in the morning, your
         routine.
03  IE:  Er my usual routine is that I check the answerphone
04       first of all
05  IR:  Uhuh
06  IE:  to see if any messages have been left on that ... open the
07       filing cabinets and
08  IR:  You unlock the filing cabinets
09  IE:  I unlock the filing cabinets
10  IR:  Right
11  IE:  Yeah. Then I open up the post that's arrived at our end
12  IR:  You say 'your end'. Was that- How many ends, how
13       many destinations
14  IE:  By that I mean that ... [Moves on to interactions while
15       taking the post round] ... Might have a little chat or
16       I might, if they look as though they're really kind
         of stuck
17       into something straight away then I'll just kind of
18  IR:  When you say you'll have a little chat, I mean, you'll
19       institute that will you, or
20  IE:  Er er, it de_pends really. Sometimes [Exchanges on nature
21       of talk continue] ... if there's maybe something particular
22       that I want to talk about I will- I will let them know that
23  IR:  Uhuh
24  IE:  and ask when it will be convenient for me to see them.
25  IR:  Right. So effectively you're signalling that things are
26       important but they're picking the time for the talk.
27  IE:  Yeah, that's it exactly. Yeah and if ...
28       [Exchanges on subject of talk continue.]
29  IR:  If we could go back a bit and talk a bit more about the
30       relationship between you are and the other
         section.
```

NB: for a note on transcription symbols, see pp. 181–4.

One way of approaching an interview is to consider the different types of question you might need to ask and the contribution these can make to eliciting the sort of information you require. The following represent the main question types.

1. Opening: In a formal interview it's often a good idea to begin by inviting a fairly lengthy response. Spradley (1979) describes this as a 'grand tour' approach (e.g. 'Talk me through that lesson'), as distinct from a 'mini-tour' ('Can you explain what you understand by 'boardwork'?). This often provides a natural springboard for further questions, which fall into the following three types [for example, Extract 2.2:01–2].

2. Check/reflect: If you're in any doubt about whether you've understood something, it's always worth checking this or reflecting a statement back to the speaker. This may also prompt the speaker to develop a point further – though it does not have that effect in this particular extract [Extract 2.2:08–9].

3. Follow-up: When the speaker has raised something or perhaps given a subtle indication that there is more to be discovered on this topic, the interviewer may decide to follow it up (perhaps in a later interview if the point emerges only when the tape or transcript is studied). Sometimes simple encouragement to continue will suffice, but it may be necessary to explicitly invite the speaker to expand and to pursue this invitation if necessary [Extract 2.2:12–13].

4. Probe: Inevitably, points will emerge during the interview that demand more careful excavation and here the interviewer will need to probe specific elements in order to build up a satisfactory picture. The most straightforward method is by direct invitation to add more detail, or through the use of directed questions. You can use Wh-questions, but too many of these produce a staccato effect in the interview and can cast it in too interrogatory a light. It's useful to think in terms of 'event' questions designed to elicit chronologies, relationships, reactions, and so on, and 'perspective' questions, which invite explanation and interpretation [Extract 2.2:18–19].

Sometimes it may be necessary to establish how the interviewee sees the world and how they structure their understanding of it, something which will involve more careful questioning designed to elicit from the speaker categorisations or rankings.

Indirect probes can be very useful, especially where topics are sensitive. Questions like 'What do people think about X?' can be even more revealing than 'What do you think about X?' and hypothetical formulations such as 'If you were principal, what would you do if...' reduce the element of personal challenge. Setting up contrasts and inviting comments on these can also be very effective.

5. Structuring: Finally, in a formal interview, it may be necessary to mark a shift of topic by using structuring moves such as, 'Can we move on to . . .'. Sometimes this will prompt an interviewee to add extra points while it is still appropriate to do so, something that is less easy to do if topics move in a series of small, natural steps (Jefferson 1984) from one to another [Extract 2.2:29–30].

The main question types are summarised in Box 2.3. Another way of looking at the development of an interview is to consider it in terms of the extent to which the interviewer is directive. Whyte (1984:99–100) offers very useful advice on the degrees of directiveness available in the research interview and the following list uses his categorisation. The options are arranged in order of increasing directiveness, with the first point representing the lowest degree of directiveness.

1. 'Uh-huh', nod of head, etc: Responses like this encourage the informant to continue without directing the form of the response in any way.

2. Reflection: This simply reflects the informant's words back to them. It involves a slight degree of directiveness because the repetition encourages the speaker to expand on the reflected utterance.

3. Probe the informant's last remark: In this, instead of simply reflecting the statement back to the informant, the interviewer responds to the statement

---

Box 2.3 Interview question types

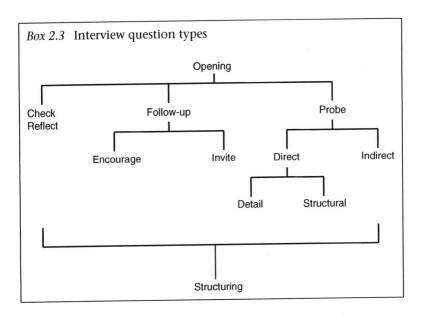

with a comment or question (for example, 'When you say you thought the teacher was wrong, was this because you think that sort of thing is always wrong or because it worked out badly in this particular case?').

4. Probe an idea in preceding turn: The interviewer probes an idea preceding the final remark but within the informant's prior statement (for example, 'You said the student's response was arrogant. What do you mean by that?').

5. Probe an idea introduced earlier: The interviewer picks up an idea from earlier in the interview (for example, 'Earlier on, you said that you thought that a sense of humour was important. Where do you think you should draw the line?').

6. Introduction of a new topic: Here the interviewer introduces a topic that has not been referred to before.

The combination of these two approaches, outlined above and summarised in Box 2.4, provides a rich source of options that you can explore in your own interviewing. A good interview, though, doesn't rest simply on the mastery of a range of different techniques, it calls for a sensitivity on the part of the interviewer that can be developed only through time and honest self-evaluation.

Box 2.4   A summary of interview prompts

Questions can be divided into those which help to maintain the flow of talk (interactional) and those which help structure the information elicited in the interview (structural).

Interactional	Structural	(leads to)	Feature
Uh-uh	Opening	⇒	Point of entry (Grand Tour)
Check	Following up	⇒	Expansion
Reflect	Probing	⇒	More detail, perspective, views
	Structuring	⇒	Next topic

Evaluating the interview

As with the development of all skills, practice is important, but without the element of evaluation there is always the risk of simply repeating old mistakes to the point of fossilisation. The best way of examining your work is to transcribe sections from the interview, but this takes up a great deal of time that you may not wish to spend. Listening to extracts is quicker and the next best option, but you'll need to press on through the embarrassment that listening to our own verbal perform-ance usually generates.

If time doesn't allow sufficient opportunity to pursue these options, even a few minutes' reflection on the interview while it is fresh in your mind will help you to spot strengths and weaknesses – though this is no substitute for listening. Box 2.5 suggests an approach to this.

Box 2.5   A guide to interview evaluation

Overall
- What was the balance of talk?
- Could you have talked less?
- If you take out your contributions does the resulting account flow naturally?
- Was it rich in detail?

Sections
- Were there any staccato sections?
- What prompted these? (Wh-questions?)
- What other strategies could you have used?
- Were the transitions natural?
- Did you close down topics early?
- Was there a sense of shared progress?

Turns
- Did you use a range of responses?
- Where might you have followed up or probed?
- Which were the most/least successful questions and why?
- Did you close down any responses too early?
- Were you too directive?

Action
- Identify at least one, preferably two or three, things that you will bear in mind in your next interview.
- Write them down and use them in the evaluation of that interview.

As you become more experienced as an interviewer, you will also develop a sense of how things are unfolding, a sort of sixth sense that will enable you to monitor what's happening while also giving full attention to the business in hand. You'll also develop a feeling for the authenticity of responses. Of course, there are some things you can check against other evidence, perhaps from other interviews or your own observation, but confirming the truth or otherwise of what you hear is never as simple as this.

There's no straightforward formula for determining accuracy because we are all at the mercy of our imperfect memories and sometimes these can even take us to the heart of events we have never known first hand. This is often a matter of human psychology rather than bad faith, but from the point of view of the interview that makes no difference. Which of these two accounts, transcribed from interviews in Part 3 of the 1964 BBC series 'The Great War', strikes you as the more convincing?

Extract 2.3   A personal experience? (A)

On Thursday the 28th of August the Z entered X. It was a marvellous sunny day but still I keep the vision of grey, grey all over the town. They arrived in long, long streams, long grey streams. It was a sinister greenish grey. Even the helmets had a grey cover. They went along in the main street of X with their equipment, with all their war material, heavy guns, their officers on horseback. And their music, that music of drum and fife, and always the same little tune.

Extract 2.4   A personal experience? (B)

We entered the village, a company of approximately two hundred men. And we were just taking off our knapsack and queuing up for the soup kitchen who wanted to give us some food when a terrific firing started. From all sides we were fired at. The cook and his mate were killed. Quite a number of our soldiers were wounded and killed, too. We stormed the houses where the firing came from but all we could find were some innocent looking peasants in blue blouses. But when we searched the houses we found infantry rifles still hot from firing.

Before giving my own views, I should emphasise that I don't know which of these is a genuine first-hand account. Both were presented as such and I am sure that both speakers gave honest accounts. I am equally prepared to believe that the incidents – or something like them – actually happened.

For me, the first has the flavour of direct experience. I know that the presentation is more poetic, less matter of fact, than that of the second, but this is a matter of personal style. Of course, if the story involved a noticeable style shift that would be a different matter, but these extracts came with no broader context against which to judge them. When people experience something they tend to seize on particular details, even to the point of distorting their account, and this is what we have in Extract 2.3. The woman reporting dwells on the overwhelming sense of greyness on a sunny day, something that must have struck her powerfully as a young woman. In fact, we learn little else about the soldiers, though she notes the small detail of the helmet covers. Notice, too, that when she refers to the music there is the telling detail of 'always the same tune'. These striking particulars are what make this account convincing for me.

Extract 2.4 is very different. We have facts: the number of men, the shooting of the cook and his mate, the blue blouses, and so on. But these are very general descriptions, none of them idiosyncratic. There is no distortion of perspective, no striking and unusual image, everything is in the form of a story that can be passed on. Actions are therefore broadly summed up ('we stormed the houses') and some of the facts are almost clichés: the firing 'from all sides', the innocent peasants, the rifles, 'hot from firing'. Stories like this were part of a propaganda war waged by both sides, and what happened to part of your regiment in the next village belongs in part to you. I think this was his story, but the 'we' is a very broad one that does not extend in this case to shared action.

Conclusion

I suggested at the start of this level that the skills of good interviewing can be applied naturally in a number of different contexts, but from a research point of view they are particularly effective when applied along with the sort of observation introduced in the next chapter. In fact, Hammersley and Atkinson (1995:141) claim that participant observation and the interview are in many ways very similar. For example, in both we have to take account of context and we need to work to build and maintain rapport.

It will hardly surprise you to find that I agree with this position and think that it makes good sense to work on observation and interviewing in tandem. In fact, in the case below I'll illustrate how a failure to pay sufficient attention to interviewing produced a distorted interpretation of a teaching situation. However, the relationship between these two methods of data collection is not simply a matter of checking interview 'facts' against our own observations, or confirming our own insights with statements from the actors themselves. If we truly seek to understand better the professional world we inhabit, we need to be sensitive to all aspects of the ways in which it presents itself to us, and aware of our place within it.

Case 2.1: the missing dimension

This is a simple story that is little to my credit as a researcher, but I owe it the telling. Some dozen years or more back, I came into possession of a wonderful videotaped extract of classroom teaching from an institution that I had visited. With the permission of the teacher involved, I used it around the world (and finally at an international conference in his presence) to confound the notion that we can easily judge another's teaching. For the extract evoked passionate, even indignant responses as audiences watched a domineering teacher harassing and apparently humiliating a luckless student who was unable to provide him with the required answers. On the surface it seemed a prime example of authoritarian teaching, a very model of pointless persecution.

However, things were not as they seemed, and there were plenty of clues pointing to this: he was popular with students and colleagues, regarded as a successful teacher and even promoted to a senior post. So how could I account for this lesson? An interview with the teacher concerned provided the context I needed. 'I'm not a teacher', he said when asked about how he saw himself in the institution, 'I'm a social worker'. I seized on this comment and developed my questioning in the light of it.

The students were military cadets, depending on this job for a lifetime's income that would support their extended families and facing the prospect of unemployment if they failed at the end of their training. In fact, the only examination they absolutely had to pass was an English language one, even though most of them would never be called upon ever to use the language. They had only three chances to pass a very basic test that boiled down to learning the contents of a set vocabulary list and performing a few basic transformations, and most of them soon mastered the necessary knowledge and skills. Others would learn as the English course progressed, until towards the end there would be just one or two left struggling at the limits of their competence. These were the ones he concentrated on. His job was not to teach English but to get them through the exam for the sake of their futures.

But why the authoritarian approach? Were there not other ways? Not with a window in the classroom door inviting the attention of passing officers who would not hesitate to punish any recruit seen presenting himself with other than military bearing. The cadets were tired at the end of a day that had begun at 4 am and were disposed to nod off – a serious breach of military discipline. Above all, then, he must keep them awake, and an energetic, badgering, authoritarian approach, peppered with simple jokes, would serve this end. Here was teaching, then, that responded perfectly to circumstances, and a good illustration of the dangers of passing judgement on the basis of a snapshot, however bold the colours.

Unfortunately, my attention had been so distracted by his initial comment about being a social worker that I had allowed this aspect to dominate the interview. Nothing he had told me was inaccurate or exaggerated, so I presented him as a teacher responding to circumstances simply because this is what circumstances demanded. I had not gone on to probe more deeply into his views of teaching and his perception of himself. Many years later, in another country entirely, I had the chance to do this and in exploring his career history I discovered that the approach I had assumed to be imposed on him against his natural inclinations was in fact consonant with these. He taught like this not only because he had to but because this was how he *liked* to teach. It certainly didn't mean he was a bad teacher, far from it – I have observed his work and have the greatest respect for it – but it did add an important perspective to a picture I had mistakenly represented as complete.

I close this level, then, with a reminder of how much can be missed when the interviewer loses themselves, however innocently, in a particular view of reality. Extract 2.5 provides a clear example of what my later interview revealed.

Extract 2.5   Fundamental beliefs

IE: Most of my experience as a professional teacher – my *formative* experience as a professional teacher – was in tough schools where you had to be- to be heard. There are certain types of teaching (2.0) I don't feel comfortable with (1.0) and I can't do. (1.5) For example, (1.5) I don't know whether this marks me down as the egotist of all time, but I like a quiet classroom, and if I talk you listen. And if you talk, I listen. That to me is elementary good manners and it's elementary behaviour in the classroom. I cannot stand being in a room where nine million different things are happening all at once because I can't concentrate on it and I can't monitor individuals' performances within that classroom. So I am a very traditional teacher. I have *tried* to do it other ways, I ain't comfortable with it and at my age I ain't gonna change.

Level 2: issues of structure

The focus in Level 1 was on the open or unstructured interview, something which can provide the possibility of deep insights into someone else's understanding of their world. But when we need to explore particular lines of inquiry or find out how different people view the same things, a more structured approach may be called for:

A disadvantage in relying solely upon the results of open-ended interviews is that this makes it difficult for the researcher to make reasonable and valid comparisons across informants. To make comparisons across people and to summarize the results in a meaningful way, the researcher must ask all informants the same questions. (Johnson and Weller 2002:499)

In this level, the nature of the semi-structured interview is considered, first from the point of view of structure itself, then with two specific practical aspects in mind: procedures for setting up the interview (which will be relevant to all formal as opposed to opportunistic interviewing) and techniques for its successful implementation. Finally, I present an example of an interview where agenda undermines purpose, to the detriment of both participants.

Structure or straitjacket?

Between the open, almost conversational, interview and the verbally administered questionnaire lies a huge territory encompassing all manner of level of structure. It's perhaps tempting to think that the most successful structures will depend entirely on question design, but this rests on a rather naïve assumption that interviewees are all being asked the same questions. In fact, there is overwhelming evidence that this is not the case. Mishler (1986), for example, points to research which indicates that the difference may amount to between 25 per cent and 40 per cent of the questions asked and demonstrates that the variation involved can have a significant effect on the responses obtained (see also Frey 1989). In fact, the circumstances in which interviews are conducted can have a considerable influence on the outcomes.

A more important reason for not thinking solely in terms of questions is that this distracts attention from the interactive nature of all interviewing. The aim of the qualitative interview, however structured, is not merely to accumulate information but to deepen understanding, and in order to do this the interviewer must be responsive to nuance and opportunity as the interview progresses. This is not best achieved by dragging an unwilling victim through every nook and cranny of an interrogatory masterplan but by *listening* to what they have to say and how they say it:

> However well prepared you feel yourself to be, however well you have tried to design the interview questions in a style that your informants would not be put off by, in the actual interview, you will need to rapidly learn the specific way this unique informant speaks to you on this unique occasion: you will need to learn their 'idiolect' (discursive practices). (Wengraf 2001:64)

The focus in any interview must always be on the person, not the programme, and all questioning is hollow unless accompanied by attentive listening. It is in the context of these essential truths that the points outlined below must be interpreted.

Setting up and conducting the interview

In the first level I introduced what I described as the informal interview, where the researcher orients talk towards general questions that will allow the respondent to reveal aspects of their experience and understanding. This can be very effective. However, if you wish to develop specific lines of questioning, with the interviewee geared up to respond to your probes, you will need to set up formal interviews, making the purpose of the interaction clear at the outset.

Interviewing is never really an 'answer' to anything; it is a journey within a journey. This means that it should not be regarded as simply a means of confirming something already known or as definitive in itself; the approach must be as exploratory as the interview itself, and it is the responsibility of the researcher to create the best possible conditions for a successful encounter. Formal interviews therefore have to be carefully thought through, with a sensitivity to person and situation.

If the researcher treats each interview as an individual experience in itself and not merely a contribution to an accumulating pile of data that will one day be sorted out and analysed, the experience should be enjoyable as well as rewarding, especially if certain basic practical guidelines are followed. These fall into four categories: preliminary questions (Who? When? Where? How long?' and 'Under what conditions?'), preparation, opening and closing.

Preliminary questions

1. Who?   Interviews take time, so the number of people you will be able to involve is limited. This means that selection is particularly important and deserves careful thought. What will constitute a representative sample, covering all the relevant perspectives? If there are particular categories, how many people in each will you interview? Does any particular order suggest itself? However careful your analysis at this stage, it's always worth making sure that you leave a few empty slots for what might emerge along the way.

2. When?   Try to bear in mind the implications of the timing of the interview, whether local or global. By global considerations I mean the timing of the interview in terms of the information sought. For example, if you wish to explore the first impressions students make on teachers, you'll need to set up the interviews at the beginning of a course, while views of student progress will need to be sought later on. Given the fallibility of human memory, the general rule for data collection is 'the fresher the better', so this needs to be reflected in an interview schedule. Local considerations refer to the timing of interviews in terms of what might influence the nature of the response. For example, an interview with a teacher at the end of a full day after a particularly difficult class will perhaps receive a less enthusiastic and optimistic response than one held mid-morning early on in the week.

3. Where?   Don't underestimate the importance of this. Apart from the obvious considerations of privacy and comfort, try to consider the possible influence of the setting on the information someone is likely to give. For example, a principal is much more likely to deliver the official line sitting behind their desk than over a drink in a nearby café or bar.

4. How long?   Decisions about the duration of the interview should be made in the light of local constraints and opportunities, but always allow as much time as you can. It's not a good idea, for example, to try to fit a half-hour interview into a break of 40 minutes: by the time your informant has made a cup of tea, grabbed a few materials for the next session and spent a 'quick couple of minutes' sorting out an urgent issue, and you've spent time to settling into the interview, you'll be in a perfect position to call things to a halt just as they're getting interesting. Wengraf (2001) advises that around three hours are needed for a 45-minute interview: a minimum of 30 minutes before (preparation), 25 during (pre-interview arrangement, warm-up and goodbyes), and 90 after (debriefing, fieldnotes). I think this to be excessive, but it gives you an idea of what could be involved.

You also have to bear in mind the likely impact on the quality of responses received if an interview goes on for too long, though sacrifices may have to be made if a follow-up interview isn't possible. Burgess (1984a) claims that about an hour and a half is an optimum time for an interview, but I always feel that tiredness can begin to creep in after an hour or so. However, one researcher (Ortiz 2001) found some respondents – interestingly enough, the wives of professional athletes – with considerably more stamina than this and reports interviews lasting between 30 minutes and 7 hours!

5. Under what conditions? There is almost universal agreement that you should record the interview, provided that the interviewee agrees. However, views on the advisability of note-taking are more divided. I belong to the camp that sees this as adding unnecessary formality to the proceedings, which might inhibit the informant and distract the interviewer. If the worst comes to the worst, notes can be made immediately after the interview and written up as soon as possible after that.

If you want your respondent to be at ease, you should settle conditions of confidentiality in advance. I normally propose that I should be free to draw on the interview for any general and non-attributable points without first checking (e.g. 'There is a feeling among at least some of the teachers that . . . '), but that the interviewee should be given all transcripts and have the right to insist on the removal of anything that is be seriously compromising, unless a suitable form of representation can be agreed. Some researchers, however, think that this degree of censorship is unacceptable.

Preparation

In order to get the best out of the interview, take time to prepare the ground. Make sure the room is ready, the tape recorder is working, water is available, and so on. In short, leave yourself free to concentrate fully on the interview itself when the time comes. If you can take time to establish rapport with the respondent in advance of the interview, so much the better, but at least take time to think about your relationship with the interviewee. Reflect on how you will present yourself. If you're inappropriately formal, this might dispose the interviewee to produce an official version, too informal and you might not be taken seriously. Are you likely to be seen as an outsider and what are the implications of this? If you're an insider, is there a chance that the interviewee will take too much for granted? You may also need to consider cultural factors (for example, the degree of formality expected) and design your approach accordingly.

Opening the interview

As with so many things, the opening exerts a powerful influence on what follows. The standard advice is to spend time building rapport, though this is very much an individual matter. Certain technical details should certainly be dealt with: explaining the purpose of the interview and confirming the value of the interviewee's contribution, confirming length and general topic, offering reassurance on ethical issues, confirming permission to record, etc. I also think it's very important at this stage to assess the interactional situation. Is the interviewee nervous? Are they loquacious? Serious? And so on. This assessment is not a matter of pre-judgement but an important element in strategic preparation. Box 2.6 provides a checklist of the points covered so far..

Box 2.6   Checklist for setting up a formal interview

<u>Prior review</u>

1. Review categories of interviewees on list (does any
   particular order suggest itself?)   ❏
2. Check timing (any global issues? local influences?)   ❏
3. Decide on setting (options? implications?)   ❏
4. Establish length (expected duration + pre- and post-
   available slots?)   ❏

<u>Practicalities</u>

5. Confirm arrangements (time and location, directions needed?) ❏
6. Agree conditions (confidentiality, editing.)   ❏
7. Check room (tape recorder, tapes, batteries, notebook, water) ❏

<u>Notes</u>

8. Points to be covered in opening (purpose, confidentiality,
   length, etc.)   ❏
9. Interview guide (main and subsidiary questions)   ❏
10. Closing points (thanks, invitation to ask questions,
    follow up)   ❏

Closing the interview

Closing receives less attention in the literature, but if things don't end on the right note this can affect future interview situations. An expression of gratitude and appreciation is essential, and do invite the interviewee to make comments or ask questions. A short note of thanks after the interview is also a politeness that many people appreciate.

Developing an interview guide

There are two expressions used to describe the design of questions in a structured interview and one of them is misleading. 'Interview schedule' is best reserved for what are effectively oral questionnaires; in the context of qualitative inquiry it suggests that interviewing is merely a matter of following a predetermined schedule, and thus encourages the sort of 'eyes down' approach that will fail to spot opportunities within the interview itself. On the other hand, 'interview guide' describes a resource that can be drawn on in whatever way and to whatever extent is appropriate.

In what follows I concentrate on the individual interview, but this is not to suggest that everything can be captured in a single encounter – far from it. In some cases follow-up interviews will be necessary anyway, because the topics to be covered cannot be fitted into a single session, but in any case a follow-up meeting should be arranged wherever possible. There will always be issues arising from the first interview, some of them only revealed by subsequent analysis, and a second meeting will provide an invaluable opportunity to develop lines of investigation, check details, compare responses, and so on. The following steps to producing an effective guide should therefore be read with this in mind.

1. Decide on what the interview is setting out to achieve: make sure that you have a clear picture of this. A good sense of purpose provides the best internal guide to developing successful lines of questioning.

2. Identify the big questions: these are the questions that will provide the framework for the interview. One approach is to derive interview questions directly from research questions (Kvale 1996:131) (Box 2.7, below, provides an example of this), but it is also possible to think in terms of main topics and subsidiary topics – what really matters is to establish a workable hierarchy. It's very important to remember, though, that the big questions for you, the researcher, are not questions that will have meaning for the interviewee. Effective interviewing depends on being able to frame questions that will elicit willing and informative responses, and in order to do this you need to be able to see things from the interviewee's perspective.

3. Decide on lines of inquiry deriving from these: the big questions will form a very useful checklist that you can carry round in your head in order to ensure that you have covered the relevant territory, but you should also sketch out in advance possible lines of inquiry from these. This involves identifying the subsidiary topics that fall under your main headings.

4. Write a suitable warm-up question: this should call for an extended response based on something with which the interviewee is very familiar, so one of Spradley's (1979) 'grand tour' (for example, 'Talk me through a typical X') questions would serve well.

5. Analyse, apply, review, revise: when you've planned your guide, analyse it carefully from the point of view of the interviewee and try to spot potential difficulties or opportunities, then conduct a pilot interview using it and subject the guide to critical review. Finally, in the light of your discoveries, revise it where necessary and be prepared to develop it further as the interviews progress.

Box 2.7 illustrates the ways in which interview questions might be derived from a research question. In this example, a researcher is exploring the relationship between two terms, EAP teaching and needs analysis, and one of the research questions is concerned with the relationship between the target discourse community and approaches to teaching. The interviewee is a postgraduate student. Consider the advantages and disadvantages, in terms of their impact on the interviewee, of the questions that have been derived from this particular research question.

Box 2.7   Interview questions (1): research → interview

Research question		Sample interview questions
In what ways is the concept of a target discourse community realised through EAP teaching?	⇒	Do you think the materials you're using are relevant to your own specialist field? → *What actual materials from your field (e.g. academic papers) do you use?* → *Can you talk me through how the teacher went about using that? etc.*

> ⇒ Can you give me example of things
> you've done in the course recently
> that would be directly useful to you
> in your work?
>
> ⇒ Do you ever have the chance in
> lessons to discuss your specialist
> field and what goes on there?

The first question is specific and invites a yes/no answer. The advantage of this is that it's easy for the interviewee to respond and to get a general sense of what the interviewer is interested in. Some interviewees, of course, will treat this as an opportunity to address this topic directly, especially if they are encouraged by a short silence following a yes/no response. However, if the respondent does not open up in this way and the interviewer moves directly to the subsidiary questions, this may create a sense of interrogation rather than exploration. More seriously, once the interviewee has taken up a position in response to the initial question, even though it may be something they have never given any thought to before, they may feel the need to justify their stance in subsequent responses. A more general prompt such as 'Tell me about the sort of materials that are used in your lessons' might offer a gentler and more open beginning.

The second question, which might also serve as a good opening question, is designed to elicit a list of things, which is always a useful way of opening up territory. The respondent can then draw directly on specific experience and the interviewee should find plenty to work from. The options are quite wide-ranging, though ('things' might be classroom activities, projects, exercises, and so on, and work could include professional activity as well as work on the relevant academic course) so the interviewer should be ready for this.

The same applies to the last question, but the point of entry here is not so straightforward. Respondents might find it difficult to come up with examples, so the interviewer should at least have one or two examples (preferably from a different field) ready as illustrations. In fact, this is the sort of question that might need to be changed radically in the light of field experience.

Elicitation techniques

The preparation of the guide, the setting up of the interview and the management of the necessary preliminaries are all matters that unfold in a fairly measured way, but once the questioning begins time compresses alarmingly, decisions multiply and thinking space disappears. In such circumstances good technique and plenty of practice are essential. The questioning strategies and response options described in the previous level are fundamental and should eventually become second nature, but there are one or two broader strategies available. This section introduces them.

A technique that offers a useful default pattern of enquiry is that of progressive focusing. The idea of this has already been introduced: begin with a general question, then gradually focus in on more specific features, deriving these from higher level interests. Box 2.8 illustrates a typical example.

Box 2.8   Interview questions (2): general → specific

<u>Views of pre-reading</u>

How do you feel about pre-reading activities?
⇒ Could you describe some of the activities you use?
  ⇒ What are the strengths and weaknesses of that activity?
  ⇒ Would you use it with beginners? etc.
If you had to recommend a particular type of pre-reading activity to a new teacher, what would it be?
⇒ What features made you choose this?
  ⇒ Examples of use from your own teaching.
  ⇒ Variations?
Etc.

Bear in mind when following this procedure that specific questions don't necessarily have to be closed questions, as you can see if you compare the final question in the first example above with, 'How would you feel about using it with beginners?' If you are worried about inviting a response that is longer and more detailed than you need, there's nothing wrong with specifying the level of detail you're looking for, for example: 'Could you just briefly outline...' or 'Could you sum up in just a few sentences...'.

Johnson and Weller (2002) describe a range a elicitation techniques, two of which are particularly worth mentioning. The first, taxonomic elicitation, is unlikely to be useful if you are researching TESOL, but it could be valuable outside this (or in needs analysis situations) where you need to develop your local understanding. It involves asking someone to develop a taxonomy, or structured set of items and their relationships, by asking a question like 'What different kinds of communicative activities can be used in the classroom?' The second technique is free recall, where the respondent is asked to recall as much as possible on a single topic. This may take the form of a list, as in 'Name all the vocabulary games you can think of'.

There is a natural tendency to work with straightforward questions in an interview situation, but sometimes other approaches can be more effective, especially where a straightforward question might elicit a stock response. For example, telling a story, offering a metaphor, quoting an opinion, or even showing a picture, might prompt reactions that would otherwise be difficult to elicit. Oblique but specific questions are often more effective than more obvious general alternatives. Box 2.9 provides examples of different ways of approaching the same question.

Box 2.9 Interview questions (3): direct → oblique

Direct	Oblique
What's your view of Communicative Language Teaching?	'If you were interviewing a candidate for a teaching post here and they described themself as a communicative language teacher, how would you check that out?'
How important do you think classroom arrangement is?	Show photographs of different classrooms with same teacher-fronted activity taking place and ask for comments on these.
Should a teacher ever get personally involved with a student?	Tell story of student with particular language learning difficulties. Teacher sees adult student of the opposite sex after class to discuss these and they agree to finish discussion in a bar. This happens a few times and they strike up a close but non-physical friendship. Invite interviewee's views on this, or 'If you were the principal of this school, what action, if any, would you take?'

It may even be necessary to rethink your whole approach to the interview. Lerner (quoted in Hammersley and Atkinson 1995) describes a deliciously oblique strategy used to interview members of French élites:

> Our first approaches to interviewing were modest, tentative, apologetic. Trial-and-error, hit-and-miss (what the French love to call 'L'empiricisme anglo-saxon') finally produced a workable formula. To each prospective respondent, the interviewer explained that his Institute had undertaken a study of attitudes among the elite. As Frenchmen do not respond readily to questionnaires, he continued, we were seeking the counsel of specially qualified persons: 'Would you be so kind as to review with us the questionnaire we propose to use and give us the benefit of your criticisms? In responding yourself, you could explain which questions a Frenchman would be likely to resist and why; which questions would draw ambiguous or evasive responses that could not be properly interpreted; and which questions could be altered in such a way as to require reflective rather than merely stereotyped answers.
>
> By casting the interviewee in the role of expert consultant, we gave him the opportunity to indulge in a favourite indoor sport – generalizing about Frenchmen. (Lerner 1957:27)

Conclusion

This level has explored approaches to the semi-structured interview and suggested ways in which you can set up and conduct such interviews. It has treated such interviews as largely unproblematic, but the next level will address some of the complex relational challenges associated with relying too heavily on this method of data gathering. In the meantime, this one finishes with a case that illustrates the more specific interactional dangers arising from a misunderstanding of the nature of the exchange taking place.

Case 2.2: well if you'd told me it was an interview...

This is a somewhat unusual case, chosen because it is effectively a complete interview illustrating the importance of establishing a proper context for the exchange and pointing to issues of identity that will be picked up at the next level. It is not a qualitative interview, but the lessons it teaches are nevertheless relevant ones.

In fact, this is a variety of interview with which you are probably familiar: the language school placement interview designed to assign new students to the appropriate level of study. The interviewer/teacher involved in this case has the usual packed schedule, with very little time to achieve the necessary goal of assessing the candidate. If the result is less than perfect, this is more a reflection of the pressure of circumstance than a comment on the teacher's competence. In any case, there will always be a chance to reassign students later.

I am grateful to Annette Gosse for this extract (Extract 2.6), which formed part of an MSc assignment, though with a different focus from the one adopted here. I have kept to her notation, most features of which appear in the list of transcription symbols in Box 4.1 on pages 173 and 174. Briefly, '(–)' denotes short pauses and '(+)' longer ones, square brackets show where overlapping talk begins, equals signs at the end of one line and the beginning of the next represent talk where one turn runs into the next with no audible pause, and underlining indicates emphasis. I have used 'T' to represent the Teacher/Interviewer and 'S' to represent the student, whom I will call 'Sada' for the purposes of analysis.

In a nutshell, the problems with this exchange arise from the fact that while the interviewer approaches it as a placement interview, the candidate has not been told the purpose of the meeting and therefore assumes that it is designed to find out about her previous experience of language learning. In reading it, you might like to look at where and how the misunderstandings arise and consider the interactional identity of the 'interviewer'.

Extract 2.6   A placement interview

```
01   T:  Have you taken English before, Sada?
02   S:  (–) Ah (+) maybe (–) not (–) good=
03   T:  =Good. Did you take English in high s-school- in school?
04   S:  (–) Yes
05   T:  How many years did you take English?=
06   S:  =Ah (–) six=
07   T:  =Six years=
08   S:  =Yes
09   T:  (–) And are you ⌈married
10   S:               ⌊Teacher (–) English (–) no good (–)
11       because speak English and Arabic=
12   T:  =Oh=
13   S:  =No- No English (–) OK=
14   T:  =Oh (–) so you didn't get ⌈enough
15   S:                            ⌊understand=
```

Extract 2.6   (Continued)

```
16   T:   = didn't get enough practice in English (–) you didn't get
17        enough practice in English speaking =
18   S:   = Practice? =
19   T:   = Practice (–) talking over and over and over
20   S:   (–) Ah
21   T:   Practice means the same many times (–) so because
22        your teacher was English and Arabic =
23   S:   = Yes =
24   T:   = you need more time with English
25   S:   Ah
26   T:   (+) More practice. I think. Have you taken classes
27        here before, Sada?
28   S:   Yes
29   T:   Is it, you've taken classes here at [name of school]?
30   S:   (+) What? =
31   T:   = Have you come here ⌈to school?
32   S:                        ⌊Yes
33   T:   To School X? ⌈Right now
34   S:                ⌊Yes, ah yes
35   T:   Have you taken classes before?
36   S:   (–) AH (–) because (–) ⌈I want
37   T:                          ⌊Ah-ha
38   S:   I would like to English =
39   T:   = OK (+) I think Level Two.
```

Source: Annette Gosse, 1998, Unpublished MSc Project, Aston
University.

Shorn of all preliminaries, the talk begins with a question about Sada's experience of learning English and the interviewer makes the goal of assigning her to an appropriate class relevant throughout the exchange through references to such things as practice (e.g. 1.16) and educational time needed (1.24). Most strikingly, the conclusion explicitly assigns Sada to a particular level, thereby announcing that the goal has been achieved.

But has it? If someone knows that the object of a particular exchange is to assess the level of their English, they will design their talk in order to achieve the best possible outcome, and if they fail to do this they will be at a disadvantage when compared to other interviewees. This case is interesting because it is not at all clear that Sada herself understands that this is a placement interview, or understands this in the sense of being aware of the relevant conventions. An examination of the way the interview unfolds will reveal the unfortunate consequences of this.

The interview begins with a question inviting a polar yes/no response, but Sada infers that what is required is some comment on the quality of the instruction she has received, a reasonable assumption if she regards this as an opportunity to discuss her previous experience of learning English. The teacher's evaluation (l.3) indicates her acceptance of this response, though as an assessment of the content of Sada's statement it would be bizarre – a gratuitously insulting suggestion that Sada's 'not good' experience of learning English was in fact a 'good' thing.

In fact, the teacher's 'good' reflects her agenda, pursued unproblematically for a few more turns but invoked with less success in the odd question in line 9: 'And are you married'. To get a sense of how odd this might seem to someone not aware of the relevant conventions, imagine it slotted into a 'getting to know you' sequence in small talk. What makes it particularly odd is the use of the connective *and*. Taking the interaction as it stands, there is no obvious link between the number of years Sada has studied English and her marital status, and therefore no justification whatsoever for the connective. However, anyone familiar with the routines of language placement interviews will know that the primary aim is to establish the linguistic level of the candidate. Ideally, this is achieved through a natural progression manipulated by the interviewer, but the constraints of this particular event allow for sudden switches of this kind. The *and*-preface (Heritage and Sorjonen 1994), then, refers not to the content of the previous question but to the question as a stage in an assessment process. It announces that the interviewer is moving on to another linguistic check.

For the teacher this is one placement interview in a whole series stretching through to the end of an exhausting day, but what of Sada? For her it is a much more unusual encounter and one with which she may be completely unfamiliar. Hardly surprising, then, that she overlaps the teacher's question about marriage in order to pursue her earlier point about inadequate teaching – and fails a linguistic 'test' she is not even aware of taking.

This mismatch of perceptions produces a distinctly odd sequence later in the talk, beginning with the interviewer's polar question in lines 26–7 and Sada's straightforward response, which is then treated as in some sense problematic. From the perspective of the teacher this may be entirely appropriate. It may be, for instance, that the teacher would expect to have the records of applicants who have previously attended the school and by this point she may also have concluded that the candidate has a poor grasp of English, although we cannot know this. However, Sada has answered the question unequivocally, so her puzzled 'What?' in response to the teacher's check is understandable. Nevertheless, when the question is reformulated in line 31, she obligingly provides a clear response and does not even balk at the further check in line 33.

The interviewer's question, 'Have you taken classes before?' in line 35, however, is a different matter. All the talk so far has centred on Sada's experience in English classes, so the question appears redundant. Talk is built turn-on-turn, and each new turn displays the speaker's understanding of what has gone before as the basis for moving the interaction forward, so Sada struggles to make sense of this. The structure of her response with its pauses and hesitation marker ('(-) AH (-) because (-) I want'), is understandable. Her efforts to grasp where the teacher wants the talk to go produce a return to the more general topic of her linguistic needs, apparently addressing the question of *why* she has applied for English lessons – all to no avail because the interaction is brought to an sudden halt by the interviewer's judgemental guillotine in response to time constraints.

Sada's pursuit of the topic of her language learning experience (for example, from line 10) and her return to it just before the end suggest that she is not behaving as a 'candidate' or 'assessee' but rather as a client. The interviewer's identity, though, is less straightforward. There is ample evidence of an assumed 'assessor – applicant' relationship, from 'good' in line 3, through judgements about Sada's language needs (l.24 and l.26), to the final assignment of level. However, for the most part this process of assessment reflects an asymmetry that is more characteristic of the classroom and invokes an institutional context where the teacher's superior knowledge of English is taken for granted as an aspect of her role. The most obvious example of this in the extract is where the teacher explains the meaning of *practice* to Sada, offering first (l.19) an emphatic repetition and a definition ('talking over and over') and then (l.21), in the absence of unambiguous evidence that Sada has understood, a less colloquial formulation ('Practice means the same many times').

However, the interviewer also responds to Sada's account so as to suggest a genuine interest in its content, consistent with Sada's perception of her as enquirer rather than assessor. The interviewer's response in lines 21–4 provides a wonderful example of potential interpretive ambiguity. Her first turn, 'because your teacher was *English* and Arabic', takes up Sada's own point, which the latter confirms, but the subsequent claim that 'you need more time with *English*' could be taken in two ways: as either a natural upshot of Sada's observation or an assessment of language needs. If the former, it emerges as an expression of understanding, even alignment; if the latter, it points towards the assessment that will soon follow. There are doubtless lessons here that bear on the process of oral language assessment, but this very short passage also serves as a valuable resource for the qualitative interviewer. Here the misunderstandings are pretty evident, some of them quite shocking, even darkly humorous. But in the longer qualitative interview they may be less apparent, the assumptions behind them subtly colouring the nature of interviewee responses and perhaps even circumscribing their content. This passage underlines the need to ensure that the interviewee understands the nature of what is involved and highlights the danger of establishing an asymmetrical interactional relationship that can obscure misunderstandings and distort interpretation. The interviewer should try to build the talk with the interviewee naturally, remaining sensitive to the fact that identity is not an unchanging given, established in advance of the encounter, but a negotiated presence that can influence the nature of the talk itself. This will be the main theme for Level 3.

Level 3: aspects of analysis

The theme of this level is analysis but the key to it is 'aspects'. Analysis is in fact no straightforward matter, a simple one-off exercise in transforming a mound of unanalysed interview transcripts into a neatly categorised set of related statements; it is an unfolding process of interactional exploration that begins with the very first interview and informs the research process through to its final representation. Because analysis is so integral to the interview process, I include it here as an essential skill that needs to be developed and not something that can be subsumed under the more general discussion of analysis and representation in Chapter 6. This level therefore begins with a survey of the challenges facing the interviewer in qualitative inquiry, then develops an approach to analysis that responds to these.

Interviews and representation

I date my own reservations about interviews to my reading of Elbaz's (1983) widely respected study of teacher thinking, based on extensive in-depth interviews with a single teacher. I found it entertaining and informative, but my own experience as a teacher made me wonder whether the processes described were *post hoc* constructs. I know that when I'm asked to talk about my reasons for doing things, I can provide a whole array of very sensible reasons why I 'decided' to do something which in fact I stumbled into almost blindly. Teachers are generally very articulate, and reliance on interview data can give a misleading impression of their thought processes.

When I came to combine teacher interviews with tapes and observation in my own research, I discovered a very complex world of representation and argumentation which reinforced my reservations and crystallised into a position that Atkinson and Silverman (1997:322) sum up extremely succinctly: 'We take at face value the image of the self-revealing speaking subject at our peril'.

Part of the problem, the authors argue, is that we live in an 'interview society', where, under the guise of 'discovering' an authentic self which is unitary and coherent, the interviewer and interviewee collaborate within one of the recognised interview types (for example, the public confession, the psychiatrist's couch) to construct the narrator as witness to his or her own biography, using these 'more-or-less standardized discursive domains' in order to 'construct the interiority of the subject' (1997:314). Although their work focuses on the life history interview, which has received particular attention (see, for example, MacLure 1993), their reservations have wider application. The two previous levels have focused on the importance of technique, but however refined this may be it does not guarantee access to the interviewee's 'real' self. The interview is a constructed event in which those involved have parts to play, and our approach to analysis must respond to this.

Analysis in talk

Analysis does not begin when talk ends but is part of the ongoing process of interviewing from the perspective of both interviewer and interviewee. On a fairly basic level, interviewers will check that they have understood certain statements, perhaps inviting clarification and expansion; at a more sophisticated level, they will make connections with earlier statements, inviting the interviewee to consider the relationship between the different articulations and where necessary make comparisons or resolve contradictions. Similarly, the interviewee will be conscious of the developing talk and may realise as a position develops that it relates in some way to earlier talk and leads towards particular interpretations or positions.

All this arises from ongoing analysis and interpretation and may affect the form or content of talk, both planned and unplanned. It is important, then, that when more formal analysis takes place it does not treat the data as representing some 'pure' pre-analytical resource: analysis is embedded within analysis.

Analysis of talk: transcription

The first step to any adequate analysis of interview data must be transcription. Other approaches are possible (Jones 1985b, for example, describes the use of cognitive mapping in order to represent interview contents), but only a transcript allows the sort of focused attention on the minutiae of talk that promotes insights into technique and content. If alternatives are to be used, it's probably best to regard them as enabling mechanisms for broad understandings rather than as a substitute for the precise analysis that transcripts allow.

The first step, then, is the production of a transcript that can serve as a basis for analysis. This is not a substitute for the tape itself but a working representation of it, and it may occasionally be necessary to return to the original. The process of transcription, whatever the level of delicacy, is a fairly tedious business and it's best to be realistic at the outset about what lies ahead:

> The outcome of, for example, an hour-long interview and seven hours' laborious transcription of that interview is, frequently, an account miserably bereft of the concrete, nitty gritty nuggets of information that would make the researcher's life easy. (Gardner 2001:192)

Chapter 4 deals at length with issues of transcription, but a system for interviews does not need to be as sophisticated as the one proposed there. In brief, it should aim for maximum readability without sacrificing essential features. Box 2.10 suggests minimal transcription features for interviews, though inevitably you will develop your own additions and amendments (for example, I use colons to indicate lengthened syllables and hyphens for words that are cut off).

Box 2.10   Basic transcription features for interviews

1. **Pauses:** these can be timed to the nearest (half) second, or symbols indicating a short (–) or long (+) pauses can be used.
2. **Overlap:** this is rarer in interviews than in conversation, so show it either by using square brackets or by relying on the layout of the text.
3. **Emphasis:** use italics or underlining.
4. **Fillers:** capture all fillers ('um', 'er', etc.) and repetitions.

Box 2.10 (Continued)

5. **Intonation:** punctuate for intonation rather than grammar (period = falling intonation; comma = contour of intonation indicating speaker will continue; question mark = questioning intonation; exclamation mark = exclamatory), which means that not all questions have question marks.
6. **Problematic features:** any words that are not clear should be put in single brackets, e.g. 'He (rescinded) that particular directive.'
7. **Non-verbal features:** can appear in double or square brackets, e.g. '((sharp intake of breath))'.

It might seem trivial at this point to discuss the niceties of formatting, but in my experience failure to address this early on can cause a great deal of unnecessary frustration later. Three things really matter when you're developing interview transcription: a reliable line numbering system, easy transfer of the main text to the final paper, report or thesis, and space for comments or notes. If you plan to make notes in pen, the last of these can be achieved by setting broad margins, but this is not workable on a computer, so it's worth going for something that can be used with either pen or machine.

For this I suggest a template based on a table with three columns, as in Extract 2.7. The first column is simply a sequence of numbers, with a consistent total on each page – a check that no numbers have been omitted. I have different templates, running from 500 lines to several thousand. The second column is for the interview itself and ideally will correspond to the size of indented quotations you will incorporate into your final text. Since the original line numbers are not needed for this, it can be lifted straight from its column. The final column is for any notes and comments, and since any column markings that are part of the computer program itself will be invisible when the text is printed out, you will be left with a natural margin for handwritten comments.

Extract 2.7   Format for interview transcript

Line	Speaker and talk	Comments/Notes
001	IE: I mean (1.5) <u>here</u> you you see things	*Job satisfaction:*
002	from start to finish,	*- whole process*

```
003
004   IR:   Yeah
005
006   IE:   and so (2.5) you get to see:: (1.0) not      - see outcomes
007         just the results and implications,           - see bigger picture
008         but it's more interesting because
009         you follow it through, so you're
010         doing it for a purpose.                      - purpose is clear
```

Other formatting such as line spacing and font is a matter of preference, and it's also possible to move to a separate row in the table for each turn in the talk, which allows comments to be related to turns. I prefer to number all lines, but you can instead number speakers, or even just 'meaning segments', though I think this imposes an unnecessary interpretive structure on the transcript. You may also decide that it's a good idea to leave a line between speakers, since the line numbering system is for reference only.

In Extract 2.7 I've used IE and IR for the those involved, but in practice I would use pseudonyms, building up a list of all these as soon as possible in the project. There are other refinements, such as including a column for notes to the left of the transcript as well as to the right, or using different coloured inks for interviewer and interviewee (Wengraf 2001). Decisions like this should be made early on in the transcription process and as far as possible finalised at the end of the first transcription. They are important not so much in themselves but as part of the sort of systematic attention to transcription quality that Poland, in his discussion of the subject (Poland 1995), claims is the exception rather than the norm. Whatever form of representation you adopt, Box 2.11 lists four maxims that should underlie all your transcription work.

Box 2.11   Four essential maxims for interview transcription

1. *Brains listen, ears are tools*
   This means that listening is an inherently selective process and we need to train ourselves to listen in a new, more closely attentive way. Repeated and careful listening enables the brain to switch to 'transcript mode'.

Box 2.11   (Continued)

2. *Talk is more than words*
   The non-verbal dimension, and its associated emotional context, is very important and very hard to capture. We need to pay particular attention to this, representing it either in brackets or in a separate column in the transcript.

3. *It's down to you in the end*
   If you must use someone else to transcribe, carefully explain what's needed, use their first transcript as a basis for further clarification, and use their text not as a final version but as a basis for your own transcript arising from further listening.

4. *Lose the tape and you lose the talk*
   It's always a good idea to transcribe from copies of an original tape, but whatever you do *never* pass on an original to anyone else.

Analysis of talk: technique

In order to be better at what we do, we need to find ways of examining what we do. In this respect at least interviews have a natural advantage because we can use the transcript not merely as a source of information relevant to our research, but as a resource for the analysis of our own performance. In this section I propose four aspects that can be addressed here.

1. Questions: this is the most basic but also potentially the most transformative aspect. If we examine the interview from the perspective of the questioning techniques and strategies described in the previous two levels, we will almost inevitably find aspects of our questioning that call for improvement: a lack of variety, perhaps, or a failure to pick up on opportunities; in certain situations possibly even a tendency to close things down prematurely.

2. Distortions: it's possible that we may also find examples in our talk of previously unsuspected bias or unwarranted assumptions that are distorting our questioning, closing down options or even leading the interviewee towards particular positions. There are two reasons why TESOL researchers need to be particularly sensitive to this. The first is the fairly obvious one that ours is a global profession where cultural sensitivities are important. We may find ourselves in situations where we are interviewing a fluent English speaker with a very different educational and cultural background from our own, which may lead us into making unwarranted assumptions about what can be taken for granted. The second reason is that we are very likely to find ourselves interviewing fellow professionals and bringing with us our own views and perspectives on our shared profession. We must be careful not to let these leak into our questioning.

3. Relationships: we cannot ignore our relationship with the interviewee and the effect this might have on the way the talk develops. Mishler (1986), emphasising the interactive nature of interviews, highlights the extent to which interviewees construct their accounts in response to the interviewer's signals, however subtle. He points to the dangers of the analyst 'filtering out' information and underlines the importance of 'relistening'. In doing this, we need to be on the lookout for signals that we might be sending out.

We should also read with an eye to the relationship that emerges from the transcript. For example, if I am interviewing a young male student, to what extent is he responding to me as late-middle-aged male teacher and what evidence is there for this in his responses? If I already know the interviewee, to what extent is our previous relationship an issue? What other relationships, if any, emerge and what are the implications of these for the outcomes of the interview?

4. The interviewee: our encounter with the respondent is fundamental to all that happens in the interview. Unless we wish to treat all that emerges as unproblematically 'factual', our engagement with it must be mediated by our engagement with our interviewees and our understanding of them. This is why Gubrium and Holstein (2002b:11) insist that the process of analysis is also that of 'collaboratively making audible and visible the phenomenal depths of the individual subject at the centre of our shared concerns'.

The authors emphasise that this implies that we should think carefully about technical matters because 'they produce the detailed subject' (ibid., p. 12). This is taken up in the next section, but what needs to be noted here is that, in examining the relationship that develops through the talk, we also need to note the ways in which the interviewee presents themself because this might have an important bearing on the way they represent things to us.

One option is to invite a colleague to comment on the transcript of one of your interviews as a means of establishing a fresh perspective on your technique. I'm grateful to my colleague, Steve Mann, for allowing me to extract the following examples from my own response to one of his transcripts (Extract 2.8). Space does not allow the full context to be established, so I have selected only the turns that immediately prompt the comments, all his except for the last which is the response of his interviewee (J). These also represent, for illustrative purposes, negative comments from a script that prompted a much larger portion of positive points; however, they do provide a flavour of the sort of thing you might note when looking critically at your own work or that of a colleague. A more detailed example, operating at all four levels, is provided in the Case shown at the end of this level.

Extract 2.8   Comments on interviewer's turns

so it's interesting and there's also a sense that it's something that makes you want to say more than you might normally want to say	*Where's this in J's response? Are you anticipating according to your own agenda?*
yeah (.) yeah	*Can sound as though you 'know' this, but there might have been an area there to explore – which topics?*
so there's a sense that the space does create an opportunity that wasn't there before- or wasn't there enough (.) for seeing the way people view a particular topic.	*[Have previously commented on the extent to which S uses 'so'.] These formulations tend to pin the speaker down and therefore close off other possibilities. Notice how it produces from J an extension/expansion of your own line.*
well it's an interesting issue (.) I'm going to step out of Reflecting mode for a second	*Why? Couldn't you have prompted J to produce her account of this?*
[J] that's interesting (.) yeah	*Problem here is that your evaluative intervention here prompts J to think of something new that may lead her off her own track*

Analysis of talk: relationships and accounts

Respondents' accounts are just that: accounts. They are knowledges generated in, partially constituting and constituted by, particular contexts – those contexts being the power/knowledge complexes of different and multiple time-spaces. At the same time, they are not naïve attempts to describe the world, but are actively constructed – through the negotiation between researcher and respondent – in the attempt to manage social identity. (Gardner 2001:196)

Whatever the technical niceties of our approach to analysis, we can never afford to treat the words spoken as a decontextualised resource from which facts and interpretations can be extracted. The systematic approach that all analysis demands must be equally in evidence in our reading of the text itself if we are to lay sound interpretive foundations for what follows.

When I said to my 14-year-old daughter on Friday night, 'We'll talk about this in the morning', I sent a clear signal that the person who would be talking to her was not the one who had exchanged light-hearted insults with her earlier that evening. And when the serious exchanges were over that Saturday morning and we'd all agreed that a grounding was in order, we sealed it with a hug and went back to the banter. Sometimes I even say to my daughters, 'I'm sorry, but on this one I'm going to have to be a dad, like it or not'. They have no problem with this because they long ago worked out that we can't wear the same hat all the time.

Most of the time, we don't need to be explicit about the shifts that take place in our talk because developing a sensitivity to the relevant signals is part of growing up. Everything we say, and the way we say it, is affected by our relationship with the people we're talking to, the circumstances in which we speak, relevant past experiences, things we might already have said, and so on. If we ignore all this in analysing an interview, we fly in the face of our everyday experience.

My wife and daughters have it easy because they've had years to get used to me, but anyone interviewing me will have a lot less to go on. The challenge will then lie in using the relatively limited resource of the interview exchanges to identify just who is speaking. For example, if you interview a colleague who has been in your institution a long time about something that is an important issue in that professional context, will they construct their responses in terms of the recognised ways of talking about this topic? This may be revealing in itself, but it would not necessarily represent their personal view, so it won't provide evidence for a claim that 'teachers in this school regard issue X as...'.

Or suppose you are interviewing a principal who is a member of a national organisation of principals and is responding to a much-debated question on which the organisation has an agreed line. Whose story will you get? How will you know to what extent your interviewee is actually acting as a mouthpiece for the organisation's standard line? And who is the 'me' to whom this interviewee responds? If the issue is one where teachers and principals have consistently adopted different positions, will you be treated here as a *teacher* rather than as a *researcher*? The issue is not an abstract one:

> The issue of how interviewees respond to us based on who we are – in their lives, as well as in the social categories to which we belong, such as age, gender, class and race – is a practical concern as well as an epistemological or theoretical one. (Miller and Glassner 1997:101)

In this section I develop a position that responds to this challenge head on by treating all interview responses as accounts rather than reports. I then set this within a broader practical context of analytic procedure and outline specific techniques that can be applied.

Interviews as accounts

Baker (1997), drawing on the ideas of Sacks, provides a stimulating discussion of the interview as a form of *accounting* rather than a matter of straightforward description. In an interview, she argues, what we have access to is not an interior set of beliefs or knowledge but a way of constructing talk that depends on category identifications and members' accounting processes (their beliefs, local understandings, motivations, and so on). Baker asks us to reflect on the difference between the same person being approached to speak as a *professor*, which would call into play such associated categories as 'students' and related properties or activities such as 'doing research', and as a *mother-of-three*, with associated categories such as 'children' and related activities or properties such as 'caringness'.

As Baker points out (1997:139), the developing interview 'serves to add to and elaborate on the categories and activities proposed in the initial description'. She argues that there are practical lessons we can draw from this in terms of assumptions and approach, beginning with the recognition of the following:

1. interviews are interactional events in which members draw on their cultural knowledge, including knowledge of how members of certain categories speak;
2. questions are a central part of the data and not merely neutral invitations to speak;
3. interview responses should be treated as accounts rather than reports.

The analytical implication of this is that we need to examine how participants make use of membership categorisation devices. In order to do this we first identify the central categories (people, places or things) which underpin the talk, including standard pairs (teacher/ student; silent student/turn-grabber); then we can work through the activities associated with these categories to fill out the attributions that are made to each of the categories; and finally we look for the courses of social action that are implied, 'descriptions of how categories of actors do, could or should behave' (ibid., p. 143). In a later paper (Baker 2002), the author notes that researchers rarely conduct interviews with this approach to analysis in mind but claims that it can open up a valuable perspective on the ways in which such interviews are accomplished. The challenge, then, lies in deciding how best to use this perspective.

Practical considerations

Somehow a balance has to be struck. Nijhof (1997), for example, claims that a focus on interactional performances can direct attention away from the responses themselves and the 'response work' that produces them. Answers to questions, he argues, should be seen as part of a performance by the interviewee and he recommends limiting analysis to 'the readings actually construed by the respondents' (1997:179). In order to achieve this, we must present not only the reply but also the question of which it is a reading, and in addition any earlier formulations to which it might be responding. His position differs from Baker's in that his focus is not on the interaction but on the individual, 'the reflecting actor' (ibid., p. 184).

Whatever practical advice might be given, the best form of preparation is the development of a feeling for talk that can only come with practice in reading transcripts. There can be no straightforward formula for what must remain an essentially exploratory experience, but most writers (for example, Holstein and Gubrium 1995, Poland and Pederson 1998, Heyl 2001) emphasise the need for careful inspection of transcripts and the tapes themselves. I underline this because in the context of a process that demands so much of the researcher it can seem one effort too many. The rewards, though, can be analytically significant.

Clues in the talk itself, such as explicit statements of position along the lines of 'speaking as a mother now' or 'wearing my professional hat' (Gubrium 1995) can help, as can a careful examination of stylistic shifts, different ways of speaking, and so on, but the best route to success is through the development of a feeling for interaction that can be fostered only through repeated practice. The approach in Box 2.12, then, is intended as no more than a guide to how things might break down in practice.

Box 2.12   An approach to establishing an analytical perspective

1. Make notes immediately after the interview, paying particular attention to relational issues. Include gut feelings.
2. Reflect on the interview from the perspective of the relationship of interviewer and interviewee, its broader context (professional setting, previous interviews, etc.) and its development. Note points to bear in mind.
3. Read the interview from an interactional perspective. How does the relationship between interviewer and interviewee develop? Highlight and comment on any key shifts or passages.
4. Look for clues to shifts in perspective or orientation (e.g. explicit comments about perceived identity, changes in the nature of the talk). Highlight these.
5. Look closely at the way the interviewee's positions develop. Where possible, relate later formulations to earlier ones.
6. Highlight problematic passages.
7. Sum up implications of the above for a developing analysis.
8. If possible, arrange a further interview to help in the process of clarification.

Outcomes of talk: analysis and interpretation

Here is a picture of analysis that most qualitative researchers would recognise:

> In his present study of community developers, Herb has collected over 2 million words of interview data, along with 12 boxes of documents. He reads the interviews, paragraph by paragraph and word by word, marking off each time a particular idea or concept is mentioned or explained, and indicating in a code the subject of each paragraph. Then he groups together responses describing the same idea or process and examines everything he has put in the same category.
> (Rubin and Rubin 1995:227)

Nothing in what follows undermines this approach, which, allowing for idiosyncratic variations, is more or less what we have to get down to at some point if we wish to understand our data. So far, to use Mason's metaphor (2002:226), I have developed a position that sees the interview in terms of construction rather than excavation, but the business of analysis has still to be done. General analytical procedures are discussed in Chapter 6, but there are considerations relevant to interviews that demand more immediate attention. In this section I refer to them in terms of the following three relationships.

Relate analysis to the process of data collection

This relationship demands emphasis for three reasons. The first arises from the advantages of using the analysis of transcripts in order to develop analytical and technical skills and hence contributing to the overall quality of the project. The second relates to the contribution that ongoing analysis can make to data collection. If analysis is introduced as early as possible, it can be related to the research questions and associated theoretical issues, thus informing the way that data collection develops.

The third reason is a much more practical one. Weaving analysis and collection together is the best defence I know against what might be termed 'data dominance', a situation in which the researcher becomes overwhelmed by the sheer weight of accumulated data, with the result that analysis may be reduced to a necessary and uninspiringly technical process rather than an illuminating exploration.

In a painfully honest and very revealing paper, Scott (1985) describes how a project designed to explore the context and processes of postgraduate research in a social science context became bogged down in just this way. Despite initial resistance from the community being studied, she succeeded in collecting a substantial body of interview data, turning over much of the transcription to an assistant. Eventually, this data proved to be not so much the materials from which she could develop a convincing research position as a millstone that impeded analytical and interpretive progress. The essential steps in her narrative are summarised in Box 2.13, which reveals how external pressures (point 1) encouraged an approach to data collection (2) which subtly shifted her attention from analysis to collection itself (3). The consequences of this were a distortion of the research effort (4 and 5) and a feeling of helplessness in the face of accumulated but unanalysed data (6). Her account serves as a powerful reminder of the need to establish a proper perspective on data and its place in the research process. More is not necessarily better.

Box 2.13   Data dominance

1. Responses from researchers working within positivist paradigms at conferences caused the researcher to feel under intense pressure to quantify.
2. Partly in response to this demand, she focused more and more on accumulating taped interviews until her data set was almost unmanageable.
3. Eventually she found herself measuring success in terms of the quantity of interviewing and this, rather than analysis, became the *raison d'être* of the research.
4. However, data gathering wasted time because no new insights were gained.
5. No interview notes were taken, so the status of the tape recordings changed. Now the tapes came to equal 'the truth' and she began to feel that she had become little more than an extension of the tape recorder.
6. Finally, she reached a point she was unable to draw a line between the data and the rest of her life.

Source: based on Scott 1985.

Relate interviews to other data sources

We have seen that analysing interviews is not simply a matter of identifying the 'facts' and checking them out in terms of internal consistency, alternative accounts, evidence from other sources, and so on. However, this does not mean that such connections should be ignored. Respondents are human, with all the defects of memory, conscious and unconscious motivations, social and interpersonal needs, and so on, that influence the ways in which reality might be represented. It is therefore incumbent on the researcher to make use of all available data sources in order to get the best possible fix on the information that is presented in interviews. Gardner (2001) provides an excellent discussion of issues of truth and memory that includes an example of a respondent claiming to take no part in the current public and political life of a parish. Subsequent analysis of other interviews and library archives revealed a very different picture and the researcher was able to identify several local positions of influence occupied by the respondent (for much darker examples of respondent deceit, see Sikes 2000).

Qualitative research calls for something of the detective in us, but our interest lies not so much in matching up different versions of the facts in order to pin down 'the truth', as in understanding the ways in which social and professional realities are understood and constructed. That someone describes themself as a 'communicative' language teacher but limits their verbal interaction with classes to lectures from the front of the classroom is something we might all benefit from understanding, but the identification of the contradiction itself is no more than the first step towards such understanding.

Relate categories to representations

All analysis will depend to some extent on categorisation, but we have seen how the categories invoked by respondents are matters of representation. We must recognise that they are merely points of view and that the interpretations they embody are those of a particular individual. The process of categorisation and analysis must therefore involve a consideration of the broader contextual issues that this level has highlighted.

This does not mean that the voice of the individual should be downgraded. The thorniest issue in dealing with any data, and particularly interview data, is the extent to which our own representation of it is also inherently interpretive. Since we cannot literally 'be' the respondents, we must appropriate their words, and in doing so the honesty we owe them is recognition of the interpretive act we are performing, even in so elementary an act as the selection and inevitable recontextualisation of their utterances. This issue of transparency is one that we should always keep in our minds as we seek to represent the voices of those who have contributed to our own understanding.

Case 2.3: you can tell me... (I'm a researcher)

In this section I use a brief extract (2.9) as a means of exploring the four aspects of analysis proposed earlier in this level. A snapshot like this cannot hope to capture the richness of an interview encounter, but in looking at this particular passage I was moved to comment on each of the relevant aspects: questions, distortions, relationships and the interviewee. My comments do not include all the observations I made but select what I think are the most interesting; your own reading may well suggest other priorities.

The background here is important. Before the interview, I had spent time in the field observing the interviewee, Sue, who worked very closely with her colleague, Penny, and had interviewed both of them previously, both together and separately. A number of interesting questions arose along the way about these two very different characters, many of them centring on the nature of their relationship and its relevance to the work they did. So when Sue applied for and was offered a new job at another institution, I seized the opportunity to arrange a final interview with her at the end of her penultimate day at work.

In the hope of getting her to open up, I decided to spend a fair amount of time in casual talk prior to getting down to business (in fact, we exchanged plumbing stories), then chat generally about her new job, before focusing in on the relationship I wanted to know more about. All talk is affected by what has gone before and this is no exception. My responses here are not typical of my usual interview technique and I think our opening informalities may account for this. See what you think.

Extract 2.9   Part of an interview

```
01    IR:   Yeah, leaving, you're obviously going to leave Penny,
02          you know, as a team, so, go on, how do you feel about
03          that?=
04    Sue:  =It's not a bad fate.
05    IR:   ((Laughs)) Go on.
06    Sue:  She drives me mad.
07    IR:   Yeah
08    Sue:  So:: that's one of the reasons I'm applying for
09          other ⌈jobs any⌉way
10    IR:        ⌊Really? ⌋
11    Sue:  Yeah.=
12    IR:   =Yeah.
13    Sue:  Oh it's a brilliant team here,
14    IR:   Yeah
15    Sue:  And apart from which I'm sure you've heard about Fiona,
16    IR:   Yeah, oh well yeah, yeah.
17    Sue:  E::m
18    IR:   Yeah
19    Sue:  And Penny and I get on really well with the (finance) but
20          she drives me potty.
21    IR:   Yeah.
```

```
22  Sue:  So, er, I won't be sad to leave that one ⌈behind.
23  IR:                                          ⌊Really? Isn't
24        that- isn't that interesting. Why is it- why is it that-
25        (3.0)
26        ((Sue sits back, smiling, but showing a distinct
27        reluctance to continue.))
28  Sue:  Oooooooooooo ((The precise sound of this suggests
29        something that it would be a bit naughty to go into
30        details. The interviewer talks over this.))
31  IR:   You can tell me, I'm not- it doesn't
32  Sue:  oo((tone changes))oooWhat isn't it. ((Sniffs)) I find her
33        disorganised,
34  IR:   ((Very quietly)) Yeah
35  Sue:  lazy,
36        (1.0)
37  IR:   ((Very quietly)) Yeah
38  Sue:  selfish,
39        (2.0)
40  IR:   Really that(?) Yeah
41  Sue:  E:r unapproachable. Really unapproachable.
42  IR:   Really?
43  Sue:  Yeah
44  IR:   Yeah
45  Sue:  If I got... ((Expands on this and give examples))
```

Level 1: questions

As an interviewer, my range of responses here is very limited. I begin with a general invitation to discuss feelings and then rely almost entirely on 'yeah', which features in two-thirds of the responses, including a long stretch between lines 12 and 21. When heard on the tape, 'go on' in my first couple of turns is intonationally very odd for an interview and seems to belong much more to the sort of exchange typically used to elicit gossip in informal encounters. This is almost certainly a leftover from the initial casual exchanges.

It's noticeable that when I go beyond 'yeah' (for example, in line 23), the interview opens up, and there's strong evidence that my lazy reliance on 'yeah' means that I miss at least one obvious opportunity to probe a statement. I fail to pick up Sue's statement that Penny drives her 'mad' (l.6) and my slightly surprised response to her statement about deciding to apply for jobs serves only to direct her away from the subject of Penny and towards a statement about how good the team is. Her almost immediate return to a reformulation of the statement using 'potty' instead of 'mad' (l.20) should have served as a strong signal to me to probe this response. Instead, I settle for 'yeah'. *What I learn from this is that I need to be more attentive to respondents' repetitions and reformulations of earlier statements.*

Level 2: distortions

My second use of 'really' (l.42) sounds distinctly surprised and its positioning brings an element of evaluation into my talk that could serve to distort what follows. Sue has presented a list of four of Penny's characteristics from her perspective: disorganised, lazy, selfish and unapproachable. They don't amount to a very pleasant description, but my response along the way is to make no comment on them, except perhaps for my response to 'selfish' where there is the slightest hint of a questioning intonation in 'really', though this is followed by 'yeah', which produces a fairly neutral effect. It's only when she produces 'unapproachable' that I show clearly marked surprise, eventually prompting the justification of the claim that begins in line 45.

Had I persisted with 'yeah' all the way through the list, then paused to review all of the characteristics presented, there would have been no evaluative implication in my response. However, my evident surprise at 'unapproachable' changes the pragmatic force of my previous responses. In themselves they appear neutral, but the surprise here marks Sue's earlier comments as unsurprising and therefore implicitly acceptable. I have effectively, if only implicitly, agreed with the description of Penny as disorganised, lazy and selfish, which was certainly not my intention. Interactionally, I suspect that the 'Really that(?) Yeah' is a transitional response pointing towards an expression of more explicit surprise meant to apply to the whole list. However, that's not how the transcript reads and it's certainly not how Sue interpreted it, which is really all that matters.

Although I eventually managed to get the interview back on track, it seems clear that my initial response produced a distorted impression of alignment with Sue's position. *What I learn from this is to be much more careful when framing my responses to items in a list, especially if they are contentious.* Responses must depend on the context in which such descriptions are produced, but as a general rule it is probably best to maintain a neutral response in order to elicit the full list, before returning to particular points.

Level 3: relationships

I've already mentioned my decision to approach this interview very informally and as a strategy this may have elicited responses that a more formal atmosphere might have inhibited, but it does produce my distinctly odd response in line 31: 'You can tell me, I'm not- it doesn't'. It's hard to characterise this precisely, but on the basis of its form I'm inclined to see it as almost a caricature of the professional/client confidentiality relationship, along the lines of 'You can tell me, I'm a doctor'. Of course, had this relationship been established at the outset there would have been no need for this altogether exceptional statement, so in a sense it represents a failure to establish the proper conditions for an interview. On the other hand, it does produce the goods in terms of blunt speaking.

My main reservation is that by allowing the 'go on' stance of a fellow gossip to stay in play alongside a formal reassurance of confidentiality, I am deliberately encouraging Sue to 'dish the dirt' rather than to explore with me the nature of her professional relationship with Penny. In fact, even when the interview took what might be described as a more conventional shape, she continued to speak openly and quite bluntly, and at the end stated emphatically that I was free to use the interview in any way I saw fit. *What I learn from this is the need to consider carefully in advance the implications of any deliberate move away from the 'interviewer' identity.*

Level 4: the interviewee

This is not the Sue of earlier interviews. She is about to leave and does not anticipate working with Penny again; she has worked very professionally for years, revealing her true feelings to only one other colleague, and now she seems to want to set the record straight, to spill the beans. Her long 'oooo' preceding the revelations is a necessary reluctance marker, inviting reassurance that what follows is acceptable, but also detectable in it is a sense of delicious anticipation. Sue's previous interview responses and comments, delivered in the rôle of responsible professional with work to do and relationships to maintain, have to be looked at again in the light of what she has said here.

Skills development

By far the best way of developing interview skills is that recommended in the course of this chapter: plenty of practice and the careful analysis of transcripts. However, it is possible to hone particular skills and identify key areas for development, and this is what the following tasks are designed to do.

The first task (Task 2.1) aims to develop the important skills involved in opening up a topic. It is based on a single topic interview and therefore tests your ability to maintain focus.

Task 2.1   Opening up a topic Setting up

Setting up
Begin by deciding on a simple topic that can be covered in a relatively brief interview, and preferably one that colleagues might be prepared to spare about 15 minutes for. A good example would be 'Setting up groupwork'.

Procedure
1. Begin with a 'mini tour' question along the lines of 'Talk me through how you...'
2. Concentrate on using follow-ups and probes in order to open up the topic as much as possible *without shifting to a new topic*.
3. Identify the most effective of these. Why did they work so well? Can you classify different types? Which work best for you?

Development
1. Repeat this with as many colleagues as possible, refining your follow-ups and probes as you go along. Record all interviews.
2. When you decide you have enough data or you have completed your quota of interviews, sum up the main lessons you've learnt about (a) your own interviewing style, and (b) follow-up and probe questions. Try to draw up a list of advice points for future reference.
3. Prepare a short presentation for a staff meeting or for your study group on your findings. If you are a member of a study group, you can all decide on different topics in advance and work towards two forms of presentation (either orally or in poster form) on (a) findings, and (b) interview questions. In the case of the latter, identify key findings. Can you agree a set of useful maxims for opening up interviews?

The second task (Task 2.2) focuses on question design and is particularly suitable for anyone considering a semi-structured approach to interviewing.

Task 2.2 Designing interview questions

Setting up

Decide on a single focus of inquiry, which could be anything you would like to know more about. It should be something that you can explore through interviews with people accessible to you (e.g. colleagues, family, friends). Examples might be, 'What are teachers' views of the coursebook used in this school?' or 'What do teachers think of staff meetings?'

Procedure

1. Write down the main question, then identify key interview questions deriving from this.
2. Use the key interview questions to work out progressively focused questions, moving from general to particular.
3. Critique the questions you have selected, then use the final versions as a basis for the design of a semi-structured interview.
4. Conduct an interview using this guide and review its effectiveness in the light of your experience. Which parts worked best and which were weakest? Can you relate this to how the questions were derived, or was it a matter of questioning technique, or both?

Development

1. Revise your guide in the light of the first interview and repeat the interview, preferably with someone with a very different character (e.g. more extrovert, opinionated). Review what you learn from comparing the two. How did your questioning change? Were there any questions that worked with one respondent and not the other? Etc.
2. Look at your questions again and see which ones can be approached obliquely rather than directly. Revise the interview guide in the light of this and, if possible, conduct another interview for the purposes of comparison and review.
3. If you are working in a group, the critiquing after initial drafting can be undertaken by others and, if appropriate, different guides can be developed. These can then be used and the results compared.
4. Another very enjoyable group activity is a challenge based on finding oblique approaches. A selection of questions is distributed among the groups and each has to try to develop the most convincing oblique approaches. (n.b. This is a useful exercise for exploring creativity in question design, but it would lead to a very odd interview if taken to extremes.)

The third task (Task 2.3) is a general one that can be used at any stage provided that a partner is available. The key to this is the recognition that no interview is perfect and that honest criticism, if offered in a supportive spirit, can provide an excellent pointer to areas that need improvement.

Task 2.3   Refining technique

Setting up

Agree a couple of topics for an interview. They should be very straightforward and potentially entertaining. 'Places I've loved', 'People who have inspired me' and 'Things I'd never do again' are the sort of subjects that can work well. This is the kind of topic that demands something of the interviewer (opening them up can represent a real challenge), but if the interviewer sets out to understand *why* these choices have been made they can be very revealing.

Procedure
1. Agree a duration for the interviews and take it in turns to interview one another. The topic can be different for each interview or the same topic can be repeated. Record the interviews.
2. Immediately after each interview, both participants write down their impressions. What was the overall feeling you were left with? Which parts went well/badly? Which parts would you like to hear again?
3. Discuss these impressions. Where do you agree/disagree most significantly? Which points would you like to explore in more depth? Are there any lessons you can agree on now?

Development
1. Explore the transcript together. Begin with the parts of the interview you identified as most interesting or problematic. Discuss your feelings/thinking at key points in the interview. Identify questions or responses that seemed to you to provoke the most interesting reactions and discuss the implications of these for interview technique. If there are parts where the interview seemed to go badly, decide why this happened and work out an alternative approach.
2. Agree a set of 'improvement points' for the next interview.
3. When you feel ready for it (this may be days or weeks later) move on to the next topic, reviewing the 'improvement points' first. When you eventually review your performance in this, make these your starting points.

The most important task you can perform is to continue to evaluate your performance using the criteria contained in this chapter. You can, if you wish, focus in on particular features and work on improving this aspect of your interviewing technique. Which ones you choose must depend on your own particular strengths and weaknesses as an interviewer, but obvious candidates are opportunities missed and lines of development prematurely closed down. It can also be instructive to try to work out your own idiosyncracies as an interviewer, or, if you are part of a group, work out one another's idiosyncracies. After all, part of the reason that interviews are such a rich source of data is that people are all so different – whichever side of the interview you're sitting.

Reading guide

Level 1
It's not difficult to find very basic introductions to interviewing, often as part of a general introduction to research, and TESOL possesses a few of these. However, they are usually so basic as to be rather more misleading than helpful. The best approach is to go for a longer treatment that's very readable and is written by someone who has used this data collection method for a considerable time.

Fortunately, there is a book that serves this purpose admirably. Rubin and Rubin (1995) have spent much of their lives doing research that is based on interviews and together they've written a book that gives you a real sense of what it's like to be involved in qualitative interviewing. None of us is likely to be as involved as they are in this particular world, and some of the positions they advance seem rather dated, but along the way they are able to pass on nuggets of practical wisdom with the sort of clarity that only long experience can provide. It's a book you can read for pleasure as well as information.

If you want the same experience but in a significantly smaller helping, the only alternative I know is Burgess (1984b:101 – 22). The chapter in the Burgess book is around twenty years old and things have moved on, but it is based on experience in educational settings and it does have lots of good examples and insights. For such a short read, it has plenty to offer and is worth tracking down.

Level 2
The literature at this level is growing all the time and offers a range of texts. My own view is that, as a practical introduction with good coverage, Arksey and Knight (1999) offers the best single text. It tends to go

for range rather than depth, but it contains plenty of useful lists and it sets out the options well.

In such a popular field there are plenty of shorter summaries to which you can resort, but the most comprehensive of these is probably the chapter on interviewing contained in Patton 1990. At times its orientation towards evaluation emerges, but never sufficiently strongly to provide a distraction, and the chapter itself is rich in detail. Alternatively, if your interest is in the semi-structured interview, Flick (2002:72–95) provides a crisp introduction with some useful recommendations for further reading.

If you are interested in interviewing using a focus group, Bloor *et al.* (2001) offer a handy practical introduction, or there is a useful brief paper by Oates (2000) and an overview in Grbich (1999:108–15). Anyone researching élites within TESOL can benefit from the experiences of others who have faced the particular challenges they bring (Thomas 1993 or a useful brief discussion in Arksey and Knight 1999:122–5). Otherwise, your explorations should be within the context of the particular traditions within which you are working, in which case the following may be useful: Wengraf (2002) for life history; Heyl (2001) or Hammersley and Atkinson (1995:124–56) for ethnography; DeVault and McCoy (2002) for institutional ethnography.

Study strategy 2.1 offers an overview.

Study strategy 2.1   The importance of interview practice

The best way of improving your performance in this area is to get plenty of practice in interviewing, but you can deepen this in either of the following ways:

1. Draw on the lessons of experienced practitioners. For this I recommend Rubin and Rubin (1995), discussed above.
2. Explore specific techniques and strategies. Patton (1990) includes plenty of these, some of them offering slightly different perspectives from the ones developed in this chapter. Johnson and Weller (2002) also provide an excellent overview of elicitation techniques.

Level 3

At this level much will depend on the research tradition within which you are working (Study strategy 2.2). As well as helping you to develop relevant techniques, the chapter itself should prepare you for conducting the interview and help you to get a perspective on analysis, but for more detailed information on content and analytical perspectives, you may need to explore literature within the tradition itself. Currently, Gubrium and Holstein (2002a) offer the best single collection of papers on all aspects of interviewing, so this might make a useful starting point. For a critical discussion of interviews from an applied linguist, you could add Block (2000).

The growing interest in the place of the teacher in TESOL suggests that life history interviews might become popular, in which case Wengraf (2001) provides a comprehensive introduction. His book is not particularly readable and it's a little too systems-based for my taste, but there's plenty of useful advice there for any qualitative interviewer – if you're prepared to work to dig it out.

Other aspects of interview technique and approach have been mentioned in the course of the chapter, but I should add that I have found myself in situations where teachers have become quite emotional about professional experiences, so I think it's also worth mentioning Ellis, Kiesinger and Tillmann-Healy's paper on this topic (1997), which includes some useful references.

Study strategy 2.2   Examining your research tradition

This guide is based on the fact that you will probably want to explore aspects of your own research tradition and consider in more depth some of the issues raised in the chapter.

1. For the former, Gubrium and Holstein (2002a) makes a good starting point and Bryman (2002) also promises to be helpful.

2. If you would like to revisit some of the issues raised here, Kvale (1996) offers a useful introduction to qualitative interviewing and a consideration of some key issues. His shorter and more provocative later paper (1999) advances the case for the psychoanalytical interview as a viable approach. However, if you would prefer something rather shorter and more entertaining, I thoroughly recommend Walford's short chapter on interviews (2001). This raises a number of provocative questions about the use of the qualitative interview and approaches to it, and draws on around a quarter of a century's experience of qualitative research in education.

3
Observation

Preview

Just because we work with language doesn't mean that we walk around with our eyes closed: teachers have to develop keen observational skills as a matter of survival. However, the instinctive deployment of such skills is not the same thing as using them to improve our understanding of the professional world we inhabit, so it is unfortunate that in the TESOL research literature the *skills* of observation are almost completely overlooked. True, there has been a good deal of work on observation systems, but these have their limitations and cannot offer the rich possibilities that are inherent in freer observation. My focus in this chapter, therefore, will be on developing observation skills and indicating how these can be deployed to good effect; I will defer consideration of structured observation until the final level.

Level 1 will introduce you to the skills of observation, showing how much can be discovered through the application of these. It will deal briefly with ethical issues associated with observation and offer some basic advice on note taking. The main practical focus of the level, though, will be on how to relate physical characteristics of a setting to the behaviours that take place there.

Level 2 aims to develop further the skills introduced at Level 1, setting them in the wider context of fieldwork. It addresses issues of access and field relations before moving on to consider how observation can be structured and to identify approaches that help develop sensitivity to setting and activity. Practical matters are concluded with a section on note taking, then the ethical issues touched on at the introductory level are highlighted in slightly more detail. The level concludes with a case raising issues of description and representation.

Level 3 focuses on structured observation. While recognising the dangers involved in this approach, it also highlights the valuable part such observation can play in fieldwork and provides advice on how to decide whether to incorporate it. Practical advice is offered on designing and applying an observation schedule and potential problems are addressed. The level also includes a section on how to calculate interobserver agreement.

Although this chapter begins and ends with classroom examples, for the most part my focus is on the school rather than the classroom. This is partly because the classroom is such a familiar place that establishing observational 'distance' can be very difficult and partly because the institutional context is ideal for discussing issues of access, field relations, and so on. It's also interesting to discover how taking the time to stand back and observe our own institutional context can reveal fascinating and unexpected aspects that we have previously taken for granted.

Level 1: learning to see

The first step to becoming a good observer is to accept that this is something you have to work at. We can all sit back and observe at the drop of a hat, but what we cannot do is work up the sort of description that will yield valuable insights – to do that we need a little guidance and a lot of practice.

Wolcott (1994:153–5) offers an illustration of just how demanding and rewarding good observation can be in a story that bears retelling. It concerns the experience of Nathanial Shaler during the time that Louis Agassiz, an eminent biologist-naturalist, agreed to take him on as a student. When Shaler arrived, Agassiz directed him to sit at a table on which the latter then placed a rusty pan containing a small fish. Agassiz told his new student to 'study it', warned him not to damage the specimen, and advised him to confine his attention to the specimen, eschewing discussion with others or printed sources. He concluded by saying that he would return to question Shaler when he thought the latter was ready. After an hour Shaler felt he had completed his task and was ready to move on to a more demanding assignment, but he was dismayed to find that Agassiz showed no interest in returning. It was only on the seventh day, by which time Shaler felt that he knew a hundred times more than was revealed in his initial inspection, that Agassiz returned and delivered a peremptory 'Well?' The hour-long explication that followed was brought to an abrupt end with the exclamation, 'That is not right!' Shaler applied himself with even more determination, discarding his original notes and working on a new description for ten hours a day over the next week. The results seemed to satisfy Agassiz, who gave him a more demanding task that occupied him for the next two months, punctuated periodically by his teacher's only comment – 'That is not right'. Shaler eventually became an eminent scientist in his own right, but he never forgot this demanding initiation or his sense of excitement as his skills of observation developed.

In his comment on this, Wolcott refers to the importance of the 'self as instrument' (1994:156), a description that seems to me to capture the essence of what is involved. Observation is more than a mechanical process to be gone through; it is a commitment to apply the full range of our perceptual and analytic skills as intensely and extensively as we are able, in the pursuit of understanding. What follows will not be as demanding as Shaler's painful immersion, but it will help you to develop your own skills of observation. To illustrate how much we can understand just from looking, consider the extracts describing a teacher's actions (Extract 3.1) in a lesson that was broadcast as part of a television series following the progress of someone just beginning their career as a teacher in a state school in England.

These three descriptions trace a teacher's loss of control and eventual humiliation. At first his movements are slow and expansive, used to exercise control over the class, and he moves freely in the students' territory. Later, he has retreated to the filing cabinet and his movements are nervous, accusing, aimed at the class opposite him. Finally, he is pressed against the cabinet, his body knotted and his hands covering his face, protecting himself when confronted by a student who displays her confidence to the class. We do not need to hear the words to recognise the teacher's failure.

I have watched the videotape of this lesson many, many times, and never without pain. I don't know the teacher personally but I have known others like him, and although he received help and advice, I can't help feeling that if this had drawn on more sensitive observation and an analysis of his interaction rather than just on rules for effective teaching, he might still be in the profession. Solutions, of course, are never that simple, but at the end of this level you should at least have a greater understanding of how to develop your own powers of observation and your sensitivity to setting, participants and interaction. First, though, we need to consider some of the ethical issues associated with observation.

Extract 3.1 A lesson

The teacher's arm signals are relatively expansive and he uses a number of directive motions, such as the one where he points to a student with his right arm while using slow up and down movements of an outstretched left palm to quieten the rest of the class. When students are on task, he moves around the class, occasionally briefly resuming his position at the front in order to make a general point.

. . . He leans his left elbow against the filing cabinet and uses his right hand to jab at the class. Eventually he moves, his arms pinned to his sides down as far as the elbow, but jerking in tight, stabbing movements below that. He reaches the desk and leans a hand on it while continuing to stab with the other, then he returns to the filing cabinet, hugging it closer.

. . . He is engaged in an exchange with the late arriving student. She sits back in her desk, body half turned to the class, arms fairly wide, head back, while he presses himself tightly to the side of the filing cabinet, elbows clenched to his stomach, his hands completely covering his face up to the eyes. He speaks through his fingers.

Access and ethics

'The cat', as the saying goes, 'can look at the queen'. The dictum, though, does not go on to sanction systematic observation or taking notes. It might also be argued that part of the contract with monarchs is that, in exchange for the considerable benefits they enjoy by virtue of their position, they should also agree to be on public display occasionally. When I choose to stand up and talk at a conference or when I take on a rôle in the school parents' pantomime, I accept similar conditions, but for the rest of the time I value my privacy. I don't mind people looking, but the thought of being observed – by cats or anyone else – makes me just a little uncomfortable. On the other hand, I know that I can't walk in the street or enter any reasonably large building without my actions being captured on hidden cameras. So where does this leave the person who wants to get down to the business of observation? One starting point is to ask whether there are any settings that can be described as 'open', in the sense that access to data collection is unproblematic. You might like to consider this before reading on.

The question is not as straightforward as it may seem at first sight. The obvious answer is that places such as parks, street corners, perhaps shops and places of entertainment are 'open' in the sense that behaviour is public. Therefore, the argument might go, there is nothing wrong in collecting data from these settings. But this ignores the relationship between the behaviour of the observer and that of other actors. In all settings there is a sense of what is appropriate behaviour, and surreptitious note-taking on the actions of others rarely fits that category – at best it is regarded as prying. There is a sense, then, in which entry has to be 'managed' if not negotiated in such settings. The nature of the management will depend on the setting and the observer's position in it. For example, it's not unusual to see people sitting in airports or public parks making notes, so this activity will be seen as unexceptional, whereas sitting and scribbling in a nightclub would be regarded as distinctly odd (though my colleague, Steve Mann, suggests the intriguing alternative of inputting 'messages' into a mobile phone in this situation).

There are at least three research issues that need to be addressed when observing: the effect on the behaviour of the observed, possible consequences for the observer, and the ethics of the observer's actions. The first of these issues raises the spectre of the *observer's paradox*: if people know they're being observed they won't act normally. The observer therefore needs to ensure as far as possible when taking notes that this is not apparent to others present, even though they may well 'know' what the researcher is doing, having given permission for it. This is largely a matter of how note taking is managed, which will be the focus of the next section. The second issue has to do with our relationship with those we are observing: if you are observing people you know, make sure that there is no risk of damaging your personal relationships with them, and when observing people you don't know, spare a thought for your physical safety. In the special situation where the researcher becomes part of the group being observed (and hence a *participant observer*), the development of this relationship is particularly relevant.

The final issue is the most complex: What are the ethics of data collection? When observing public places, it is impossible to ask permission of all those involved so this issue doesn't arise, and in any case the actors will remain anonymous, but note taking still needs to be unobtrusive and non-threatening. However, in some private settings such as the classroom, where the observer's presence and activities are clear to all, permission is essential. Between these two extremes lie difficult grey areas where hard thinking is needed. For example, when undertaking needs analysis in an ESP (English for Specific Purposes) project that involves observation of insider-client interactions in a semi-public place, is it sufficient to have permission from senior managers or should everyone involved know what is happening? These are difficult matters to settle, but the questions in Box 3.1 are designed to help in the decision-making process.

Box 3.1   Deciding on permission for observing (semi-) private places

1. Is it feasible to ask general permission to observe from those involved without compromising the observation? If it is, ask permission.
2. If you have received general permission from someone in a senior position, is observation something that plays an accepted part in the activities of the setting? If so, go ahead.
3. Will the results of your observation be made public, albeit in disguised form? If so, ask permission.
4. If in doubt, how would you feel in this situation if you discovered that someone had been observing you secretly?

The observation activities proposed below need not be part of any larger project, so any notes you make need be seen only by you and can be destroyed when they have served their purpose. If this is this case, permission may not be an issue, provided that the observation is discreet.

Just looking

Pick a convenient setting (for example, look out of your window at the street below, observe what's happening in your staff room, your living room, the bus, the train) and observe for as long as you possibly can, aiming for between half an hour and an hour if you can manage it. Don't take notes, just fix your attention on the scene in front of you and try to build up a clear picture of what is happening. When you've done that, sit back and reflect on the experience, jotting down notes if you feel that helps. Then read on.

There are no straightforward rules for observation, but you can learn a lot from practice and reflection on that practice. For example, if you tried that observation task you will probably have encountered some of the observation problems with which all researchers wrestle. Most of these have to do with attention, although they take different forms. The first and most obvious is the difficulty of maintaining attention. You begin with every good intention of keeping your attention fixed on the scene in front of you, but before long you've drifted off into thoughts about the furniture, your partner's new job, or that raindrop trickling down the window. Usually the shift is quite subtle, beginning with a consideration of some aspect of behaviour that interests you, and moving away by degrees. The only protection against it, unless you are in the very fortunate position of being able to take notes on the spot, is to develop resistance through experience and establish some sort of inner monitoring system. It's also worth remembering that the challenge lies not so much in preventing your attention from drifting away – that's probably inevitable – as in making sure that it drifts back again.

A second problem of attention has to do with what you observe. Your first experience of observation in the task above was probably a sense of confusion about *what* to look for. The word 'observation' itself has built into it the idea of purposeful looking, so it doesn't really make sense just to sit down and look; you want to know what to look *for*. All effective observation could perhaps be described as the continual refinement of this issue of focus, which cannot be resolved simply by fixing on one particular object at the expense of others. The danger in looking for something particular is that you may be able to find it only at the cost of ignoring what is genuinely interesting. One experienced researcher's comments on the value of observation direct attention to the importance of an open mind and an eye for the unexpected:

> Participant observation offers the advantage of serendipity: significant discoveries that were unanticipated. In contrast to the survey, which is planned on the basis of what the researcher expects to find, participant observation opens up possibilities for encountering the completely unexpected phenomenon that may be more significant than anything the field worker could have foreseen, suggesting important hypotheses worthy of further study. (Whyte 1984:27)

This, more than anything else, is what makes observation worthwhile. Even if you don't have any plans for a larger project, simply developing your eye for detail and your awareness for what is happening in your own context can generate insights that are professionally valuable.

The third thing you may have experienced after observing for a few minutes is the sense that 'nothing is happening'. You observe 'actions', but they seem meaningless because they are either random or entirely predictable. This is as it should be. The *starting point* of observation is this entirely unexceptional world, but if the observation is successful it will succeed in 'making it strange', opening up perspectives on behaviour which the ordinary eye misses. Achieving this is not easy, and though there are no simple rules for observation to help you overcome the problems I've identified, it is possible to develop strategies designed to dig beneath the surface of things. Two key perspectives are introduced below and others are discussed in Level 2.

A sense of place

Sometimes I get tired of the way my neighbourhood supermarket keeps shifting the location of its foodstuffs, but I understand that the manager has a job to do. Like others in his trade, he knows that settings are not neutral; they both reflect and influence the way we go about our business. For the manager of a shop this balance is important: if the arrangement is too alien to our experience we might avoid the store, but within reasonable parameters of expectation the manager is free to design the layout in a way that encourages us to buy more. The desire for financial reward ensures that those in retailing invest time and money in matters of design and display, but other settings might be influenced by different motivations. For example, offices might be arranged with employee productivity or client impression in mind, while living rooms are often laid out to facilitate social interaction. Because these arrangements are part of our everyday world it is all too easy to take them for granted, so if we wish to succeed as an observer of the social world we must cultivate and sustain a proper sensitivity to the presence of setting.

If you would like to work on developing your observation skills, it would be worth deciding now on a setting that will be the focus for your work. Once you've settled on a place, you'll be able to experience a gradually deepening understanding of what happens there as your observation skills develop. Just a couple of simple observational activities should open your eyes to things you have so far taken for granted, though to get a full sense of what is possible, you'll need to follow up your work here with the activities suggested in Level 2. If you decide to do that, the setting won't change, so your decision here is an important one. I would suggest that you choose somewhere you have access to on a daily basis and where your presence is unexceptional. Ideally, it would also offer you the possibility of taking notes without drawing attention to yourself. The most obvious example would be a staffroom or a common room, but you might also consider a café/restaurant/bar, a waiting room, or some other place where people gather and where you have to spend time. For example, if you have to pick up your children from a playgroup and spend time waiting for them along with other parents, this might represent a good opportunity to observe. Take some time in choosing the setting and try to settle on something you are comfortable with and would like to know more about.

When you have decided on a setting, work on building up as full a description as you can, paying particular attention to the objects in it and the way they are arranged. Don't worry about people at this point – it's the stage not the actors that you're interested in. Draw a sketch of it and think carefully about the things there. Note down as much as you can and don't just settle for the obvious (chairs, tables, etc.), let your eye settle on smaller objects: notices on the wall, piles of books, somebody's glasses case and hat, a sandwich box, etc. Study the arrangements. How are things grouped? What's fixed and what's moveable? What *does* move? What stays put? Take as many visits as you need to build up a detailed picture of the physical setting. Remember Shaler and the fish: look hard and, if you can, look long.

When you're satisfied with the description you've produced, stand back and ask yourself what it tells you about the setting. Consider both *space* and *objects*. What space is available and how is it distributed? Which spaces encourage particular activities and which spaces discourage them? This may be important if you wish to assess the significance of a particular action. Are there any spaces or rules relating to spaces that allow people to define their rôle by occupying them (e.g. 'I'm on duty when I'm standing here')? Here are three areas I noted in one particular staffroom:

Kettle and coffee machine:	Brief social exchanges usually confined to time spent waiting for the kettle to boil or coffee to filter through.
Armchairs:	Longer periods of casual talk; reading books/papers/magazines; occasionally sleeping.
Desks facing the wall:	Private study, marking or preparation.

In this staffroom, sitting at a desk facing the wall might announce 'I'm at work', so a person who constantly initiates exchanges with people at their desks, thus breaking into their working time, might be an authority figure, or a pest, or both. Similarly, waiting outside the staffroom door might define someone as a student.

The same sorts of questions can be asked of objects. Ownership of or access to particular objects might be a sign of status; certain objects might be associated with particular activities. For example, a notice board with a timetable on it and announcements for the day will attract different attention from one with local information or conference announcements; a particular desk might have extra features (e.g. a lamp, a telephone, personal objects such as a glasses case) identifying ownership. Look carefully at the nature and arrangement of objects and think about what they might mean. If you do a thorough job here, you're already moving naturally to the second stage of observation.

The inhabitants

The conventional term for the people you are observing is 'actors' and for the most part I'll follow this convention. However, I've chosen 'inhabitants' for my title here to capture the sense of inhabitation, of *living* within the space and hence *using* it for particular activities. I know that inhabitation represents a more extended activity than might be appropriate here, but it's the relationship I'm interested in. To take an example with which you will be familiar, a teacher walks into a classroom and, seeing that the desks are arranged in rows facing the front, asks for them to be rearranged in clusters or in a circle. The relationship between layout and activity is fundamental, and most semi-public settings will represent a compromise between institutional arrangement and individual initiative sanctioned by group usage. If you have already formed a clear picture of the physical setting, you should be in an excellent position to explore how its inhabitants interact with their environment and their fellow actors, as in this example from Whyte:

> When evening activities were going full blast, I looked around the room to see which people were talking together, playing cards together, or otherwise interacting. I counted the number of men in the room, so as to know how many I would have to account for. Since I was familiar with the main physical objects of the clubroom, it was not difficult to get a mental picture of the men in relation to tables, chairs, couches, radio, and so on. When individuals moved about or when there was some interaction between the groupings, I sought to retain that in mind. In the course of an evening, there might be a general reshuffling of positions. I was not able to remember every movement, but I tried to observe with which members the movements began.

And when another spatial arrangement developed, I went through the same mental process as I had with the first. (Whyte 1984:86)

Begin by observing and taking notes from the point of view of the relationship between actions and setting. Ask questions such as the following: are particular activities related to particular spaces? How do people make use of the setting in their everyday activities? Are there distinct territories? Who inhabits them, who are the visitors and who is excluded? Do this on more than one occasion if you can, then review your notes and ask yourself what you have learned about: (a) this particular setting; (b) the relevance of space and objects; and (c) the process of observation.

By now you should be developing an interesting picture of an environment you had previously taken for granted, and it's possible to enrich your description – and your understanding – further if you wish. You may already have noted many of the things that follow, but they will at least serve as a useful checklist. How closely did you look at the people themselves? What are their names? How are they addressed? How do they present themselves, etc.? Extract 3.2 on p. 115 illustrates how a difference in dress may be significant: the two male ('General English') teachers were casually dressed, while the two female ('Business English') teachers dressed quite formally – a reflection, as it turned out, of more than their teaching responsibilities. Take this a stage further and try to form a picture of relationships. What are the groups? How do they relate to one another? Are there hierarchies? How do people move from one group to another? How are relationships defined? Can you spot any unwritten rules? And so on. Of course, it is through interaction that such relationships are established and developed, so try to note down topics, summaries of what is said, snatches of talk. Ideally, you could combine this with the sort of recording and analysis discussed in Chapter 4.

Finally, and most importantly, reflect on your observations. Try to stand back from your descriptions and examine them from different perspectives to see whether this generates different insights or different ways of understanding what is happening. And don't forget that even changing your vantage point as an observer can help you to see things with a fresh eye. Insights will be more likely to develop if you reflect not only on the content of your notes but on the act of observation itself. The awareness of becoming a better, more sensitive observer is reward in itself, but it also offers the prospect of a richer relationship with the world around you. Box 3.2 summarises the basic steps towards that end.

Box 3.2 Summary: steps in building a description

1. Resolve ethical and practical issues.
2. Build up a full description of the setting: objects and spaces.
3. Consider what these arrangements encourage/enforce.
4. Note how actors use the objects and spaces.
5. Describe the actors and their relationships.
6. Note down any relevant exchanges.
7. At all stages, review what you have learned about the setting and about observation.

Note taking

The way we approach note taking is influenced to some extent by our view of what observation involves. To illustrate this I begin with a position very different from the one I subsequently go on to develop. In a section on procedures for observation, Grbich (1999:134) says that '[t]he researcher acts largely as a camera, scanning and recording detail wherever she/he happens to be focusing, while also recording sounds and spoken language from a broader range'. This comparison leads to interesting claims and ones that I do not think can be sustained. She goes on to say that it is preferable that no notes are made on site but as soon as possible after leaving it. However, the level of detail she demands would require a super-human memory – or a videotape. For example, she advises that '[a]ll verbal language (agreement, disagreement) should be recorded, including topics of conversation and time spent on each' (1999:135). Anyone who has ever tried recapturing even five minutes of conversation after a gap of ten minutes or so will recognise the impossibility of her prescription – in fact, you might like to test this for yourself.

My purpose here is not so much to disagree with Grbich, who also provides a useful picture of how description can evolve over time, but to point out that our view of ourselves as observers will colour the way we go about observing and note taking. I see observation as essentially a human activity and believe that many of the challenges it brings derive from a need to overcome our natural inclinations. In order to do this, we need to approach observation not through the undiscriminating lens of the camera but consciously and systematically. Adler and Adler

(1994:377) sum up the position perfectly: 'What differentiates the observations of social scientists from those of everyday-life actors is the former's systematic and purposive nature'.

Box 3.3　An order of preference for note taking

1. Find a way of disguising the note taking so that it is possible to make notes as events unfold. When I was a participant observer in a language school, I made detailed and extensive 'lesson plans', which were in fact little more than obvious and visible headings under which I scribbled tiny and barely legible fieldnotes.
2. Find a location on-site where notes can be made as soon as possible after the events. There might well be a room or corner available where you can take brief notes while the memories are still very fresh.
3. Make all notes off-site. If you have to do this, get brief notes down as soon as possible, perhaps at a nearby café on the bus or train home.

Box 3.3 presents three approaches to note taking in descending order of preference. There are, in fact, three stages in the writing process, of which note taking (perhaps 'jotting' would be a better word) is the first. The next step is to move from basic notes to a fuller description, usually referred to as *fieldnotes*. This has to be done back at base, but it should be tackled as soon as possible, allowing as few events (especially inter-actions with others) as possible to get between notes and fieldnotes. When writing up notes, try to recall as much as possible, aiming above all for richness of detail, but don't worry about style – the notes are for you and you alone. In fact, one researcher (Jackson 1990:20) has said that a fieldnote is 'something that can't readily be comprehended by another person'. Only if you decide to make your findings public do you need to move to the third stage, where the fieldnotes are used as the basis for a final version. Often this will include extracts from the fieldnotes themselves, as Extract 3.2 illustrates. The fieldnotes here (in italics) were written up from a jotting, 'n.b. clothes' and are now embedded in a broader account derived from other notes and interpretations.

Extract 3.2   A published version

The first thing likely to strike a visitor to the school, though, is the difference in their appearance:

Louise, like Jenny [and Annette] is smartly dressed. Well made up, comfortable but serious blouse, short dark skirt and black tights. Attractive and friendly clothes, but definitely appropriate to business. Paul and Harry present a much more casual picture: crewneck jumpers, jeans (denims for Harry) and open-necked shirts. The contrast is clear but not stark.
(F–12/1/94)

This difference is to some extent a reflection of personal preference, but it is also in line with the division of responsibilities in the school. Harry and Paul teach general English, which tends to attract younger and more academically or socially oriented learners, while Annette and Louise concentrate on business English and attract corporate clients, many on a one-to-one basis. As principal, Jenny deals with both sets of clients. The division is, coincidentally, also along gender lines and, less coincidentally, territorial: Annette and Louise are based in the upper staffroom, where business materials are kept and where they discuss aspects of their shared professional interest in this area, while Harry and Paul have their base in the general staffroom.

Case 3.1: whose topic?

On my way back from a recent visit to Japan I was sitting in Narita airport thinking about this book and it occurred to me that the best way of illustrating how you could fit observation into all sorts of situations would be to do just that. I therefore looked around and spotted a group sitting nearby whose conversation I could not hear. What conclusions do you draw about their interaction from reading the skeleton description in Extract 3.3?

You might have noticed a number of things about this, but for me what is interesting is the role that A plays. I don't know what they were saying and I don't know if A is the leader of this group – it's more likely that her rôle here has something to do with the topic and her 'ownership' of it – but it seems clear that she is the dominant figure in these exchanges. She is the only one who holds the floor on her own and when

Extract 3.3 Narita Airport 10:00 21/2/02

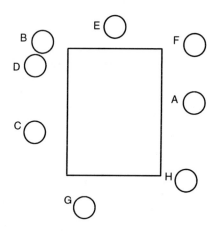

Setting
Coffee area in Narita airport departure lounge. Low table, comfortable chairs, plenty of space.

Participants
8 Japanese young adults (c.20 years old), all female except for one (H). All sitting on own seats except B, who is perched on the arm of D's chair.

Events
C films throughout, moving the camera around the table, sometimes focusing on speaker, sometimes on listener.

1. A talks. All orient to the talk. B's ice cream spoon remains suspended, empty, between mouth and tub.
2. A stops talking. B resumes eating.
3. D talks. E&F and G&H hold separate conversations. A and B orient to D, B continues eating.
4. H and E talk across the table. B stops eating, all listen. A leans forward and nods repeatedly as talk continues. Occasionally participants orient briefly to A.

she does everyone listens to her; in fact, B even stops eating her ice cream. When D talks she does not hold the floor. A and B pay attention to her, but two other conversations have started up and continue as she talks. Eventually, two of the other interactants engage in talk across the table, which once again becomes the focus of the group's attention. Even so, A feels able to lean forward into the central space that represents the shared floor and to nod in response to the talk. This sort of behaviour acknowledges and encourages the talk, but it also represents A's investment in the talk, almost in a proprietorial sense. Given the way that other listeners orient to her responses as well as the talk itself, this does not seem an unreasonable assumption – though it remains no more than an assumption.

I admit that this is hardly an exciting episode, but it was an entertaining way to pass the time while also honing my observational skills. I recommend it as an airport activity.

Level 2: participant observation

Participant observation, according to Adler and Adler (1994:378), 'enjoys the advantage of drawing the observer into the phenomenological complexity of the world, where connections, correlations, and causes can be witnessed as and how they unfold'. This complexity makes participant observation perhaps the most challenging but certainly the most involving method of data collection in qualitative inquiry. However, it demands engagement, and this engagement has to be carefully negotiated, so it would be inappropriate to treat observation as something that you can simply sit down and do. I adopted that approach in Level 1, where I was concerned to develop basic skills, but here I offer a broader view of the fieldwork experience. Aspects of this also apply to the methods of data collection discussed in Chapters 2 and 4, but they have a particular resonance in the case of observation.

This level follows a very rough chronology from entering the field through to the production of a written account and covers the following topics:

- negotiating entry to the chosen setting and representing your research;
- the establishment and maintenance of relationships on which successful data collection will depend;
- a structure for observation, identifying key elements of a setting;
- general and specific strategies for observation, designed to hone your skills;

- approaches to note-taking and different types of notes;
- discussion of a case focusing on the issue of description as part of a final text.

Access and entry

The negotiation of entry is an aspect of research that is sometimes neglected in discussions of qualitative methodologies and yet it is the element upon which so much depends: a failure here might mean that an ideal opportunity is missed altogether. Conversely, success at the expense of goodwill can fatally undermine data gathering. Public settings, by their very nature, are not likely to represent a problem provided that a suitably open standpoint is available and care is taken with appearance, but temporary membership of a particular group is a different matter, and here access may need to be carefully negotiated. In what follows I discuss the chronological stages in gaining access and building relationships in the field, summarised in Box 3.4.

Box 3.4   Stages in fieldwork

1. Making contact
2. Arranging consent
3. Representing your research
4. Establishing your rôle
5. Building relationships
6. Leaving the field

Making contact

This is one of those obvious but easily neglected factors when looking for a suitable research site. I have known people fire off any number of letters to official representatives and decision-makers in the hope that a door will be opened to them, and with a single exception they might have saved themselves the expense of the stamps. All the evidence of the literature points unequivocally to the conclusion that it is personal contact which is likely to open doors (for a powerful example of this, see Hoffman 1980).

So once potential research sites have been identified, it is well worth thinking hard about whether there is a point of contact via an intermediary known to both parties, or even via a chain of intermediaries. Apart from the advantages of personal contact, this might along the way turn up opportunities the researcher has not previously considered. However, it might also sow the seeds of problems further down the line, as my own experience with a language school confirms (Richards 1997a, 1999a). I've written this up as a series of extracts and as the story begins (Extract 3.4) and starts to unfold, you might like to identify the source of the problem.

Extract 3.4 The Pen School 1: next door via Mexico

My experience when looking for a school in which to research staffroom talk underlines the value of personal contact, however unexpected. I was interested in a particular type of staffroom and had made contacts with various institutions around England, some nearly 200 miles from my home, but without success. Eventually, at a conference in Mexico, I met the owner of a school that was exactly what I was looking for – and it turned out to be just a five-minute walk from my home.

Arranging consent

Whether directly or via a mutual acquaintance, negotiations should eventually lead to someone who is in a position to provide access to the research site, aptly known as a *gatekeeper*. In the context of TESOL, gatekeepers are likely to be school owners and principals, education officials, and so on, all with their own particular axes to grind and territories to protect. It's all too easy to forget this when you are negotiating with them and as a result to focus only on your own concerns.

When dealing with gatekeepers, try to be aware of the rôle they might play in your research; accounts of fieldwork are rich in examples of gatekeepers who have, for good or ill, made all the difference to the outcomes of the research. Where the gatekeeper is a popular and influential individual, the association can be entirely positive, but where there is suspicion or resentment the researcher may find it an uphill struggle to establish genuinely close relationships with other participants. The process of consultation itself is likely to involve what Dingwall (1980) has called a 'hierarchy of consent' and it is vital to ensure that all parties concerned are fully involved in the process of negotiation, because any one of them might be able to undermine the researcher's efforts.

When meeting gatekeepers (Extract 3.5), thought should be given to issues of presentation and appearance: what will seem warmly casual to some may represent to others a lack of respect for due formalities. If possible, it is also a good idea to offer something in return for their cooperation, though again the views of all interested parties will need to be considered – contributions can also be interpreted as challenges. My contribution to the Pen was to teach and catalogue materials during my stay and to offer teacher development sessions when the research was completed.

Extract 3.5   The Pen School 2: first meetings

On the basis of my Mexico contact, I phoned the principal of the local school, Jenny. My initial meeting with her lasted about an hour, and at the end of it she agreed to my coming to the Pen school in the role of participant observer, subject to the approval of the teachers there. A Friday lunchtime meeting was arranged about a fortnight later, during which I introduced myself and explained that I was interested in studying the way teachers work together and talk to one another. I emphasised that if they invited me to join them I would remain only as long as they were happy for me to be there. I explained that I would like to do some teaching in the school and to interview them about their lives and work, suggesting that eventually I might also ask if I could tape some of their staffroom talk, although I would fully understand if they felt that this would not be appropriate. We discussed the likely products of the research and I left them with some examples of my own work on teacher development to think over their response.

Representing your research

Inevitably, at some stage in the negotiation process you will be expected to explain the purpose of your research, and you should make sure that you have thought carefully about the implications of what you say. The issue is sometimes represented as a matter of whether the researcher resorts to deception, but this suggests that a simple choice is available. In fact, a full description of the project from the researcher would probably not be welcome even if such a thing were possible; the real challenge lies in choosing how much to leave out and how to represent what is left in. Erickson's position (1967:373), that it is unethical to deliberately misrepresent your research, is a compelling one and should always be borne in mind, but it is usually possible to offer a description that is honest but general enough not to give the game away.

Negotiation must also address the way in which the data may be used and the extent to which it can be edited or otherwise controlled by people other than the researcher (Extract 3.6). Some researchers claim that once permission to observe and record is given, participants should not be allowed any editorial control, but in the case of taped data this may be an unreasonable imposition. In my own case, staffroom talk occasionally included unguarded comments that might have compromised professional relationships and it would have been unreasonable to have insisted on publishing these – anonymity is never absolute.

Extract 3.6   The Pen School 3: ground rules

The teachers responded positively to my request but asked for another meeting the following week. This allowed me to meet one of the teachers who had been absent from the original meeting and gave them the chance to ask more probing questions about the nature of my work. I replied honestly but in general terms, keeping the subject of the study as 'teachers' lives, work and talk'. I sought to reassure them that if at any stage they felt my presence was an intrusion, I would withdraw from the school without any recrimination. I also reassured them that if I did eventually tape anything, they would have the right to decide whether this could be made public. I also promised to show them any work based on this research which might be published or presented at conferences, and though I did not allow the right of veto on such work, we agreed that they could check it for accuracy and I would take into account their responses.

Establishing your rôle

Viewed simplistically, the establishment of the researcher's rôle is something that is managed at the outset and can be summed up fairly neatly, but this fails to capture the multiple possibilities inherent in the negotiation of identity through the research process or the extent to which this is embedded in the wider research experience. As Burgess points out (1992:ix), each fieldwork setting offers a learning experience, not just about a particular culture and about research methodology and techniques, but about oneself. This last, 'crucial element' (ibid.), under- lies the discussion which follows. It is, says Stenhouse (1984:218) a 'classic position on fieldwork' that 'you learn by getting your hands dirty', but each research swamp seems to have its own particular varieties of mud, some stickier than others. Much will depend on the way the researcher is viewed:

> Qualitative researchers notice that folks in the field receive them dif- ferently depending on what the participants see as the research pur- pose. Evaluators may be given red carpet treatment but doors often remain closed; university researchers are either ignored or collared by those who have a particular interest in the topic; and action researchers are expected to move in and 'go native'. (Rossman and Rallis 1998:95)

As a researcher, then, you will need to evaluate your perceived rela- tionship with the group from the outset and, as far as possible, adjust the way you present yourself in order to facilitate productive data gathering. For example, the observer of students who presents in the manner of a teacher or authority figure is unlikely to establish a close relationship with them (Geer 1999:36).

The literature of qualitative inquiry offers various ways of categor- ising 'overt' and 'covert' roles (for example, Whyte 1984:30), ranging from 'complete participant', through 'participant-as-observer' and 'observer-as-participant', to 'complete observer' (for example, Gold 1958). Angrosino and de Pérez (2000:677) offer a useful historical summary of different positions and current thinking on the observer–participant relationship. The important distinction in TESOL contexts is probably that between an observer, who remains outside the situation being studied, and a participant–observer, who joins the group to be studied as a participant in their activities. It is possible, for example, to observe classroom behaviour as an outsider who sits at the back of the class and takes notes or as a participant involved in the activities in the lesson. In the case of the Pen School I was able to join the group as a part-time teacher, although with a special status.

TESOL researchers may also wish to study their own contexts, which presents particular problems, partly because of the difficulty of overcoming the taken-for-grantedness of much that goes on but also because of the need to negotiate an appropriate relationship with colleagues. However, as Angrosino (1997, quoted in Angrosino and de

Pérez 2000:684) shows, it is possible to go from being a full insider to an 'interested-but-ignorant bystander' by a process of reinvention through the research process.

Building relationships

The process of negotiation shades imperceptibly into that of gaining acceptance, and potentially into project definition itself (Burgess 1984b). In long-term research, building relationships is very important, but it is less likely to be a prime concern in smaller projects. Nevertheless, you do need to be aware of how people are responding to you and your presence since this may have an important influence on the way they react when you are collecting data. If you are seen as a 'spy' for the principal, for example, responses to your presence will be very different from the ones you would expect as 'fellow teacher'. The message here is a simple but important one: never let your focus on the process of collecting data distract attention from your relationships with those around you.

Early days in the field are particularly important and may significantly affect the relationship between the researcher and actors. Geer (1999), for example, claims that just three days in the field were enough to change dramatically her concept of the college students she was observing. It is at this early stage that a guide might emerge, especially if the setting is an unfamiliar one, but the immediate benefits of having someone to show you the ropes has to be set against the long-term implications of such a relationship. For example, an individual who makes particular efforts to attach themselves to the researcher might do so because they feel isolated from other colleagues or because they have political motives for doing so.

A more usual process of exploration and discovery evolves through one contact leading to another, a process known as *snowball sampling*, and as contact with different aspects of the field unfolds researchers will take opportunities to collect data as they arise (*convenience sampling*). Burgess offers a valuable insight into the possible impact of this on data collection:

> During the course of any ethnographic project researchers get to know individuals in different degrees of intensity. In this respect, friendships are established that influence the extent to which access is granted to one group and simultaneously closed off to others. (Burgess 1991:50)

The process of discovery is often an exciting one, but the researcher needs to be sensitive to the inevitable shifts in research interest that accompany evolving relationships (Shaffir and Stebbins 1991b:17). As the project moves into a more interpretive phase where major issues and themes begin to emerge, linked to broader theoretical perspectives, these will also inform data collection (and therefore involve an element of *theoretical sampling*). This development parallels a general shift from a very open approach to observation to a more focused orientation, which Spradley (1980:34) characterises as a shift from descriptive, to focused and then to selective observation. As with so many other things, it is largely a matter of feeling your way, but a good research diary can make an invaluable contribution to your decision-making.

The process of building relationships in the field is a delicate one requiring great sensitivity and constant awareness of the effects particular actions might have on very different interested constituencies. However, there seem to me to be three areas that represent particular challenges to TESOL professionals researching their own field and these are outlined below.

1. Pre-formed ideas: you will probably be undertaking this research on the back of several years of teaching experience, and will bring with you views about teachers and teaching that have formed in the course of your professional encounters. Properly developed research procedures and constant reflection on the process of data gathering will help to reduce the impact of background assumptions and expectations to an acceptable level, but the process cannot be an entirely internal one: being an ESOL teacher is part of our identity and will influence the nature of our interactions with those we encounter in the field:

> [T]he ethnographer may need to realize that what *he* or *she* observes is conditioned by who *he* or *she* is, and that different ethnographers – equally well trained and well versed in theory and method but of different gender, race or age – might well stimulate a very different set of interactions, and hence a different set of observations leading to a different set of conclusions. (Angrosino and de Pérez 2000:689; original italics)

2. Perceived investments: one consequence of our professional identity as a teacher is that we are unlikely to be seen as a neutral presence by the teachers we are observing. Observation in TESOL is so much bound up with evaluation that it will be hard for teachers not to see the teacher – researcher, possessor of sufficient relevant professional knowledge for the purposes of judgement, as someone to be regarded warily. The establishment of trust is something that has to be worked for, and lingering suspicions may lead to the creation of *fronts*:

> Where subjects do not trust 'outsiders' they may create their own 'fronts' to impede the researcher's progress. Occasionally we read of concealment and deception being promoted by the researcher adopting a 'front', not revealing that participation was under cover and negotiated for the prime purpose of observing the practices of others. 'Fronts' conceal by ensuring the researcher has only a limited opportunity to observe what is going on. (de Laine 2000:49)

Although de Laine also notes that length of exposure tends to diminish the impact of such fronts, she does not draw attention to the fact that their effects are often only visible retrospectively, which may have serious implications for the nature of the data collected up to that point and the anticipated length of the project. These considerations were brought home to me through a significant shift in my relationship with the Pen team (Extract 3.7).

Extract 3.7   The Pen School 4: a shift of perspective

The relationship of the Pen teachers with the main gatekeeper was not as close as I had assumed. I joined the Pen about two months after my initial meeting with the staff there and it was only six months later that they told me they no longer thought of me as a 'spy' from their sister school, headed by my initial contact in Mexico. The teachers had naturally assumed that I was a friend of hers and that therefore anything they said might get back to her. I also discovered later on that the school's recruitment had fallen to its lowest point just before she introduced me to them, and that everyone was worried about the potential impact of this on jobs. My arrival seemed suspiciously well timed, so the 'front' that teachers presented was one of success, which involved hiding from me any negative aspects or criticisms of higher management.

3. *Professional identification*:   perhaps the commonest warning issued to researchers new to the field is that they should not stay long enough to 'go native'. The normal development of the researcher's perspective

moves from that of outsider to insider through a golden period where they can see things from an actor's perspective and yet still maintain something of the outsider's detachment. The process is made particularly difficult for the teacher–researcher, who must always beware of identifying professionally with the actors to the extent of sharing their taken-for-granted assumptions. As Delamont notes in an illuminating and informed discussion of the challenges facing the educational researcher:

> It is a fine line between doing excellent research, which enables the researcher and then her readers to see the world as the actors see it, and becoming so over-identified with that viewpoint that the others in the setting become stereotyped, or are ignored. (Delamont 2002:39)

Leaving the field

If data collection reaches the point where it is difficult to resist this identification, it is time to hang up pad and pencil. Sometimes this will coincide with leaving the field but there may be situations where initial commitments have to be fulfilled. Taylor (1991) identifies three questions that come to mind at this final stage:

1. How and when should the study be concluded?
2. How should personal relationships be managed?
3. What are the social, political and ethical implications of the research?

The first will depend on a number of factors, while the second can perhaps best be desribed as a process of 'easing out'. It is never acceptable simply to dump those with whom you have shared such valuable time, so thought needs to be given to how contact will be phased out. In the case of the Pen I kept in contact up to the point where the school was unexpectedly closed and felt a strong sense of loss for the profession of TESOL as well as for the sake of my own happy memories of the team.

The third question raises broader ethical issues that are discussed at the end of this level, but first it will be necessary to look at techniques of observation and note-taking. As this section has shown, these techniques cannot be considered in isolation because their application is part of a much wider relational context to which the researcher must respond. The summary in Box 3.5 offers a very basic checklist of considerations that will facilitate effective field relationships:

Box 3.5 Access and relationships: some considerations

1. Make use of contacts.
2. Assess the interests of all gatekeepers.
3. Take care when representing your research.
4. Assess perceived relationships with different groups.
5. Be sensitive to your own views and the development of these.
6. Don't 'go native'.

As a final reminder of perceptual shadings, Extract 3.8 offers a glimpse of how the Pen teachers saw me, based on the descriptions offered to visitors or new staff.

Extract 3.8 The Pen School 5: representing the researcher

I began data collection in January and by the summer I was referred to as 'one of us', but with additional labels attached. I was never described explicitly as a 'teacher' but rather as 'our researcher' and on one occasion as 'our tame academic'. My role always demanded some explanation when visitors were introduced and recordings of staffroom exchanges more than a year into the research revealed different views of my role. For Harry I was 'doing research about how teachers operate', while Paul was keen to point to a focus on experienced teachers and 'how they cooperate with each other'. Only three weeks before the end of my stay Jenny, the principal, explained to a visitor that 'Keith's been attached to us ... Keith's researching us' and that my subject was 'how a quality organisa-tion operates' – thus demonstrating how the representation of research and the researcher can be used as a resource for different ends.

A structure for observations

Observation in itself can be infinitely fascinating, but the focus in this section is on the more extended and demanding process of data collec-tion, where allowance must be made for the weight of imposition that commitment brings. Fieldwork, done properly, is a mixture of intense excitement and 'rigorous, time-consuming, and often boring, tedious work' (Berg 1998:129). The researcher must be prepared for both.

Karp (1980:93), in a fascinating paper on observation in Times Square, places observation in its proper perspective as a data gathering tool: 'Researchers who develop and eye for detail in observing settings can collect an enormous wealth of data'. However, the data need to be captured systematically, and in order to do this the eye and mind must be trained so that it will be possible to follow standard procedures while at the same time holding on to an openness of viewpoint that snatches the unexpected and unguarded moment. It's a tall order.

The best starting point is to select a setting for frequent and systematic observation and then return to this again and again as you hone your skills. Level 1 includes suggestions on how to choose a setting and begin observation, but if you already have a project in mind it would make sense to choose a setting relevant to this. Once you have done that, try to work up a description using the elements described below, then explore the strategies for observation in the next section. Don't worry too much about note-taking at this stage, but when you are confident that your observational skills are sufficiently honed, address the issues of note-taking in the final section which deals with practical issues.

The most widely known checklist of things to consider is provided by Spradley (1980), who identifies space, actors, activity, object, act, event, time, goal and setting as key elements. Numerous writers have drawn on this and the structure proposed in Box 3.6, although different, owes much to Spradley's original system.

Box 3.6   Key features for observation

Setting	space	**Systems**	formal
	objects		informal
People	actors	**Behaviour**	times
	relationships		routines
	interactions		processes
	feelings		events

---

1. Setting

Level 1 focused on the setting and its inhabitants, but observation at this level will be more fine-grained. The importance of the setting is obvious enough – staffroom interaction will be different from meetings in the principal's office and encounters in the corridor – but for observation purposes we also need to look closely at aspects of this as it bears on other features such as relationships and status. I have selected two features that can be considered separately, even though they are connected.

1.1 Space: it's always a good idea to draw a sketch of your chosen setting and use this as a basis for exploring the relationship between actions and setting. Ask questions such as the following: What space is available and how is it distributed? (*Distribution*) Are there distinct territories? Who inhabits them, who are the visitors and who is excluded? What are the rules relating to them? (*Territories*) Are particular activities related to particular spaces? Which spaces encourage particular activities and which spaces discourage them? How do people make use of the setting in their everyday activities? (*Activities*) Are there any spaces or rules relating to spaces that allow people to define themselves or their actions (e.g. Jo sitting at the resources desk means 'I'm being the co-ordinator')? (*Rôles*)

1.2 Objects: the same sorts of questions can be asked of objects. Ownership of or access to particular objects might be a sign of status, certain objects might be associated with particular activities, and so on.

2. Systems

I've separated this out from routines (see below) because systems, whether formal or informal, are explicit and can be dealt with quite straightforwardly. If there are systems in operation, it's important to find out what they are so that you can observe how people orient to them. It's also worth distinguishing formal systems which participants are constrained to follow (although *how* they follow them is interesting in itself), from informal systems that are socially but not formally binding. What I have in mind here is the difference between, for example, a formal system for recording materials taken from the staffroom, and an informal system for making sure that such materials are distributed fairly. You might like to reflect for a moment on the systems that apply in your own staffroom, then spend a break watching how different people fit in with them.

3. People

It goes without saying that people are the objects of your observation, but to refer to them as 'objects' is clearly inappropriate, and the real challenge before you is to find ways of describing them and their behaviour which will help you to understand their world. To this end, four particular aspects deserve attention.

3.1 Actors: these are the people themselves. Who are the actors? What are their names? How are they addressed? What do you know of their history? How do they present themselves?

3.2 Relationships: it's important to pin these down. What are the groups? How do they relate to one another? Are there hierarchies? How do people move from one group to another? How are relationships defined?

3.3 Interactions: the relationship between this and the former category is an intimate one, since it is through interaction that such relationships are established and developed. It is possible to capture interactions in fieldnotes, but there are obvious advantages in using recorded data, which may reflect subtle alignments not immediately apparent to the observer.

3.4 Feelings: the final element is feelings. Obviously, the observer has no direct access to these, but it's important to record actors' feelings as manifested in their behaviour or talk.

4. Behaviour

A sense of this usually emerges over time, and there's a real danger of jumping to premature conclusions about what is going on and what labels might be attached to this. The explanation of particular class-room activities, for example, will be found in the relationship between teacher and class, established over time and constantly evolving. Behaviour is something that needs to be observed carefully and though its description is neither straightforward nor definitive, there are particular aspects (outlined below) that can guide observation.

4.1 Times: noting the timing of activities is very important. What takes place unexceptionally at the beginning of a lesson or break, for example, may be more significant if introduced at the end. Times provide a convenient set of co-ordinates for locating activities. Remember, though, that these are not cut-off points: the 'beginning' of a lesson is not necessarily 9 am, or the point at which the teacher enters the room; some lessons may 'begin', in a significant sense, in the corridor or even the staffroom. For example, if the principal makes a comment in the staffroom to a teacher about the class the latter is about to take, this might send the teacher into the classroom in an angry or very cheerful mood.

4.2 Routines: routines provide a useful way of orienting to behaviour in a particular setting. In all but the most temporary of contexts, routines quickly become established, some of them idiosyncratic and others shared by a number of actors. Unlike systems, they are not formally established, but they are none the less powerful for that. It can be very instructive to identify such routines in order to discover what they represent, and if routines are broken the results can provide valuable insights into relationships, shared understandings and social organisation.

4.3 Processes: these are harder to pin down but need to be distinguished from routines because the order of acts is less rigid. It can be useful, to note what processes (interactional, professional, and so on) need to be gone through in order to achieve certain goals, and it may be possible to identify common processes, or shared characteristics of different processes, as part of building up a picture of a particular world.

4.4 Events: Spradley (1980) distinguishes *acts* (single actions), *activities* (sets of related acts), and *events* (sets of related activities), but I've opted for only the highest level. It can be very helpful to identify specific events and the characteristics of these, because this may make it easier to distinguish patterns and norms. I don't think it matters too much *how* you choose to identify events, so long as you develop a fairly consistent approach to this. It's also interesting to note that as observation progresses, events become 'richer', their roots and ramifications more obviously extensive. This is both encouraging and rewarding.

Strategies for observing

Having a structure for observations and following the advice offered in Level 1 will provide you with a solid grounding for observation activities, but there are particular strategies that will hone your skills and open up the possibility for discoveries and insights that might otherwise elude you. In this section I divide these into general strategies and orienting strategies, though this does not imply a hierarchy – the best advice is to regard them all as options but go with what works for you.

General strategies

The best advice I know is offered by Wolcott (1994:161–4), who recommends four strategies for ethnographic observation. They are not meant to be exhaustive, but they deserve serious consideration. You might find some or all of them valuable in your own development as an observer.

Strategy 1: observe and record everything.   Wolcott recommends this as a useful starting point and argues that it leads to two useful realisations:

1. Because you can't observe everything, you're likely to be struck by the evidence of what you do actually record.
2. This selection can provide valuable clues to your own observing habits. You may find that you need to expand your gaze, that you focus on some things at the expense of others, and so on.

He also points out that 'a broad look around' can itself be valuable and may be appreciated by readers. A sense of place is very important and I always try to get a good feel for the setting before turning my attention to what's happening there. It can also be interesting to compare impressions at the beginning of data gathering with those occurring when the setting has become a familiar one.

Strategy 2: observe and look for nothing – that is, nothing in particular.   The advantage of looking for nothing in particular, of treating a setting as 'flat', is that certain elements may then stand out, like 'bumps'. This strategy can be particularly valuable in very complex situations where too much is happening for the observer absorb at once, or excessively familiar ones. Wolcott offers the classroom as a typical example of the latter, and says that it can be useful to treat a lesson as 'business as usual', keeping an antenna out for anything that disturbs this. For example, student interruptions might break into the orderly flow of things and provide a focus for attention.

Strategy 3: look for paradoxes.   This strategy offers a means of focusing observation and can be particularly useful in educational contexts, where paradoxes and contradictions are common. Wolcott (1994:163) quotes the example of the 'paradox between the frequently heard opinion that it is hard to get teachers to try new things and the teacher-expressed belief that teachers have insufficient opportunity to show what they already are capable of doing'.

Strategy 4: identify the key problem confronting a group.   Wolcott suggests that sometimes a group is presented with a particular problem and that this can provide a useful focus for observation. He offers an example of education administrators whose main problem is conducting teacher evaluation. In my own research, most staffroom stories centred on the problem of dealing with specifically interactional challenges in class (for example, the quiet student), and identifying this provided a valuable focus for my observation of such stories and the analysis which followed (Richards 1999b).

Orienting Strategies

In addition to these general strategies, there are also particular means of orienting in a new way to what is observed. Whether or not these particular strategies are used will depend on the situation, but it's certainly worth knowing about them. Here are three that you might find useful:

What if? As observers, we invest all our attention in what is happening, but it can sometimes be valuable to stand back and ask hypothetical questions. Lofland and Lofland (1984) provide a list of possible questions that includes examples such as the following: Why doesn't X happen? What would happen if X happened?

Maps. Whyte (1984:86) mentions watching and noting in map form the movements of the people in a club he was observing. He built up a large collection of such maps and the information they provided enabled him to form a clear picture of the relationship between movement and interaction so that eventually when an issue arose he could predict who would stand where.

Spot the leader. This simple approach, also developed by Whyte (1997:22), was based on a distinction between *pair events* (involving two people) and *set events* involving three or more. In the latter, the person who initiates a change in interaction is the leader and over time a stable pattern emerges that the researcher can use to work out groupings and their ranking structure. Case 3.1 on p. 117 illustrated this approach.

Note-taking

Fieldnotes are all things to all people. Dip into the relatively limited literature of note-taking and you'll find plenty of confident statements about what fieldnotes should be, but few of these will make happy partners. Here are a couple of uncomfortable bedfellows:

> After reading ethnographers' full field notes, it should be possible for a person to visualise exactly what the ethnographers saw and heard during the field session. (Berg 1998:150)

> [Fieldnotes are] something that can't readily be comprehended by another person. (Jackson 1990:20)

What are we to make of this? I see it as an affirmation of the importance of the individual researcher in the research process. The challenge and glowing reward of fieldwork is to come to know yourself honestly enough to discover with equal honesty the ways of others, and the process of recording is the balance by means of which this relationship can be weighed. Whatever else they might be, fieldnotes are one person's version of their encounter with the world:

> [F]ieldnotes are an expression of the ethnographer's deepening local knowledge, emerging sensitivities and evolving substantive concerns and theoretical insights. (Emerson *et al.* 2001:355)

There are no rules that will enable us to fashion this expression, and we must be aware of the mutability and the limitations of what we are about. We need to recognise, for example, that the act of writing itself imposes shape and substance; in Atkinson's (1992:6) words, 'What may be generated as "data" is affected by what the ethnographer can treat as "writable" and "readable"'. Within the broader context of such limitations, I now explore the practical issues involved in note-taking, but first wish to underline the importance of good practice (Sánchez-Janowski 2002:148): *It matters very much how notes are taken.*

Procedure

Procedures for note-taking may change as the project develops, but a useful general distinction is that proposed by Wolfinger (2002) between approaches to note-taking based on a *salience hierarchy*, in which the observer begins with what is most interesting, noteworthy or telling, and those aiming for *comprehensive note-taking*, an approach that would draw on the categories identified above. Whatever the particular approach, there are certain basic considerations that are fundamental to the production of accurate notes:

1. Limit exposure to field: serious observation is exhausting anyway, and the longer spent in the field, the longer the time needed at the desk afterwards. Berg (1998:147) suggests a 1:4 ratio of field: writing up, which is probably not a bad guide, but much depends on the nature of the setting (for example, a change of settings will involve a lot of description), degree of movement and interaction (for example, the staffroom when everyone is quietly reading will demand less than a break busy with talk and action), style of note-taking (narrative takes longer than jottings), typing speed of the researcher, and so on.

2. Minimise the gap between field and note-taking: the advantages of this are obvious and some researchers recommend trying to avoid becoming involved in conversation between leaving the field and settling down at the desk.

3. Train your memory: again, the benefits are clear, but I prefer to interpret this more broadly than simply improving recall: 'Knowing what to record comes from experimenting with one's memory' (Delamont 2002:138).

4. Jot down notes, key words and phrases: a small pocket notebook and pencil are very useful, provided that the notes can be made in secret; otherwise it's best to exploit any blank space on a convenient document in order to remain unobtrusive (which is a good reason to keep a pencil handy).

5. Seize opportunities in the field: a few moments alone, when engaged in an activity that involves writing anyway, even a visit to the lavatory (Whyte, 1984:86), can provide valuable moments.

This list embraces the three sorts of notes identified by Lofland and Lofland (1995:89–97): mental notes, jotted notes and full fieldnotes. In the case of the Pen I was lucky because I could disguise my notes as lesson planning, writing headings that referred to the latter and a text that captured what was happening in the staffroom around me (Richards 1997b). Ideally, I should have liked to keep all my notes and findings to myself, but it was important to balance the importance of not influencing the nature of staffroom interaction against the need to become a trusted member of staff. I soon discovered that this was a fairly open environment and decided that strategic openness on my part would offer an acceptable compromise. Although my note-taking was covert, I would occasionally make a comment about an idiosyncratic aspect of someone's behaviour or interactional style. The teachers seemed to enjoy this and I was careful to release only details that would not bear on any analysis I was likely to undertake.

Form of fieldnotes

Up to this point I've discussed fieldnotes as though it is sufficient simply to register in writing what is observed, in so far as this is possible, but fieldnotes can take different forms. The difference between notes in the field and written up versions is obvious enough, but analytical and relational issues also need to be taken into account. The former make it necessary to include what are usually called memos, pointing to analytical insights, possible connection with theory, methodological points, and so on. Relational issues are those that connect the researcher with the whole process of research and with actors and these will involve personal reflections and resonances.

While some researchers are happy to integrate memos with the fieldnotes themselves, many recommend that they are kept separate. In the

Pen project I began with the former approach but soon decided to write up my notes in two columns, the main one for description only and a thinner column to the right for memos. Perhaps unsurprisingly, when I introduced these two columns in my own notes, I found that the temptation to fill the 'comments' column more than doubled the space taken up by this element – an interesting reminder that not even the form notes take is analytically neutral.

When considering how your notes will be represented (columns, file cards, computer files), it's also a good idea to develop a coding system that will enable you to cross reference efficiently (see Box 3.7). However notes are stored, though, Delamont's advice (2002:67), to keep analytical notes out of the field, is wise counsel – in the wrong hands they could easily lead to distress or conflict.

An essential part of any fieldwork is the research diary. This is much more than a mere record of daily activities. It is an opportunity to reflect on all aspects of the research process and your place within it. Because no one need ever see the contents of your diary, it can also serve as a means of letting off steam or venting spleen. If your project is likely to continue beyond a year, I recommend a narrow-line page-a-day A4 diary divided into two columns, the first taking up two-thirds of the width of the page and used for the first year's entries. In the second year, entries can then be made in the narrower column (preferably in a different ink), next to the previous year's comments, which can be read and reflected upon. This process can generate interesting insights and serve as an encouraging reminder of progress made.

Box 3.7	Different forms of fieldnotes			
	Notes	*Memos*	*Diaries*	*Texts*
Purpose:	Data	Analysis	Reflection	Representation
Site:	Field	Desk	Drawer	'Podium'
Status:	Core	Supplementary	Personal	Public

The notes that most people will see are the final version and here, too, there are choices to be made but no simple formula for delivering a finished text. How much, in any case, should fieldnotes be edited and polished? How literary should they be? What place is there for dialogue, contrast, tension? Will there be a place for visual evidence (see Banks 2001 for an excellent introduction to this)? QI offers no answers, only the prospect of further discovery. Box 3.8 represents what I take to be, broadly speaking, two different ways in which authors articulate differences of approach. Like so much else in QI, they are not necessarily exclusive and they are certainly not exhaustive, but they are steps towards representing understanding.

Box 3.8 Approaches to writing up fieldnotes

Emerson *et al.* (1995:60–3)	*Real time* (from the perspective at the time, knowledge is incomplete)	*End point* (writer has relatively full knowledge)
Emerson *et al.* (1995:60–3)	*Sketch* (impressionistic representation using detailed imagery)	*Episode* (focus on action evolving over time)
Abrams* (1988)	*First person* (involved insider, limited view)	*Third person* (detached outsider, omniscient view)
van Maanen (1988)	*Confessional tales*	*Realist tales*
Atkinson (1992a)	*Transcriptions* (actors' own words)	*Inscriptions* (written accounts by the observer)

*Quoted in Emerson *et al.* 1995

Ethics

Good QI discovers things about people they didn't know themselves and might not want others to know. It can hurt; a lot; and for a long time. This means that no researcher should ever duck ethical issues. Some academic communities have ethical committees that help in the decision-making process, but there is no licence on earth that takes away the personal responsibility each of us carries:

> It is the responsibility of the ethnographer to try to act in ways that are ethically acceptable, taking due account of his or her goals, the situation in which the research is being carried out, and the values and interests of the people involved. (Hammersley and Atkinson 1995:285)

What follows is no more than a thumbnail sketch of the territory. If you would like to know more, de Laine (2000) offers a broad and balanced discussion, but the ultimate arbiter of what is right and decent is your own conscience.

Consent

Some of the issues here were discussed in the context of gaining entry to the field. It is the researcher's responsibility to decide – or discover – where consent for entry, observation, action, and so on, is required and to ensure that it is properly obtained from all concerned parties on the basis of honest representation. The ethical issues here centre on the relevance and limits of consent, and on representation. When is consent needed? How far does it extend? Has it been freely given, or was there an element of coercion?

Honesty

A condition of informed consent is honest representation, but no representation is ever complete, so how much is enough, and who should be told what? If the information given compromises the research then the project has failed before it begins, but how far should the researcher be prepared to reveal their aims? The ethical issue here is the fine dividing line between limited description and deliberate deception.

Privacy

I mentioned in Level 1 that 'public' places may nevertheless carry with them the idea that some actions count as prying; the same applies to places to which we have been given access. Are there assumed/understood/ agreed limits on what we might legitimately do there in terms of observation and recording, and are there particular acts which count as private? It's important for the researcher to keep these things in mind and not to assume that the matter of privacy is closed once permission is obtained.

Ownership

Considerations such as those above shade into issues of ownership. To what extent does the data 'belong' to the researcher? The degree of control (for example, with regard to editing, restrictions on access, release) to be exercised by those involved in the research needs to be carefully considered and negotiated. There are no guidelines on acceptable procedures here, but all decisions should be based on respect for the other parties involved and a recognition of the importance of their voice.

Harm

If all the above issues are properly dealt with, the chances of harm are small, but the researcher should always be aware of these and careful not to be the inadvertent cause of harm to others. There is a sense in which research is not a natural thing, at least in as much as the researcher has to 'make strange' the events that occur; and the outcomes, which cast a penetrating light on ordinary events, have the power to hurt. The researcher needs to be aware of this.

Conclusion

Like so many things that anyone can do, observation makes its demands on the researcher in subtle but pervasive ways, demanding a level of sensitivity that can be exhausting. Nobody properly engages in participant observation without learning more about themselves as a person as well as a researcher, and once skills of observation have been developed the world never looks quite the same again. It's been a long time since I sat in an airport lounge or on a train platform and simply read a book – and life gets richer by the day.

Case 3.2: adequate description

This particular case is based on two short descriptions that I think raise important issues. Polkinghorn (1997:14) has argued that research cannot be considered complete until it has undergone the transformation from a 'list or sequence of disconnected research events into a unified story with a thematic point', but it would be a mistake to see this as a particular stage in writing up. To illustrate how this process of transformation inhabits the whole data gathering process, I use description, something that is usually presented as important but essentially unproblematic:

> I hope I offer useful advice in suggesting that novice researchers who feel uncertain about how far to go, how much interpretation to offer, should err on the side of too much description, too little interpretation. (Wolcott 1994:36)

> Describing involves a set of issues to do with categorizing into classes of things, formulating as something, providing detail or not, making judgements and so on. (Potter 1996:5)

The term 'description' suggests a matching relationship between a particular state of affairs and a corresponding verbal representation such that the former is identifiable on the basis of the latter. It is almost as though the description might be 'laid over' that which it describes and any issues resolved on the basis of the closeness of the match. This seems to be the position implicit in Wolcott's advice, where the novice is encouraged to think of description and interpretation as separable elements. However, there are fault lines in this assumption that are evident in Potter's reference to 'formulating as something' and 'making judgements', which open a window onto the investment of self underlying all description.

It might be thought that description of social events inevitably implicates the author more deeply than does mere physical description, but consider these extracts (Extracts 3.9 and 3.10) from my own written up fieldnotes.

Extract 3.9   The Pen School

In choosing this building and adapting it as they did, the Pen teachers aimed to create the atmosphere of a home rather than a school.... With the exception of a sign to the left of the door, there is little to indicate that this is not a substantial town residence: downstairs windows are curtained, upstairs windows have blinds, and the front door, with its bell in the middle, is typical of many in the town.... Tucked away next to this ['comfortable' self-access centre] is a small room shared by the two teachers of business English.

Extract 3.10   The Centre

There is nothing of the domestic about the Centre, perched at the top of an anachronistic brick-built block that declares its dated institutionality to visitors and passers by alike.... The Centre is located on a floor which, without rising or falling, manages to move from the tenth to the seventh and back up to the ninth floor via a serpentine corridor which almost, but not quite, completes a circuit around the buildings.... The Centre is strung out along a meandering corridor, the stretch it occupies best described as an elongated 'S' with a double kink on the downstroke.

Nothing here is *merely* the opinion of the writer; all descriptions come complete with the stamp of member validation. Furthermore, the physical facts are checkable – the overlay will work. And yet the two accounts are massively informed by the writer's unstated interpretation of what these two places *are*. The Pen is essentially a 'home' in itself and the Centre is part of an institution; the images are of domestic comfort and institutional harshness, of warmth and cold, wholeness and dismemberment, togetherness and isolation. The above examples each contain three sentences: the writer's position is made explicit in the opening sentence, the second one achieves its aims by means of the selection of examples, and the final sentence relies on linguistic choice ('tucked away' is redolent of a cosy world with its warm nooks and crannies, while 'strung out', 'meandering' and 'stretch' achieve the opposite effect, with the added suggestion of distortion in 'kink'). None of this was conscious – I just wrote the way things seemed to me – but the resulting description could generate expectations that bear on the analysis itself. For example, the creation of a collaborative identity in the context of domestic unity might seem a much more straightforward business than its achievement in the face of institutional separation.

For a different perspective on neutrality, consider the final sentence in Extract 3.11 and what it *might* suggest about the meetings that take place in the room – assuming that writers include only what is relevant.

Extract 3.11   The meeting room

The UM (Unit Meeting) room is used as a teaching room and so has a whiteboard, plastic chairs and laminated tables arranged in a solid block. There are book cabinets and a video and television on a large trolley. Staff arrange themselves around this block of tables. As UM is a 'lunchtime' meeting where sandwiches are provided, there is a food and drinks trolley under the whiteboard. Staff have copies of the agenda and usually bring a pen and a diary as well as various other documents depending on the agenda. There is a clock on the wall.

Source: (Mann 2002:38–9)

Recognition of the investment of self in description is what informs the new ethnographies whose interpretivist orientation embraces amongst others autoethnography, fictional accounts and ethnopoetics, all recognising the significance of the creative act of description. Goodall (2000) captures emphatically the research experience as an aspect of selfhood, embracing the authenticity of the lived experience as a legitimate representational resource:

You write what you have been *attracted to* and *convinced by*. You write what you have read as *meaningful*; you interpret what you have read as a meaningful *pattern*. The story you write will be part of the larger story of who you are, where you've been, what you've read and argued over, what you believe in and value, what you feel compelled to name as significant. (Goodall 2000:87; original italics)

Goodall's position has much in common with Pollner and Emerson's ethnomethodological stance (2001) that confronts the researcher's positional dilemma by insisting on the legitimacy of embodied presence. The analytical perspectives may be radically different, but both approaches provide a clear statement of their response to the issue of adequate description.

Level 3: structured observation

All researchers want results and new researchers probably want them more desperately than older hands, who can rest easy in the faith engendered by earlier successes. But the desire for tangible outcomes, convertible currency in the professional and academic market, can distort the research process, turning it away from the search for understanding and towards an obsession with the meaningless accumulation of detail. One of the most important decisions you may need to make at this level of research is what part, if any, the systematic use of predetermined categories will play in your approach. Writers in the field of qualitative inquiry usually distinguish between *participant observation* and *structured observation*, the subject of this level. Structured observation is sometimes also referred to as systematic observation, but this misleadingly implies that participant observation is not systematic, so I shall avoid the term.

I actually prefer to think in terms of a continuum between *open observation*, which might characterise the early stages of participant observation where the observer tries to get a general sense of the setting and the activities associated with it, and *closed observation*, where the observer is strictly coding behaviour on a low-inference schedule, or instrument (the former is the term usually employed to describe what is actually used). This less categorical approach recognises the range of decisions and sensitivities that the qualitative researcher can respond to and does not imply a simple contrast that invites the assignment of evaluative labels. My emphasis in this level will therefore be not so much on the relative advantages and disadvantages of the two standard approaches but on how to reach a decision on the appropriate balance and how to approach structured observation in a way that will contribute to a qualitative project. I will begin, though, by highlighting the dangers of settling too quickly for a more closed approach.

The hidden dangers of closed observation

The success of an open approach to observation relies very much on learning how to do something skilfully that we all do in a fairly slapdash fashion as a matter of course. It depends on cultivating ways of seeing, developing new sensitivities and disciplining the mind to attend to particular features of situations both strange and familiar. It therefore seems deceptively easy but demands much in terms of mental stamina. In addition, once fieldnotes are written up their discursive nature does not lend itself to straightforward analysis. A closed approach, on the other hand, demands much more in terms of preparation but delivers the goods by the bucketload: once you've developed the system and become practised in its application, you can accumulate information at an inspiring rate. The dangers are still there, but they are hidden and may not make themselves apparent until a later stage in the project. Early awareness is therefore very important and the following points consider potential trouble spots from four angles: perspective, design, procedure and interpretation.

Perspective

One of the strengths of closed observation is that it allows researchers to focus on those areas and characteristics that they wish to know more about. Therefore, when it is introduced at the right stage and with appropriate consideration, it can make a very powerful contribution to the development of understanding. However, in my experience many novice researchers tend to introduce it at the beginning of their projects and without giving proper consideration to the implications of these for the project as a whole. Wolcott (1994:159) captures very effectively the limiting effects of an observation schedule: 'If you direct me to observe eye movements, gait, proximity, and so on, then we can talk about reliability, but, when you so direct me, I become your observer, an extension of your senses or your system'.

Language teaching has seen its fair share of observation systems, often used as part of large-scale quantitative projects, and it serves little purpose to criticise projects so far removed from our own concerns. Wolcott's point, though, is a different one: what concerns him is that electing for such a system can serve to conceal more than it reveals. The researcher must therefore be alive to the fact that the introduction of a closed system brings with it a necessary narrowing of focus and perhaps even an element of instrumentality.

Design

Matters of design will be addressed in a later section, but at this stage it is worth extending Wolcott's point to consider the issue of labelling.

Fundamental to any category system, and characteristic of closed approaches generally, is the assignment of descriptive labels allowing behaviour to be categorised with a view to developing a overall picture of the events taking place. If this is done with limited ambitions and with a view to deepening the researcher's understanding of particular features of behaviour, it can serve the project well, but attempts to capture precise teaching 'activities' in a single set of descriptive terms can produce a plethora of labels and a deal of confusion. Thirty years ago a researcher (Adams 1972) took the trouble to survey the many labels on offer in the area of classroom observation and produced a daunting list of available terms. Box 3.9 presents the 'A' entry alone – sufficient to indicate the size and scope of the full collection:

Box 3.9 Perceptions of teacher role in observational studies

The following list is taken from the 'A' entry in a collection of descriptive terms appearing in research papers based on teacher observation (Adams 1972):

Term	Occurrences
Abstracts	(2)
Abuses	(1)
Accepts (behaviour)	(6)
Accepts (feeling)	(14)
Accepts (idea)	(13)
Accepts (general)	(11)
Accuses	(1)
Acknowledges (approves, confirms)	(3)
Acts	(7)
Admits	(2)
Affects	(7)
Affirms	(4)
Agrees	(3)
Analyses	(7)
Answers	(11)
Appeals	(2)
Applies	(2)
Assigns	(5)
Assists	(5)
Associates	(2)

Attends to	(3)
Avoids (defends)	(1)

Procedure

I enjoy fiddling with things. Messing about with a chart or a table is my idea of a pleasant distraction from the rigours of my normal academic routine, and if I can see something taking shape I get a real sense of achievement. I doubt if everyone shares my particular delights, but I think it's likely that the preparation and administration of an observation schedule has something for everyone: the opportunity to tinker for people like me, the appeal of the systematic for those who enjoy creating order out of chaos, an opportunity to establish fixed routines for others, and so on. But the range of its attractions makes it a dangerous instrument:

> There is a tendency for structured observation to generate lots of bits of data. The problem here can be one of trying to piece them together to produce an overall picture, or one of trying to find general themes that link fragments of data together. (Bryman 2001a:173)

Interpretation

Bryman's observation points to the associated problem of interpretation. Because the accumulative potential of structured observation can undermine its analytic purpose, it is possible to become swamped with information that has distorted the shape of the original project, leaving the researcher with no clear sense of the co-ordinates that inform effective decision-making. Even where this doesn't happen, it can be all too easy to settle for facts *as* explanations rather than as a means to understanding.

This is not to say that quantitative representations can't provide intriguing insights into the nature of classroom behaviour, as the following simple statements, derived from a study of three Canadian ESL teachers (White and Lightbown 1984), demonstrate:

- Teachers ask up to four questions a minute.
- 40 per cent of questions receive no response.
- 64 per cent are repeats of earlier questions.
- There are up to nine repetitions of the same question.

I find this description both amusing and intriguing (try saying the same thing nine times in a row), and it stimulates me to want to understand how and why this comes about. Simple statements like this can provoke such responses, but more complex and detailed quantitative representations are sometimes left to stand as explanations in themselves. The qualitative researcher needs to remember that description, whether in narrative or categorical form, is not the same as interpretation and that the search for understanding always takes us below the surface of things.

Good decisions are made in the light of evolving needs and the context of the project as a whole, and it helps to have an overall picture of how participant observation compares with structured observation. Box 3.10 provides a brief overview of the main lines of difference. Participant observation, where 'the human instrument is a most sensitive and perceptive data-gathering tool' (Fetterman 1991:92), lends itself to the narrative representation of events recorded retrospectively. Its open orientation means that coding takes place later, as part of the analytic process, though categories may emerge as the process develops. In the case of structured observation they must be determined in advance as part of a clear coding system designed for cotemporaneous application. The limitations of this approach usually make it unsuitable as a primary data collection method in qualitative research, though the existence of a clear system means that observations can be replicated by other researchers in a way that is not possible in the much more open orientation of participant observation. Properly used where the situation allows it, the two approaches can make a potent combination.

Box 3.10   Participant and structured observation

	Participant observation	*Structured observation*
Orientation	Open	Closed
Foundation	Event-based	Category-based
Form	Narrative	Descriptive
Observer status	Observer-as-instrument	Observer-through-instrument
Coding	Post-observation	Pre-observation
Recording	Retrospective	Cotemporaneous
Format	Notebook	Observation schedule
Replicability	Non-replicable	Replicable
QI status	Main or supplementary method	Supplementary method

Standard observation schedules

Although the development of an observation schedule should be informed by the wider project, anyone seeking to design one should familiarise themselves with the standard schedules that are available. In practice, most researchers develop their own (see Rees 1993 for an account of this process), but it can do no harm to understand the thinking behind successful schedules. These range from the relatively straight-forward (e.g. FIAC), to much more complicated beasts (e.g. TALOS) and a lot can learned from studying them carefully and comparing them. The reading guide at the end of this chapter offers advice on useful sources, but the briefest summary of alternatives I know of is to be found in the appendixes of Allwright and Bailey (1991). In the meantime, a brief sketch of the best-known system, FIAC, will provide a flavour of what is involved.

The groundbreaking contribution to the structured observation of classrooms was made by Flanders (1970), who developed a ten-category observation schedule, the Flanders Interaction Analysis Categories (FIAC). Designed specifically to identify direct and indirect teacher influence, its coverage and simplicity broadened its appeal beyond this relatively narrow focus, so that many subsequent systems have their roots here. Box 3.11 presents the main categories in the FIAC system.

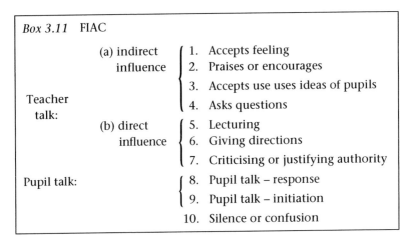

Box 3.11	FIAC		
Teacher talk:	(a) indirect influence	1.	Accepts feeling
		2.	Praises or encourages
		3.	Accepts use uses ideas of pupils
		4.	Asks questions
	(b) direct influence	5.	Lecturing
		6.	Giving directions
		7.	Criticising or justifying authority
Pupil talk:		8.	Pupil talk – response
		9.	Pupil talk – initiation
		10.	Silence or confusion

FIAC was later adapted by Moskowitz (1976) for use in foreign-language classrooms and the addition of a number of sub-categories extending its total number of categories to over 20. There have been a number of other systems devised with different ends in mind, but with detectable similarities at the most basic level. Broadly designed to cover aspects of classroom behaviour, they generally have an interactional orientation.

Deciding whether to use structured observation

The progression from 'What do I want to find out?' to 'What schedule do I use?' is not as straightforward as it may at first appear. We view new situations in the light of our current knowledge, and it often takes creative insight of a very high order to free us from the domination of taken-for-granted perceptions. We can't look at what goes on in a classroom without carrying as part of our mental baggage assumptions about the ways in which events there are organised; in fact, on the most basic level, we couldn't make any sense of things at all if we didn't have some framework for organisation. But a consequence of this is that one way of seeing can easily become the *standard* way of seeing, which is why preliminary participant observation is so important. We can use techniques associated with that to generate new ways of seeing that will in turn prompt fresh questions, a vitally important preliminary because the value of the schedule we eventually devise will depend on the quality of the questions we ask. The process looks something like that outlined in Figure 3.1.

The sorts of questions that can best be answered by structured observation are those related to particular behaviours about which we need specific information, such as the following:

- How often do students initiate interaction with the teacher?
- What's the distribution of teacher initiations to male and female students?
- How much lesson time is taken up with teacher talk?

Working up a schedule

If the decision to use structured observation has arisen from a genuine research need, the researcher should be in an excellent position to respond to the questions that arise in designing an effective observation schedule. Quantitative research tends to rely on a deductive approach, starting with a particular theoretical perspective, which may be behavioural, as exemplified by the FIAC system, or linguistic, as with the Sinclair and Coulthard system (see Chapter 4, Levels 1 and 2). However,

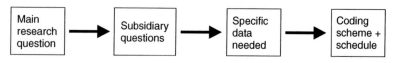

Figure 3.1   Contribution of an observation schedule

qualitative inquiry generally prefers inductive reasoning, which is why structured observation has to be considered in the light of the wider discovery process. Its design represents a creative challenge but also offers the prospect of a flexible and evolving system that allows for substantial revision at the trialling stage. Box 3.12 summarises some purely practical considerations proposed by Evertson and Green (1986:165) and the rest of this section will focus on the design issues that should inform the process of decision-making outlined there.

Box 3.12 Practical considerations in approaching structured observation

1. **Research question(s)**
   e.g. What is the occurrence of different types of student self-repair and other-repair in teacher-fronted activities and in group work?
2. **Focus**
   e.g. particular group(s), event, strategy
3. **Setting**
   e.g. classroom, staffroom
4. **'Slice of reality'**
   e.g. group work, teacher questioning
5. **Observation instrument(s)**
   e.g. category system, descriptive system
6. **Observation procedures**
   e.g. When? How often? Number of observers?
7. **Analytical procedures**
   e.g. frequency count, event structure
8. **Presenting of findings**
   e.g. written summary, tables, pie charts

Source: based on Evertson and Green 1986:165.

Basic decisions

The fundamental aim of any structured observation is to provide specific information that the researcher needs in order to answer the research questions posed, so the decision-making process should not be a mechanistic one. The most basic decision of all is what behaviours will feature in the observation. It is possible to cover all behaviours (the FIAC system does this) but it may well be that the observation will focus on specific behaviours or events (for example, teacher questions or group work). Box 3.13 on pages 152–3 summarises other options.

Once the focus of structured observation has been established, a number of choices have to be made, four of which are particularly important:

1. The researcher will need to decide whether a *descriptive system* or a *category system* is more appropriate. This will probably depend on the extent to which numerical information is required and whether the relevant behaviour can be broken down into a reasonable number of discrete categories.
2. It may also be necessary to decide whether a *rating scale* is to be used. Rating scales evaluate behaviour according to agreed criteria (for example, 'high, medium, low') and rating systems are particularly suitable for purposes of evaluation (a good example is the RSA Diploma Check List for Practical Tests, reproduced in Malamah-Thomas 1987:73), though rating and non-rating systems can be combined.
3. The degree of inference involved (i.e. the extent to which observers are required to use their own judgement in applying the system) will also need to be assessed. Where the structured observation involves one observer and is essentially descriptive, *high-inference categories* are perfectly acceptable, but if more than one observer is involved *low-inference categories* are preferable.
4   When the categories have been identified, the researcher must decide on how behaviours will be sampled, and there are two options available: *event sampling* (or event-based coding) and *interval sampling* (or time-based coding). In interval sampling behaviours are coded at predetermined intervals (e.g. every three seconds), while event sampling codes behaviours as they occur, regardless of the length of time that elapses during their occurrence.

Box 3.13   Options in structured observation systems

Descriptive	*Category*
Open. May be some (general) preset categories. Entries may extend over a number of paragraph, resembling fieldnotes.	Closed. Sample specific behaviours and events. Coded concurrently with events and therefore depend on small, precisely defined, easily coded low-inference units.
Rating	*Non-rating*
Relatively open. Involve element of assessment, and therefore retrospective judgement. More	Scalar rating not needed. Task is to assign behaviour to preset categories.

high inference than non-rating systems.

High inference
Direct attention to important aspects of behaviour and offer the chance to capture a sense of its richness. Descriptive systems usually high inference but might have low inference elements.

Event sampling
Focuses on events and can be used with low frequency behaviours. Decide on events to be observed and ensure all instances are captured. Provides details of events and can address questions such as 'How often does X occur?' and 'How long does X take?'

Low inference
Low-inference approaches tend to be atomistic, artificially dividing up complex events. But can be used by teams and provide precise, detailed information. Category systems should be low-inference.

Interval sampling
Best used with high frequency behaviours. Divide specified period into shorter time segments, then code behaviour at onset of each segment. No record of exact time taken up by particular activities, but gives general picture of time distribution throughout period.

Illustrations

A comparison of extracts from two (hypothetical) approaches, one based on a rating scale and the other on a non-rating scale, will illustrate some of the points made above. In the first example (Extract 3.12), which involves interval sampling but no rating, coding takes place every five seconds, at which point the user enters the relevant code in the box under the time shown, working across in the 5-second units then down through the minutes. The best way of handling the practicalities of such fine tuning is not to rely on a watch, which doubles the observation tasks, but to make a tape on which you record a click every five seconds; this can then be played back quietly through a single earphone and used as a prompt.

Extract 3.12 Four minutes of coding on a 10-category system

	5	10	15	20	25	30	35	40	45	50	55	60
1	2	2	2	6	6	2	2	6	6	6	6	5
2	2	2	10	2	2	6	2	2	2	10	5	5
3	5	3	3	5	3	3	6	6	4	4	4	6
4	2	2	6	6	6	6	6	5	3	6	6	9

If we assume that 2 stands for student talk, 6 for teacher talk and 5 for silence, we can see that in the first minute the talk is divided roughly equally and there is at least one example of silence. Although teacher talk seems to predominate slightly, the system doesn't allow us to state this with certainty (though a clearer picture of unequal distribution emerges over the four minutes), nor does it allow us to be certain about the number of turns because it is possible for a very brief turn to occur with a 5-second segment but not be recorded.

An alternative form of interval sampling would involve identifying activities on one axis and time periods on another, as in Extract 3.13, though in practice the time periods in this example would probably be longer and might run down the page, allowing the ten categories to go across the top.

Extract 3.13   Example of non-rating system (interval sampling)

	5	10	15	20	25	30	35	40	45	50	55	60
TT				√	√			√	√	√	√	
ST	√	√	√			√	√					
Sil												√
Oth												

A rating system (Extract 3.14) looks very different from either of these two and although it allows us to make general comments about (in this case) aspects of teacher delivery, it gives us no indication whatsoever about how often this occurs or how long it lasts.

Extract 3.14   Example of rating system (event sampling)

Feature	Aspects	R	Comments
	Clarity	4	*Speed often too fast. Big*
Delivery	Loudness	4	*ability range in class, but T*
	Speed	2	*made no allowances when*
	Appropriateness	2	*speaking to weaker Ss.*

Defining the units

When basic decisions have been made, attention turns to the design of the observation schedule itself. As with all such systems, it is best to think

first about higher order categories and then work out lower order definitions in terms of these. Trialling is absolutely vital if the categories are
to do their job, but the considerations below should help you to avoid
some initial pitfalls. They can be applied to all structured observation
but are designed with category systems particularly in mind.

1. Within category:

- *Make sure the category is as clear as possible.*
  'Teacher doubt' would be a difficult category to code because it's not
  clear what it refers to in classroom terms.
- *Check that the category is related to observable behaviour.*
  Even if we knew what 'Teacher doubt' referred to, it would be hard
  to code because we can't see into the mind of the teacher.
- *Be as precise as possible.*
  'Uses a wide range of target language structures' is clear enough but
  doesn't specify what constitutes 'a wide range'. If this is to be used as
  a category, there will need to be accompanying specification.
- *Consider the range of each category.*
  'Corrects fellow pupil in group work' covers two complementary
  categories. It might have been more effective to separate the two,
  so that 'corrects fellow pupil' can be assigned to whatever category ('group work' would be one option) applies at a particular
  time.

2. Among categories:

- *Ensure that all definitions are clear and exclusive.*
  Categories should be defined clearly enough to allow the observer to
  assign classroom events to individual slots. Overlapping categories
  make effective coding impossible.
- *Check that there are no gaps in the coverage of chosen behaviours.*
  Taken together, the categories must cover all the instances of behaviour
  that fall within the parameters of the study. This may involve including
  an 'other' category (notice how the FIAC system in Box 3.11 above,
  includes 'Silence or *confusion*' as a category), but where too many
  behaviours are assigned to this category it is a sign that something
  more specific is called for.
- *The schedule must be practicable.*
  However good the schedule may be on paper, it's useless if coders
  can't apply it in practice. For example, where real time coding

applies (i.e. when the coding takes place 'live', in the lesson), the observer must be able to apply the system effectively in the time available.

Box 3.14 Summarises the essentials.

Box 3.14 Essential characteristics of an effective category system

- Clearly definable categories related to observable behaviour
- Mutually exclusive categories – no overlap
- The category set is exhaustive
- The system can be operationalised

Some practical problems

I began this level by indicating some of the dangers of closed observation, but there are also practical challenges to be overcome. Four of these are particularly important and these are outlined below.

1. Observer effect: if you have established yourself in the setting to the extent that your presence is almost taken for granted (which may mean setting aside data from earlier observations), observer effect will be minimalised. Nevertheless, you should not underestimate the effect that filling in a form (which is what completing an observation schedule amounts to in the eye of the beholder) can look like. In establishing a vantage point from which you can observe all events in the setting, you should therefore consider whether it is also possible to hide or disguise the writing or coding you are doing. In any case, it is not a good idea to rely on a single observation so you can, if possible, discard early sessions.

2. Expectancy effect: observation schedules are designed with specific purposes in mind and these cannot simply be erased from the memory. They may well create a tendency to 'see' particular features, so in order to reduce the strength of this expectancy effect you should reflect very carefully on your initial assumptions, however slight these may be. The higher the degree of inference involved in the observation, the more important it is to be aware of factors that might influence your coding.

3. *Observer drift*: this arises from the fact that observers become familiar with the schedule they are using and begin to 'see' things in expected ways, which creates a drift away from the original coding. To some extent this is inevitable, but awareness can help to reduce it and where teams of coders are involved periodic checks on inter-rater agreement can direct attention to emerging problems.

4. *Central tendency*: this applies only to rating scales and refers to the tendency for opt for something at or near the middle. Keeping options to a minimum can help to reduce it, as can clear criteria and, as in the case of observer drift, awareness and monitoring.

If you are working as an individual, awareness and reflection are probably your best defence against these problems, but if there is a team of observers an additional check is available in the form of inter-observer agreement. The next section describes a relatively straightforward way of establishing whether the level of this is acceptable.

Calculating inter-observer agreement

If, as is often the case, more than one person is involved in a structured observation project, it is very useful to be able to determine the level of agreement between observers. The natural temptation (and therefore the approach that novices tend to adopt) is to look at the raw figures and settle for something that looks convincing. So, for example, if coding has taken place on 100 occasions and in 90 cases two observers have agreed on the appropriate code, this gives a figure of 90 per cent (a percentage known as the *index of agreement* or *index of concordance*), to all intents and purposes a pretty solid outcome. The problem with this approach, though, is that it doesn't take account of chance agreement: the likelihood that two observers will choose a particular code not on the basis of pre-determined criteria but because that code is simply one of a number of options that could be chosen. If two people sit down and code a lesson without any idea of the criteria determining the choice of codes, they are almost certain to agree in at least some cases and allowance must be made for this in any calculation of overall agreement.

Fortunately, there is a very straightforward method of making allowance for such chance agreement that does not depend on a sophisticated grasp of statistics or probability theory – which is another way of saying that even I can use it. Known as Cohen's Kappa (Cohen 1960), it is based on records of agreement (where coders mark the same code on the same occasion) and disagreement (where they mark different codes) and it can be used as the basis for a fairly rough but convenient assessment of performance.

If we take the case mentioned above and assume that two coders have been involved in coding on 100 occasions and have agreed in 90 per cent of cases, we will need to go further than this and identify patterns of agreement and disagreement, that is, what codes have been chosen in each case. For the sake of simplicity, let's assume that in this case there are two observers and only four categories: A (teacher talk), B (student talk), C (on-task activity), and D (other). One way of representing the choices made is in the form of what is sometimes called a 'confusion matrix' (Extract 3.15).

Extract 3.15 A confusion matrix					
Obs 1 / Obs 2	A	B	C	D	Totals
A	40	0	0	0	40
B	1	16	1	0	18
C	2	0	30	4	36
D	0	0	2	4	6
	43	16	33	8	**100**

If we look at the matrix, we can see that in the case of teacher talk (A), the observers agreed on 40 occasions, but while Observer 2 did not mark this category on any other occasions, Observer 1 chose it on three other occasions (once[1] instead of B and twice[2] instead of C). The situation was reversed in the case of student talk (B), where there were 16 agreements and where Observer 1 did not choose it on any other occasions, unlike Observer 2 who chose it once[3] instead of A and once[4] instead of C. Here's an imaginary extract (Extract 3.16) from their completed schedules showing the differences just indicated:

Extract 3.16 Sample codings

Obs 1	A	A	A^2	A	A	A	A^1	A	B	B	A^2	C
Obs 2	A	A	C	A	A	A	B^3	A	B	B	C	B^4

Going back to the confusion matrix, we can see that the sum total of all choices made in each case is 100 (that is, Observer 1's totals along the bottom row and Observer 2's totals down the right-hand column should each add up to 100). If we also add up the total number of agreements on the matrix (shaded areas), we end up with a total of 90. This level of agreement (90 times out of 100 possibilities, or 90 per cent) gives us a raw figure, but it does not account for the fact that some of these agreements might have occurred purely by chance. We need to go further.

The first step in establishing Cohen's Kappa is to calculate the proportion of agreement between the two coders (P_{obs}) by dividing the total number of agreements by the total number of tallies:

$$\frac{\text{Total number of agreements}}{\text{Number of agreements} + \text{number of disagreements}}$$

In this case we have 90 / (90 + 10) = 0.90   So $P_{obs} = 0.90$

We now need to calculate the proportion that can be accounted for by chance (P_{exp}). We know the probability that a particular observer will chose a particular code (whether by chance or not) from the figures. Observer 1, for example, chooses category A 43 times out of a possible 100, while Observer 2 chooses it 40 times. So the probabilities are 0.43 and 0.40 respectively. Probability theory says that the likelihood of these two observers choosing this category *by chance* is simply the product of these two individual probabilities, that is, 0.40 × 0.43 (which equals 0.172, a much smaller figure than the individual ones, which of course reflect a combination of chance *and* design). In terms of our matrix, this means we simply multiply each pair of figures from right-hand and bottom rows, then add the products together for an overall proportion expected by chance:

$$(0.43 \times 0.40) + (0.16 \times 0.18) + (0.33 \times 0.36) + (0.08 \times 0.06) = 0.1696$$
$$\text{So } P_{exp} = 0.1696$$

An alternative method is to simply use the totals in the columns and divide these by 100 × 100 (= 10,000):

$$(43 \times 40) + (16 \times 18) + (33 \times 36) + (8 \times 6) = 1696/10,000 = 0.1696$$

The formula for Cohen's Kappa (K) is $K = \dfrac{P_{obs} - P_{exp}}{1 - P_{exp}}$

In our example, this reads as $K = \dfrac{0.099 - 0.1696}{1 - 0.1696} = 0.87957$ **So K = 0.88**

As you would expect, this is lower than our original figure of 90 per cent, but if we use the rough guide suggested by Fliess (1981), it is still very respectable indeed:

Fair:	Kappa of 0.40–0.60
Good:	Kappa of 0.60–0.75
Excellent:	Kappa of above 0.75

In fact, with so few categories and such simple ones, we would expect a result something like this, but in a more likely situation with a number of categories and perhaps less agreement, the difference between the index of agreement and Cohen's Kappa could be enough to move us from the impression of healthy agreement to a less secure assessment of 'fair'. A little time spent on this relatively straightforward calculation is a worthwhile investment for any situation where more than one observer is involved, and if you are planning to undertake research featuring team structured observation, Bakeman and Gottman (1997, Chapter 4), on which my summary is based, provide an excellent discussion.

Case 3.3: describing activities

I began this level with a flavour of the wide range of descriptions that can be attached to teacher actions, which perhaps gives some idea of just how daunting the prospect of pinning down the concept of 'activity' might be. However, this is precisely the challenge that faced a group of relatively inexperienced researchers involved in a project in Mexico. I'm grateful to Nora Basurto, Paula Busseniers and Barbara Scholes for allowing me to use our exchanges here. I've chosen a slice of their experience as an illustration of some of the issues raised in this level, partly because of the serious attention they gave to matters of data collection and partly because my advice was offered from the other side of the Atlantic

Ocean and therefore addresses the data in very much the same way as any detached reader might. Closer involvement on my part would have brought into play all sorts of unrecorded responses, from tacit understandings and offhand observations, to barely registered non-verbal clues. What follows is paint on damp plaster – immediate and fixed in the moment.

Background

The classroom observation that features here was part of a project that also involved interviews and open observation. At this point, the core team of three researchers was trying to develop an observation schedule that their research assistants would be able to use and had decided to work from scratch. The segment of a longish process that we will examine is based on a single exchange at a crucial stage. The team had begun by designing a very open, descriptive schedule based on a rating scale, on the assumption that this would direct them immediately to the 'successful' activities that the project aimed to identify. Unfortunately, as Extract 3.17 (taken from one of their emails) demonstrates, their assumptions were incorrect.

Extract 3.17 Mistaken assumptions

The first attempt at an observation sheet was a dismal failure, probably due to the fact that our original idea was to try and make it as easy as possible for the observer to fill in. However, it was useful in the sense that it made us realize that we had different ideas about what an activity is; where it begins and ends; what is meant by 'good,' etc.

After further discussion and reflection, one of the team designed a less open schedule that did not incorporate a rating scale. Having trialled it using a taped lesson, the team were reasonably satisfied, but they still thought that it 'included too much detail' and were particularly concerned about one of the sections. The designer sent me a sample page (Extract 3.18), completed by one of the team in the trial, and invited my comments (Extract 3.19). Before reading these (which refer only to the main columns and not to the details at the top), you might like to consider what your reply would have been and predict

Extract 3.18 Observation sheet

Name of School: _____   Name of Teacher: _____

Group no.

Step	*Time interaction*	*English level* Teacher activity (procedure/role)	*Time of day* Acid Resources	*Age* Skill Student activity and responses	*Number of boys* Objectives	*Number of girls* Other comments and observations
1	2 mins T/W/Gr	Asks ?s and elicits R about telephone calls, e.g. Do you like telephone calls? Do you phone a lot? Etc. T controls interaction		Sp L S's answers T's ?s Ss don't show much interest	• activate Ss schemata +interest about topic: phone calls • share opinions and experiences	
2	5 mins WGr	• T gives 2 slips of paper to each S – each has a part of a different phone call. asks Ss to stand up+find the people with the other part of the conversations. • T puts more slips on the table • T monitors, reminds Ss of instructions, gives encouraging comments	Slips of paper parts of 2 T. calls	Sp R Ss stood up slowly Try to find the parts Mainly huddle in big groups, a couple are on their own 1 says it's difficult In general appear to be confused Use Sp.+some Eng.	• identifying • ordering/sequencing • discuss • input topic	This activity seemed to be too difficult for the Ss and so disconcerting possibly due to unclear instructions and/or complicated by the fact that they were only given half of conv. but they weren't told this

which of the columns gave the most trouble. I present my comments exactly as I made them at the time but add some additional observations in italics.

Extract 3.19   My email in response to Extract 3.18

...going across the form it's possible to 'read' it cumulatively, but things start to unravel in the 'objectives' column. This is how I see it:

Step
This gives you a simple and useful reference device. But it is only a reference device because no criteria have been agreed.

Time/Interaction
A slightly higher level of detail providing important information which will allow you to get an idea of the breakdown of the activity in terms of time distribution and interaction type. *Potentially useful, depending on how the analysis develops.*

Teacher activity
This is where you get a more detailed breakdown of the activity itself in terms of what the teacher does. The response demanded is basically descriptive and although some observers will be better at this than others, everyone should be able to cope at a level that will provide you with essential detail. Can I suggest that in this section you also note at the end of each element whether it was in English (E) or Spanish (S). For example, if most of the botched introductions and explanations are the ones delivered in English, this alone could lead you to offering a very simple but potentially invaluable piece of advice. *The use of Spanish in these classes is widespread.*

Aids resources
Essential additional information, especially in terms of the final outcome of this project.

Skill
Another handy element for basic descriptive purposes. These smaller columns are useful: though they don't take much time to complete, they provide valuable information.

Student activity and responses

An obvious complement to teacher activity, but you're absolutely right to distinguish activity from responses (this is a subtle but fundamental distinction, so congratulations on making it). *I don't see any problem with including these in the same category.* The distinction that will need to be made clearly to the observers is between (a) activity in the sense of the activity associated with the task, and presumably set up by the teacher and (b) the responses the students make to this, which may not be predicted by the task or expected by the teacher. The distinction is important because, while both are descriptive, (a) is essential for the basic description you want to build up while (b) is invaluable in helping you to assess what happens in particular classrooms when this activity is done. Although, as your completed example shows, this sort of information is best entered in this column here, it may well be that some observers will include it in the final (comments) column. That doesn't much matter so long as the essential points are noted. *Though I actually think that the issue of where to enter this should be resolved before observation proper begins.*

So far all the description has contributed to a description of the task itself and is based entirely on an observation of events or temporal/ physical conditions in the classroom. Of course, no two people will describe things in exactly the same way, but (and you should be able to show this if you're training people using the video) it should be possible to point to things in the classroom that are the basis for the description you've entered on the form.

In the 'Objectives' column this changes because these are not visible in the same way and the degree of inference required means that you'll end up with a huge range of possibilities. For example, if you take something like step 2 in your description, what's to stop someone legitimately adding: 'motivate students by providing simple first task; get students interacting; break down shyness; provide clear break between this activity and previous desk-bound work; practise questions and answers; practise suggestions; practice agreement and disagreement; vocabulary revision; and so on and so on...' There is in principle almost no limit on where you could end up, and the problem with that is not just that you end up with widely differing lists but that it places terrible time pressure on the observer.

I don't disagree with your comments in the covering letter about what makes something 'good', but these are areas not criteria. (*From B's message: 'In my opinion for an 'activity' to be 'good' it should include and/or reflect a few of the following considerations (not necessarily in this order): linguistic; awareness of the learning process – what students need plus provision of the necessary conditions; motivation – which is part of the above, but which for me is the essential ingredient.'*) For example, there will always be a linguistic element (however indirectly realised) because this is a language lesson, the awareness you mention is not an objective but part of the process of teaching – effective teachers need to be aware of their students' needs and what's happening in the class, but this applies to all teaching and is not a particular objective for any one class. Finally, as you say, motivation is essential but it is not an objective in itself for precisely this reason. Any comments in this respect, and in respect of awareness, can appear in the final column.

If you're going to keep this column, I suggest you keep it very simple. I don't think that you need to mention task objectives because in your sample lesson these emerge clearly from the description of teacher activity in the third column, which is always likely to be the case. Neither do I think it's safe to infer teacher objectives from the activity, unless you restrict this to explicitly stated objectives in the lesson (e.g. 'At the end of this you should be able to do X') which I would suggest is very rare and not essential for the descriptions you want to end up with. It would be much better in this respect to do what you suggest and use interviews with the teachers involved in order to find out what they took the objectives to be. All you're really left with, then, is the key language elements covered. This, I think, would be useful because if you could include this information in your final bank of activities and materials it would help the teachers who will make use of them and will also provide a valuable element in your own referencing system.

That said, a description of key language elements is itself much more difficult to come up with than it seems. In the sort of activity you describe in the sample, many, many different language items will be covered and it may well be extremely difficult to identify the ones that stand out. And what are you going to do about grammatical items and functions? Both? Neither? You can try this but I don't advise it.

If you do want something here I would suggest that you try something like 'Key language or activity focus'. *I think this is still risky, but it's probably worth trialling.* Here, observers would be expected to identify any essential, common and precise features. For example in point 2 'identifying and ordering/sequencing' seem to me to be clear enough. If this had focused on, for example, the openings of a telephone call you could have 'greetings and personal identification'. You could also imagine an activity where the main point was to practise the third conditional, in which case this would go down. Yes, these would also be the key elements in objectives, but, more practically from the observer's point of view, they would be identifiable features of the lessons. Whether you want these or not is up to you, but I think you should discuss this and try it out before deciding.

Finally, let me just say how valuable that final column is. When you train the observers make sure they recognise this. It's here that you can identify factors that might account for the failure of an otherwise excellent task, or where you might identify key pedagogic areas (in your example, the need for clear instructions stands out). There's no need to think of this as evaluative, but it will contribute massively to the sort of evaluation you want to do.

I hope these comments have been useful, but please do remember that they're delivered at a distance and you're the ones who have to decide whether they amount to anything. Please do get back to me if you want to discuss any of this, and let me know how your discussions go.

This was not quite the end of the story because the amended schedule had to be trialled and further refined, but in its final form it provided valuable data for the project. It's worth bearing in mind how far the team travelled more or less under their own steam (my contribution was a very minor one that did no more than confirm what they'd already discovered) and how important the trialling process was in developing a schedule that did the job for which it was intended.

Skills development

As I have already suggested, opportunities for observation arise in all sorts of situations, so the best approach to skills development is to increase our awareness of observation opportunities and improve our ability to engineer time in order to make the best of these. The sort of thing I have in mind is arriving early for a social function and perhaps finding yourself alone (or with a sympathetic partner). In a situation like this, there is nothing untoward about watching people arrive and using this as a focus for observation.

With this in mind, I have adopted an approach to skills development here that is slightly different from that in the other two skills chapters. Rather than offer a set of tasks, I have provided guidance on using every-day activities as a means of skills development, offering some basic advice and useful approaches. If you would rather adopt a more structured approach, Janesick (1998:13–28) provides an excellent sequence of exercises.

Janesick also underlines the importance of ongoing evaluation and reflection. My own recommendation for approaching this are similar to hers and are based on the importance of identifying what has been learned from any observation experience. Reflections can be entered in a development diary or collected on loose sheets of paper and appended to the relevant observation notes, but I think it's important that they should at least be capable of standing alone. For this reason, I recommend including at least basic details of the observation (subject, location, and perhaps participants) as well as a code linking it to the notes themselves, perhaps along the lines shown in Study strategy 3.1.

Study strategy 3.1 Possible categories for observation tasks

Observation topic:
Location:
Date and time:
Lessons learned:
Points to work on:
Personal reflections:
Literature (connections/ideas):

Ideas for observation tasks

The best way of developing ideas for observation tasks is to use your own reviews and reflections, but there are approaches that will help you to see things from new perspectives or perhaps get a firm hold on some aspect of your observation technique that needs development. The ideas outlined below are suggestions as to how you might do this.

Comparisons

Identify an element that differs in two otherwise similar observation situations and observe these, noting the effects on other elements. This might be the presence or absence of a particular individual, the same event in a different setting, and so on. For example, is there a difference between morning and afternoon breaks at your institution, even though the same people are involved?

Changes

Where opportunities arise for observing changes, plan your observation with this in mind. For example, a new system is introduced to your institution. What are the initial responses (effects on routines, response of actors, and so on) and how do these compare with responses when the change is 'bedded in'? What processes have taken place? This would work equally well with the introduction of a new colleague to the staff.

Challenges

Change something in a setting and observe the effects of this. For example, if you can get agreement to change the arrangement of furniture in your staffroom, try this. Or if you have an office, move things around. Or change your own approach to something in a way that challenges conventional routines and observe how others respond to this.

Everyday organisation

Keep an eye open for situations where people have to organise themselves on the spot in order to achieve their ends. Queues provide a good example of this, or situations where people have to organise themselves to work together (for example, a project at home or work). How do they adjust their behaviour in the light of the actions of others and unfolding events? How are rules oriented to, routines established, and so on?

Something unusual

Look out for the opportunity to observe something unusual. One of Janesick's exercises (1998:22) involves observing an animal – an interesting and potentially enlightening challenge.

Some of these ideas are summarised in Study strategy 3.2.

Study strategy 3.2 Some simple observational rules

- Remember Rock (2001:32): 'There is no part of the social world that will remain boring after the application of a little curiosity'.
- Length doesn't matter – 10 minutes will do
- Note if you can, but don't worry if you can't – it's also important to train the memory
- Don't chase the unusual – the everyday is strange enough
- Nothing is at stake – abandon rather than offend
- **Always give careful consideration to ethical issues**

Reading guide

Level 1

I know of no books that get to grips with developing the fundamental skills of observation, but if you want a very readable introduction to classroom observation in general you can do no better than Wragg (1999). Chapter 3, on the use of qualitative methods, is particularly relevant to the topic of this chapter, and his discussion of the use of critical events is particularly interesting.

Level 2

My own preference is for the writings of those who have spent the best part of their lives in the field, educational or not, and particular recommendations are Whyte (1997) and Wolcott (1994), writers who might seem a touch dogmatic to some but who are never less then entertaining. The former covers less than 150 pages and is eminently readable, Wolcott is longer and slanted more towards representation than data collection, but Part I (also less than 150 pages) focuses on the educational context and has plenty to say about observing. An alternative is Delamont (2002), who approaches the research process as a voyage of discovery and introduces the different stages of progress from initial reading through to writing. Its educational orientation is a particular recommendation.

Tales from the field

- Shaffir and Stebbins (1991a) is a first rate collection of papers from researchers who discuss aspects of fieldwork in the context of their own projects. The papers are short and entertaining.

- Hammersley and Atkinson (1995, Chapters 3 and 4) provide a more succinct summary of the relevant issues, also drawing on a wide and interesting range of experiences.

Fieldnotes

If fieldnotes are going to play an important role in your data collection, it would also be well worth investing in at least one of three books on this topic.

- Lofland and Lofland (1995) explicitly covers both observation and fieldnotes.
- Emerson *et al.* (1995) is a first rate introduction to the writing of fieldnotes.
- Sanjek (1990) includes some excellent papers on the subject.

Overviews

- May (2001, Chapter 7) provides a useful brief overview of the main traditions of participant observation and a taste of some different views.
- Berg (1998) has a slightly more experiential orientation.
- Emerson *et al.* (2001), at a shade under 15 pages of text, is for my money by far the best single treatment of participant observation in terms of value per word – packed with useful information.

Study strategy 3.3 summarises the skills needed for fieldwork.

Study Strategy 3.3   Getting to know fieldwork

An excellent way to launch your reading would be to study Emerson *et al.* (2001), following this with Delamont's research journey (2002), before tackling the practical issues raised in Lofland and Lofland (1995). Once you've got a real sense of what's required and have begun to put it into practice, read as many first hand accounts of the field as you can. Delamont's references include plenty of books based on fieldwork in educational settings, but my own preference is to approach this reading in much the same way as I do any literature: find an author you enjoy and explore their work.

Level 3

There's no shortage of books on structured observation, so the choice boils down to your particular needs in this area. The best brief overview I know, despite its relative age, is that of Evertson and Green (1986), a meaty offering packed with tables and diagrams that summarise different positions and approaches.

If you'd prefer to review the contents of this chapter, there are a couple of very readable summaries that cover much the same territory. Chapter 8 of Bryman (2001a) offers some useful lists and crisp summaries of structured observation, but there is more detail to be found in the section on structured observation in Robson (2002:324–45).

Closer to home, Malamah-Thomas (1987) is not a book to sit down and read but there are plenty of useful observation systems and tasks in there, and if used properly it can be provide a valuable taste of structured observation. If you're interested in how this approach was used within a very different research paradigm, you could also read Allwright's fascinating survey (1988).

Study strategy 3.4 summarises this section.

Study strategy 3.4   Structured observation

If you decide to use structured observation, it's probably best to get hold of Bakeman and Gottman (1997) as a source of advice and information. On the other hand, if you feel that you'd simply like to explore this form of observation, Malamah-Thomas (1987) provides an excellent selection of standard systems and associated tasks. This is very much a book to dip into, but it will give you the chance to feel your way. It's not designed for work at this level, so I would advise setting Evertson and Green (1986) alongside it as a source of information on broader research issues.

4
Collecting and Analysing Spoken Interaction

Preview

In this chapter we'll look at ways of collecting, transcribing and analysing spoken interaction. On a fairly basic level, this is something that anybody can do with relatively little effort, and it can be surprisingly rewarding. But it's not quite as straightforward as it seems. The chapter will help you to avoid the basic pitfalls in data collection and will show you how to focus successfully on interesting features of talk, transcribing these at a level of delicacy appropriate to your needs (for a note on transcription conventions, see Box 4.1). By the end of the first level you should have the confidence and skill to undertake the sort of analysis that can transform your understanding of your own teaching. Readers who pursue their studies into Level 2 will find ways of honing their transcription and analytical skills, while more advanced researchers will have the chance to deepen their understanding of the way talk features within different traditions in QI and the relevance of this to broader issues.

Level 1 will explain how to make successful recordings and will highlight some of the important considerations and main sources of frustration for novice researchers. It will also introduce you to transcription and suggest ways in which you can decide, fairly economically, what to transcribe. Finally, it will show you how to approach basic analysis by a process of progressive focusing.

Level 2 is designed for those who would like to take their analysis to a slightly deeper level. It will offer a more detailed procedure for developing an adequate transcription and analysis, paying particular attention to sequences and patterns in talk, and showing how the identification of these can deepen our understanding of the nature of spoken interaction.

Level 3 will be slightly different from previous levels in that it will be built around a single case. It will involve the analysis of a transcript using three different analytical traditions: conversation analysis, interactional sociolinguistics and critical discourse analysis. The aim here is to capture at least a flavour of how these different approaches would treat the same text. The analysis will be followed by a brief discussion of another tradition, the ethnography of communication, and a summary of common features; the chapter will conclude with a brief discussion of issues associated with context.

I have tried to adopt a fairly neutral approach to the process of analysis in this chapter, but readers already familiar with the territory will recognise that Level 2 owes a great deal to the conversational analysis (CA) tradition. I think this is appropriate, not because CA can make an important contribution to QI (though it certainly can), but because its focus on sequences develops analytical skills that can be utilised to good purpose in all forms of analysis. Anyone interested in seeing CA in the context of other options will find this discussed in Level 3.

Box 4.1   A note on transcription conventions

.	Falling intonation	That was foolish.
,	Continuing contour	I took bread, butter, jam and honey
?	Questioning intonation	Who was that?
!	Exclamatory utterance	Look!
(2.0)	Pause of about 2 seconds	So (2.0) what are we going to do?
(...)	*Pause of about 1 second	In front of (...) the table
(..)*	Pause of about 0.5 second	Then (..) she just (..) left
(.)	Micropause	Put it (.) away
[]	Overlap	A: He saw it ⌈to ⌉ and stopped
		B: ⌊oh⌋
[[	Speakers start at same time	⌈⌈A: And the-
		⌊⌊B: So she left it behind.
=	Latched utterances	A: We saw her yesterday.=
		B: =And she looked fine.
–	Emphasis	Put it <u>away</u>.
:	Sound stretching	We waited for a lo:::ng time
(xxx)	Unable to transcribe	We'll just (xxxxxxxxxx) tomorrow

Box 4.1 (Continued)

(send)	Unsure transcription	And then he (juggled) it
(( ))	Other details	Leave it alone ((moves book))
↑	Prominent rising intonation	It was ↑ wonderful
↓	Prominent falling intonation	That's the end of ↓ that
-	Abrupt cut-off	If you go- if you leave
(x)	Hitch or stutter	I (x) I did
CAPS	Louder than surrounding talk	It's BILL I think
hhh	Aspirations	That's hhhhh I dunno
·hhh	Inhalations	·hhhh well I suppose so
° °	Quieter than surrounding talk	Let him see it °why don't you°
> <	Quicker than surrounding talk	>I'd just< leave it where it is

* Conversation analysts time to tenths of a second, e.g. '(0.6)'.

Level 1: getting started

My first tape recorder was a second-hand reel-to-reel machine, bought as a Christmas present by my parents from a small corner shop down the road that sold electrical goods. My first bicycle excepted, it was the most exciting present they ever bought me and I can still remember many details of that Christmas morning. Two things stand out: the first is that Christmas day was long past before I learnt how to use the machine properly, and the second is a memory of how odd my recorded voice sounded and how strange 'ordinary' conversation seemed. Since then I have made thousands of recordings and transcriptions, but neither of the issues has gone away: I continue to explore the possibilities offered by the equipment I use, occasionally making new discoveries, and I continue to use the tape recorder as a means of making strange what might otherwise be lost in the ordinariness of our everyday doings. In a sense, much of this level is about these two aspects of recording because they separate the conscious use of the tape recorder as a research instrument from its function as a recreational device.

The man in the corner shop had been very helpful. He'd spent half an hour recording detailed instructions on how to use the tape recorder and given the tape to my parents, explaining how to play it. They must have listened to the tape, removed it, turned it over and then replaced it on the recorder, so when I came to use it there seemed to be only a blank tape, and since I assumed that tapes had only one side it was not until a few months later that a casual experiment revealed the lost – and by now redundant – instructions. This explains why it took so long for me to get to grips with the functions of the tape recorder, and it highlights an important relationship between instructions and exploration. Most of the things I will explain here you can probably discover by yourself through practice, but along the way you might waste much valuable time. On the other hand, this is meant to serve as an introduction and you should always be prepared to explore for yourself the limitations and possibilities of the equipment you use.

How to make successful recordings

In making recordings for research purposes there are three areas that require particular attention: the selection of equipment, ethical considerations and procedures for recording. This section will deal with each of these in turn and the following section will start from the assumption that you already have some recorded data under your belt.

The equipment

The golden rule here is a simple one: inadequate equipment makes transcription difficult if not impossible, frustrating and demotivating the person doing the research. That said, you don't need sophisticated equipment in order to do good research; what matters is getting the right equipment for the job. Roughly speaking, there are four sorts of recording instrument you might use (these are summarised in Box 4.2):

1. *A 'walkman' style tape recorder:*   most people own or have access to one of these, and they vary greatly in quality. More expensive models may have facilities such as voice activation and speed settings and may come with an extension microphone. In fact, however sophisticated the hand-held recorder, it is not designed for large-scale recordings. These recorders are perfect for capturing interviews and small group exchanges around a table or desk, but they are rarely successful when used for recording classroom interaction.

2. *A minidisc recorder:*   these are even smaller than the hand-held tape recorder and they have two advantages: they can record for much longer periods and generally speaking they make better quality recordings.

Most minidiscs will record uninterrupted for around 75 minutes, and if your recorder has a long-play facility this can be doubled. Extension microphones supplied with these machines tend to be rather good, so you may find that, if necessary, you can use them to make classroom recordings. However, it is very difficult to transcribe directly from cheaper minidisc recorders because, unlike a tape recorder, they do not offer the user full control over spinning back the recording. In order to transcribe, therefore, you may need to transfer the data to either a computer or a tape recorder.

3. A large tape recorder: most institutions have these and in many cases they make very good classroom recorders if the right microphone is used. It's important to use an omnidirectional device, and I particularly recommend a pressure-zone microphone. These microphones are about 10 cm square and no thicker than the cover of an average ring binder, so they sit unobtrusively on a desk or, for long-term projects, can even be screwed to the wall. An omnidirectional microphone will pick up all the exchanges that take place in a classroom, but it is an indiscriminate beast and will also willingly devour all the bumps and scrapes that accompany such exchanges, not to mention the noise of crowds and passing traffic outside the classroom.

Box 4.2 Summary: recording devices

Recording individuals or small groups:
- Walkman' style recorder
- Minidisc recorder (data transferred to computer or tape recorder for transcription purposes)

Recording large groups such as classes:
- Larger, mains recorder with omnidirectional microphone (a pressure zone microphone is ideal)
- Minidisc recorder, if necessary

Recording situations where non-verbal behaviour is important:
- Video camera, supported by audiotape recording

---

4. A video recorder: the obvious advantage of a video recorder is that it captures non-verbal as well as verbal features and it may therefore be essential for some projects, but it has two drawbacks. The first is that it is relatively obtrusive, which means that it can significantly affect the behaviour of the people you are recording and therefore needs to be used with care. The second drawback is that, generally speaking, more attention is given to the quality of the picture than the sound in the design of video recorders. You will therefore need to back up your video recording with an audio recording.

Ethical issues

The tape recorder and video camera have become so associated with public scandals and/or media intrusion that people are perhaps even more suspicious of them than they used to be. In addition, where the recorded material could – legitimately or otherwise – be evaluated by employers or line managers, with potential consequences for career progression, allowing access to the recordings made can represent a genuine and very serious risk to those involved. In any case, most teachers feel uncomfortable in the presence of an observer and this applies equally well to a tape recorder. I strongly advise you to begin by recording your own classes, since this produces data that you can use to aid your own development as a teacher and a researcher. However, eventually you may wish to record others, in which case the following points (directed to classroom research but applicable more generally) may help you to negotiate permission. If you prefer, you can begin with the first and work down the list, stopping at the point where permission is given, though I prefer, as the following list shows, to put everything on the table at the outset.

1. Explain roughly why you wish to record the lesson(s), but don't be too specific in case the teacher adjusts their teaching style in response to this. For example, it is better to say that you're interested in teacher-student exchanges rather than to explain that you wish to focus on questioning strategies.
2. Assure the teacher involved that the recordings will remain absolutely confidential and that you will not make public (e.g. via publication) any of the data without their explicit permission. You may also need to discuss the conditions under which the tape will be stored. Ideally, there should be a signed, written agreement.
3. Offer to let the teacher see the transcripts if they so wish.
4. Offer to share any findings or insights that might be of use to the teacher. The teacher may even be interested in becoming involved in the investigation itself.

5. Tell the teacher that if they feel the lesson has gone particularly badly they can ask you to tape over the recording (or even retain the tape themselves).

Procedures

Having settled on the appropriate equipment and obtained permission to record, you are now in a position to collect your data – and this is where most people hit problems. There seems to be nothing more straightforward than setting up a tape recorder or video camera and letting it do the business; ten Have (1990:32) even talks of 'delegating' data collection to a machine, as if it took full responsibility for its actions. I suppose it's comforting to think in terms of mechanical perversity rather than our own incompetence, but the results are the same: the sad fact is that most people new to research fail to get the recording they want at the first attempt. I have supervised hundreds of research projects at Masters and PhD level and I would estimate that over 50 per cent of these have encountered recording problems somewhere along the line. And even experienced researchers make mistakes: less than a year ago, having double-checked my equipment, I replaced the microphone jack in the wrong socket and lost 45 minutes of data. So be prepared for problems and treat them as valuable learning opportunities.

The first step to successful recording is choosing the right equipment for the job, but whatever machine you choose, it is essential to try it out. Familiarise yourself with it in a private setting where you can test its range and limitations, then take it to the place where you plan to use it and test it there, preferably in similar conditions to the ones you will encounter. This still won't guarantee success, but it will reduce the likelihood of problems. To help you look out for some of the difficulties you might encounter, I've included a small selection in Box 4.3 – all of them genuine examples. But quality is not just a matter of sounds, it also relates to the quality of the interaction itself, the extent to which the recorded talk is 'natural'. The fact is, speakers will probably be aware that they are being recorded, at least some of the time, and this raises what has become known as the *observer's paradox*. Labov proposed this term to represent the paradox that in order to observe, the observer has to be present, but when they are present the other actors do not act in the same way as they would if they were not there. The same applies to a microphone: if people know it's there, they don't act normally.

All you can do is aim to minimise this effect as much as you can. If your microphone has been secretly placed in a hidden location and the speakers have been unaware of its presence throughout, the problem

Box 4.3 Things that can go wrong.

- The 'play' button is pressed, in place of 'record'.
- The batteries run out.
- The microphone isn't switched on.
- The microphone is placed next to a noisy OHP, which drowns out everything when switched on.
- The microphone jack isn't pushed fully into the proper socket.
- The microphone has a separate battery that runs out during recording.
- The pause button is pressed and not subsequently released.
- A late arrival occupies an empty seat in front of the video camera and blocks everything.

does not arise, but this is generally regarded as unethical. An acceptable alternative is to obtain general permission to record and then, having waited for a few days or weeks, to conceal the fact that you are taping even though the speakers 'know' about this. In a classroom this may be difficult, but a form of 'concealment through familiarity' is possible if you allow the tape recorder to become part of the furniture. Aim to record not just once but many times, until those involved cease to adjust their talk to accommodate an 'overhearer'. In that way you should be able to obtain recordings that capture fairly typical classroom exchanges, though if you are the teacher involved you may have to make the procedure for switching on the recorder so much a matter of routine that it is quickly forgotten, and if you are recording groups you will have to place 'walkman' style recorders on the desks. A video camera is also a rather prominent object, but its impact can be minimised if you place it in the same corner of the room every lesson and switch it on before the students arrive.

As with most things, making a recording may require a relatively heavy investment of time and effort the first time you do it, and once that's out of the way you can look forward to reasonably trouble-free recording with all the rewards that follow from it. In my experience, many first time researchers find it psychologically demanding to approach someone else in order to ask permission to record their lesson, and for this reason I usually recommend beginning with one of your own lessons. This will give you the chance to familiarise yourself with technical issues and will provide you with the sort of practical knowledge that can be very valuable when you do decide to record other people, who are usually more impressed by those who are able to speak confidently about what they are setting out to do. It's also true that most teachers who take the time to study recordings of themselves at work find it a richly rewarding experience. In any case, I strongly advise you to record one of your lessons so that you can move to the next section with some interesting questions of your own, ripe for examination. You might even find that some of the things you've noticed emerge in the discussions in later sections. Box 4.4 sums up the steps you can take to obtain a good reading.

Box 4.4   A procedure for recording your own teaching

1. Towards the beginning of term, ask permission of your class to record them. Explain that you will be focusing on your teaching but that if they wish you would be happy to show them extracts from the transcript where these might help them in their own studies.
2. Set up your tape recorder, concealing this as far as possible. You may be able to put it on a shelf or even in a cupboard, hanging a pressure zone mike from the wall, but the most convenient location is beneath the teacher's desk, with the microphone on the desk.
3. Begin every lesson by switching on the tape recorder, until this becomes a matter of routine.
4. Listen to part of the first recording and decide whether you need to experiment with the position of the microphone or perhaps even a different recorder.
5. If you are satisfied with the quality of the recording, use the tape again in the next lesson and repeat this a few times. Eventually, you'll need to set aside the tape and use a new one rather than risk degradation in recording quality.
6. Continue this until you reach a point where you come to the end of a lesson and decide, 'Interesting things happened there' or 'I think that was pretty typical of my teaching.' At this point, you're ready to move on to the process of listening, transcribing and analysis.

Listening to find a focus

Talk is designed to be heard, not read, so never move straight from recording to transcribing: always take the time to listen carefully – and listen again. If you've recorded something with a particular feature in mind, the business of settling down to examine it in more detail is relatively straightforward, but not all research begins with a focus that is precise enough to allow this. You might have a much more general idea of what you'd like to explore, or you might simply have followed my advice for recording one of your classes, in which case you'll need to decide what you want to transcribe and examine in more detail. If so, you can use a process probably best described as 'progressive focusing': gradually homing in on an interactional feature of interest. To do this you need to develop your listening skills.

If you listen to the tape you've made, your first reaction will be, 'Nothing's happening'. In my experience, this is *always* the case when someone new to analysis listens to a tape for the first time – and it can be very disheartening. It's only natural to think that there really *is* nothing there and to want to give up, but you should resist the temptation because there's a very simple rule that applies to this sort of analysis: *the more you listen, the more you hear.*

What you need to do, then, is listen to your tape over and over and over again (with the tape counter set at zero at the start of the tape) until you find a part of the lesson where something interesting is happening. This doesn't mean sitting down and working through the whole tape every time; it's much better to leave the tape in an accessible place so that you can listen to it whenever and for however long is convenient. Sooner or later you will identify a part of the tape where something interesting is happening. When you find this, note the number on the tape counter and spin it back to this after each listening. Again, listen as many times as you feel you need to, until you have an idea of what's going on – and when you do, it's time to get down to transcription.

Basic transcription

Two hours before writing this I talked with someone who had recently completed his first transcription and had moved on from this to transcribing a number of relatively brief exchanges. His comment on the change between his first experience to his current situation speaks for anyone who has trodden the same path:

> When I first started transcribing it took me a few hours just to record about ten minutes of talk, but I've now got it down to less than half that time and I'm really beginning to enjoy getting into the data.

The first thing that might strike you about this is that it still takes an hour or so to deal with ten minutes of talk. This is why it's not a good idea to begin by trying to transcribe a whole lesson – it could put you off classroom research for life. Your aim should be to find something interesting, perhaps lasting no more than five minutes or so, and then to transcribe this using a fairly straightforward system. This is what we'll concentrate on in this level, leaving more complicated transcription issues until the next level, though if you're the sort of person who likes to take the bull by the horns you could try using the more extensive range of symbols included in Box 4.1 at the end of the preview section (p. 173).

Transcription symbols

The aim in any transcription is to describe the talk as fully but as simply as possible. If you include too much detail the transcription will be very difficult to read, but if you settle for just the words you hear this may fail to capture important aspects of the interaction. The decision about what level of delicacy to aim at is something I'll discuss in Level 2; what matters here is that you familiarise yourself with the most important conventions. If you transcribe using the symbols recommended below and include line numbers for ease of reference, your text should be perfectly adequate for most practical purposes. You should also be in a position to read most of the transcripts published in academic papers.

Here, then, is a description of a transcription system, divided into the two fundamental aspects of talk that need to be addressed: delivery and turn-taking.

1. Aspects of delivery:　intonation is an important feature in all talk, and this can be captured by using symbols with which you will already be familiar. The *period* is used to indicate falling intonation, such as would be used to mark the end of a sentence when reading. In talk, it indicates a point where it would be legitimate for another speaker to take a turn without being seen to interrupt. (Notice, though, that some perfectly grammatical utterances end without falling intonation and so do not require a period, or any other symbol.) A *comma* indicates exactly the opposite. This represents a 'continuing' contour, the sort of intonation that shows the speaker wishes to carry on speaking. This contour may take a number of forms, but the message is clear: 'I have more to say'. Typical examples would be a list ('We bought apples, pears, plums...') or a conditional statement, ('If that's what you think, ...'). Any speaker taking over the turn at this point would be seen as interrupting, which is why this contour is so popular with politicians who want to prevent an aggressive interviewer from pursuing a point: by using a continuing contour at a point where a falling contour would be syntactically appropriate, they can force the interviewer to concede the turn or appear as rude and interruptive. The final two marks of intonation correspond exactly to their written equivalents: a *question mark* signals questioning intonation, though of course not all questions are accompanied by this, and the *exclamation mark* indicates an exclamatory utterance.

In addition to these basic symbols, you may also need to use *underlining* to indicate any words or syllables that receive particular emphasis. You might also want to show any word that is cut off short by using a *hyphen* (note that this might apply even if the whole word is uttered but ends abruptly) or to show the lengthening of syllables by using *colons* (the longer the sound stretching, the greater the number of colons). If there are any words or phrases that you can't hear, you can show this by including empty *brackets* or brackets with a row of crosses or question marks. Similarly, any words you are not sure of should be included in *single brackets*, while other actions or descriptions should appear in *double brackets*.

2. Turn-taking: all dialogue depends on turn-taking, so it's vital to capture the essential features of this. The first thing to decide is where a new turn starts. In most cases this will immediately follow the prior speaker's turn, allowing for a natural micropause between the two turns. In this case you simply begin the new turn at the beginning of the next line. Sometimes, though, a new speaker will begin before the current speaker's turn has ended, in which case you will need to show where the overlap occurs. You can use square brackets for this, if necessary including the final bracket to show where the overlap ends. Dealing with overlaps can be one of the most frustrating transcribing tasks, but I've found the following approach very effective:

1. Ignoring the overlap, transcribe the first speaker's turn to completion.
2. Transcribe the second speaker's turn at least beyond the end of the first speaker's turn.
3. Listen for where the overlap begins (and, if necessary, ends) and insert brackets.

In some cases the new speaker won't interrupt but will come in so quickly at the end of the current speaker's turn that there is no gap whatsoever between the new turn and the previous one (i.e. it is almost as if there is just one speaker). When this happens the two turns are described as 'latched' and equals signs are used at the end of the first speaker's turn and at the beginning of the second speaker's to show the lack of any pause between them.

Pauses are also important in talk and have been dealt with in a number of ways. The system suggested by Brown and Yule (1983:xii) is very straightforward: use a dash [–] for 'short pauses', a plus sign [+] for 'longer pauses' and two plus signs [+ +] for 'extended pauses'. I recommend a system along the lines of van Lier's (1988:243), using periods in brackets. I use three of these as equivalent to about one second [(...)], two for about half a second and one for a micropause, detectable but very short. Anything above a second can be timed in full or half seconds.

Armed with these symbols, you should be able to produce a good transcription of a short passage from your data. If you'd like to see how a finished version appears, have a look at Extract 4.1 on p. 186. Alternatively, you might like to try your hand first and then compare. You may not want to try all of the above transcription symbols the first time you transcribe, in which case just use the basic intonation symbols, together with conventions for pauses and overlap. This will shorten the process slightly and produce a reasonable transcript. The best way of deciding just what symbols to use is to get down to the business of transcribing in order to gradually develop your familiarity with the system and your sense of what needs to be captured in the talk. This will be helped if you use a good quality machine and practise judging the right length of pressure on the reverse button to produce a spin back that suits you. If you have access to a transcribing machine, you might like to try using this, in which case successful transcription depends on your control of the foot pedal and your adjustment of the 'spin-back' setting. Once this has been adjusted to a time that suits you, it should be possible to develop a fairly productive rhythm. The rest is a matter of practice and knowing when tiredness is beginning to set in: transcription usually benefits from a 'little and often' approach.

An introduction to analysis

Careful listening sets up good analysis. In our profession we're used to working with written texts, so there's a natural tendency to want to get stuck into the transcript as soon as possible, but it pays to remember that the tape is your primary source. A transcription is simply your best attempt to represent this on paper, so if there's anything you're not sure of you should always be prepared to go back to the tape.

When I talked about my first experiences of using a tape recorder, I mentioned how strange recorded voices seemed to me, and this sense of strangeness has never quite disappeared. In fact, it's a very valuable device to help us get under the skin of interaction. Our daily encounters for the most part go unnoticed, a part of general routines and experiences that we take for granted, but when we remove them from that everyday context they take on a very different complexion and we may have difficulty in recognising them as representations of what actually happened. Don't be downhearted or too self-critical if your first impressions suggest a much less coherent state of affairs than you expected – this is quite normal. The process of distancing that produces this impression gives us the chance to look at our work in a new way, and this can be invaluable. The aim of analysis is throw fresh light on aspects of our talk, illuminating features and patterns that have previously been hidden to us. Paradoxically, this is at the same time more simple and more complicated than it seems. It is simpler because all it really requires us to do is to look at the most basic and obvious things in our talk. If we can identify these and say how they work, they will reveal things to us that will enable us to develop a better understanding of activities achieved through the talk. The complication arises from the fact that it's not always easy to spot what is most obvious. There is a – perhaps apocryphal – detective story in which a man is murdered in his house on a morning when many of his neighbours are in the street outside. There is only one entrance to the house, so the murderer must have been seen by the neighbours, but when they are questioned they all insist that nobody visited the house during the morning in question. Eventually it transpires that the milkman committed the murder, but he, like the postwoman who also visited the house, was 'invisible' to the residents because he was so much a part of their daily routine. Good analysis depends on training ourselves to see these 'invisible' features in our talk.

Level 2 develops a structured approach to analysis, but the effectiveness of this will depend to some extent on your ability to take time in order simply to listen and look in order to discover what is going on. This is what we will concentrate on in this section, working through four steps in preliminary analysis:

- Step 1   Providing a general characterisation;
- Step 2   Identifying grossly apparent features;
- Step 3   Focusing in on structural elements;
- Step 4   Developing a description.

The first step involves getting a general sense of what is happening, so that we are in a position to say what sort of exchange is taking place. In some cases there might even be a conventional label that we can assign to it. Read the extract that follows (Extract 4.1) and decide how you would characterise it.

Extract 4.1   Question and answer

```
01   T:   But the writing is on 'weekends' which tells you::
02   S1:  When
03   T:   Whe::n. Ye:::s. ((To S2)) So would you like to give me the
04        question again.
05   S2:  When do: when do you go: (.) to on: ⌈weekends
06   Ss:                                       ⌊(xxxxxxxx)
07   S2:  When do you (..) when do you go: (..) er
08   T:   to
09   S2:  to er (..) er (.) er (...) weekends
10   S3:  ((Whispered to S2)) Taif
11   T:   When do you go to where? Banana Street?
12   S2:  When do you (.) when do you go (.) to Taif.
13   T:   Ye:::s!
```

Step 1   *Providing a general characterisation*

I would describe this as an extract from a lesson where a teacher is trying to elicit a correct response from a student.

You may have chosen to give it a slightly different label, and my general characterisation by no means captures the full range of what is happening here. However, we now have a framework within which to work and can move on to the identification of any grossly apparent features (the term is borrowed from a seminal work on turn taking by Sacks *et al.* 1974). By this I mean obvious things like the relationship between the speakers, who says what to whom, how the turns are distributed, and so on. To do this we need to form a general impression of the passage and then read it carefully, making sure that we understand just who is speaking and how each turn relates to the previous one. Try this and compare your response with mine.

Step 2   *Identifying grossly apparent features*

There are a number of speakers in this extract but the teacher has the most turns. He is the only one who asks questions or invites responses, to which the students reply. Of these, S2 has the most turns.

This is a very basic description, but Step 2 is there to ensure that we haven't missed anything obvious. You might also have included comments about how the teacher controls the interaction and is the sole arbiter of what is acceptable, though it's best to hold back on interpretations at this point if you can. (Incidentally, the length of turns in this extract gives no particular cause for comment, but if you look ahead to Extract 4.3 on p. 190 you will see that they are by no means always equal.)

In the next step attention shifts to any features or patterns in the talk that might be of particular interest. What can we say about the way in which turns are constructed, the floor is managed, topics are negotiated, and so on? This demands a close line-by-line reading.

Step 3   Focusing in on structural elements

It is clear from this extract (Extract 4.1) that it is the teacher who controls the floor and the topic. He asks the questions (e.g. l.1), decides on the activity (ll. 3–4), offers assistance where this is required (l.8) and is the arbiter of what is acceptable (ll. 11 and 13). Apart from the student directly addressed by the teacher (S2), the only one to speak makes his contribution in a whisper (l.10), not offering it for public consumption. On a more local level, we might note the use of the lengthened syllable as a prompt inviting completion in l.1 and the pauses in S2's responses in ll. 7 and 9.

In producing this description I have focused on what appear to me to be the most salient characteristics; you may have chosen others. Whatever the fine detail, once we have a picture of the features characterising this passage we are already well on the way to a description. This will consist of a straightforward representation of the event, drawing attention to the features already noted. It might start something like this:

Step 4   Developing a description

This is an example of teacher-fronted classroom talk in which brief and successful exchange with a student is followed by a more extended exchange in which the selected student fails to produce the expected answer in the first instance and succeeds only when offered support. The first exchange consists of incomplete teacher statement with sound stretching on the last word, inviting completion. S1 provides this and the teacher confirms that his response is accurate by repeating it (effectively therefore completing his initial statement) and offering an emphatic 'yes' by way of further confirmation. . . .

It is not necessary to work through a whole transcript like this: some characteristics will be immediately obvious anyway and many parts will not require close reading. However, when you have chosen to look at an extract in detail, this approach will help you to train your eye and organise your thinking – a basis for all effective analysis. Sometimes, though, our analysis does not need to be at all sophisticated in order to generate interesting research questions and provide the basis for professional development, as the following case demonstrates.

Case 4.1: giving instructions

One of the most unfortunate, although perhaps inevitable, outcomes of the excellent investigations that have been conducted into classroom talk is that many teachers feel that it is necessary to be an accomplished analyst in order to say anything worthwhile. In fact nothing could be further from the truth: all that is necessary in order to discover new aspects of classroom practice is a willingness to collect spoken data, the patience to listen carefully to it and transcribe it faithfully, and a commitment to close reading with an open mind. When it comes to describing your findings, familiarity with the literature and appropriate terminology is an advantage, but this will not produce the insights in the first place – only hard and painstaking examination of the data will deliver these.

For this reason, I've chosen a feature of classroom talk that you may have identified in your own data and my discussion of it will draw on only the most obvious features of the data. The topic is giving instructions and the data set consists of passages from two different teachers, both teaching at intermediate level. In Extract 4.2 the teacher is preparing the class for a rôle play where one student interviews another for the post of tourist guide. The extract focuses on the preparation required of the interviewee and is followed by the start of the activity. Extract 4.3 also immediately precedes the start of the activity, in this case a written task in which the students have to mark the stress in words in a text in order to identify whether they are nouns or verbs.

My brief discussion of these two passages will draw attention only to the most obvious features and will point to how this might form the basis for further investigation or for professional development.

The most striking feature of both passages is the length of the teacher's turn, and this in itself may be an important discovery. It would be interesting to discover whether all teacher instruction-giving is based on such extended deliveries, unrelieved by any attempt to involve the listeners. In the case of Extract 4.3 this may be less significant than in the first extract because most of the teacher's first turn is taken up with comments on the text that students have in front of them. Even the barely coherent 'If you couldn't really know what they meant' is relatively unimportant because the only absolutely essential information is contained in the sentence beginning, 'What I'd like you to do...'. How far is this extended prefacing typical of instruction-giving and how far is this a matter of focusing attention rather than giving information?

Extract 4.2 presents a slightly different problem because the information load here is heavy in comparison. An examination of ll.10–22, for example, produces a considerable list. It would be interesting to explore just how much information is given out in instructions and how much of this is accompanied by understanding checks. There are plenty of these in this extract ('OK?', 'Yes?', 'Right?') but in the absence of non-verbal evidence we are unable to determine whether they receive encouraging responses. All we can say for certain is that they are not followed by any pause in the flow of talk and there is no verbal feedback. It would also be interesting to see how common such 'empty checks' (I invent the term for want of a better description) are in extended teacher turns. Nor are these the only common feature of the teacher's delivery: repetition also plays a prominent part. Comprehension checks aside, there are five sentences in ll.1–7, all of them beginning with 'so', and between ll.5–7 'think of' appears four times. Much of this teacher's talk has the quality of a list, and it might be worth finding out whether this is a common feature of instruction-giving.

Extract 4.2   Giving instructions (1)

01	T:	So: the people who are the applicants, you think of the
02		<u>an</u>swers that you are going to get. So you might like to write
03		a few things down. OK? So you know that the Board are
04		going to ask you ab<u>out</u> e:m knowledge of local places. So
05		think of local places in your area that people could visit?
06		Yes? So you think of Spanish places, you think of Turkish
07		places, you think o:f
08		(..)
09	LL:	(xxxxxx)
10		<u>Thai</u> places. OK? Local spots so you can give the <u>name</u> right?
11		So people come here they could visit <u>this</u> because it's
12		interesting this because it's interesting or what<u>ever</u>.
13		Secondly, e:m (..) think of whether you've ever been a
14		tourist guide before. If you <u>have</u> you have to tell them,
15		what you <u>did</u>, how long you worked for, who you worked
16		for and so on. Right, em you need to show them that you
17		can deal with problems. (..) Right? And that you can that
18		you can <u>organise</u> small groups of people. Right? And

19	T:	personality, well that's something that they will have to
20		assess themselves because your personality is your
21		Personality that's ((xxxxxx)). OK? But try to be friendly
22		and <u>nice</u> and cooperative. OK?

Extract 4.3 Giving instructions (2)

01	T:	So, now what you could do is turn over the page (as usual).
02		Have a look at these two exercises. The way they mark
03		the- the verbs and the nouns are written on your paper,
04		you don't really have an idea of- of what the meaning is.
05		If you couldn't really know what they meant. As they are
06		now you've got 'suspect' 'produce' 'permit'. What I'd like
07		you to do is read the sentences and from the context work
08		out the meaning and mark the stress, so that the sentence
09		makes sense.
10	S1:	Yes
11	T:	OK? Erm Didier what are you doing. Can you tell me
12		what you are doing what you have to do
13	S2:	To- to find which syllable?
14	T:	Yes
15	S3:	Of the stress points. Nouns
16	T:	Yes. And?
17	S3:	Verbs
18	T:	Yes yes good. And mark it. Mark it.

Source: Adam Bevan, 1995. Unpublished MSc disertation, Aston
University.

From the perspective of professional development, it might be worth
exploring ways in which such long turns can be broken down and
methods of incorporating the sort of checking we see in ll.11–18 of
Extract 4.3. As teachers we tend to concentrate on the tasks themselves
and the language they generate, but deliberate awareness of the options
available to us in instruction-giving and a determination to reduce the
length of teacher turns in this might be invaluable. In the second level
I take up some of the issues already raised in this level at a slightly more
sophisticated level for those who wish to take their analysis a stage
further, but it is not necessary to look beyond this first level or even to
develop more sophisticated analytical skills in order to make an important contribution to our understanding of professional practice. In the
example above, the simple recognition of the length of teacher turns in

instruction-giving may be sufficient on its own to stimulate professional growth:

> The powerful moment, the moving insight (though sometimes just from one person or even a handful) is sometimes enough to create dynamic involvement in those who have access to it. (Schubert 1990:100)

Level 2: developing an analysis

Approaches to analysis

This level will build on the foundations laid at the previous level. Whatever the research tradition you eventually choose to work within, there are certain fundamental skills that are the mark of a successful analyst and what follows is designed specifically to develop these. It begins by focusing on the value of looking closely at the sequential development of talk, moves on to suggest how you can identify and exploit patterns in talk and concludes with a discussion of transcription issues.

Success here will depend on a careful examination of the transcript as the basis for a painstaking step-by-step description that calls for time and patience. There are certainly quicker ways of going about the business, but sensitivity to the subtleties of spoken interaction can be gained only through meticulous attention to detail. Approaches based on assigning pre-determined categories may seem 'easier' (though good analysis is never really easy), but if you begin with them you can miss so much else that is important to your understanding of what is happening. For example, at the most basic level you might simply divide the talk into teacher turns and student turns in order to get a picture of their relative distribution – usually a sobering experience. Or you might look at particular functions such as 'asking questions' or 'giving instructions' or more general features such as 'repetition'. This sort of work can be very revealing, but it can also blind an inexperienced analyst to what is actually happening in the interaction because it offers an immediately accessible representation of the talk and even provides, on a fairly superficial level, the basis for an explanation. By concentrating attention on surface features at the expense of the more subtle ways in which interactional outcomes are achieved, it can lead the inexperienced analyst into the sort of easy generalisation that offers little by way of insight. It pays, then, to develop the skills of fine-grained analysis as a basis for understanding talk.

Dealing with sequences

This section and the next together build towards the analysis of a short and very straightforward extract from a lesson. I have chosen it precisely because it is so unexceptional: it is easy to see what is fascinating in an unusual extract but the challenge of discovering what is interesting in ordinary exchanges is a much better way of developing analytical sensitivity. The challenge here is simply to be able to provide a sound description of a very ordinary activity – you may find it much harder than you think to resist the temptation to hurry through it.

The importance of taking time to examine sequences in interaction is no more than a reflection of the nature of the talk itself: whenever more than one person talks, the speakers have to take turns and each turn builds on the ones before. If we look carefully, we should therefore be able to see and describe the relationships between every step in the developing interaction. Of course, we don't need to lavish this degree of scrutiny on extended transcripts, but when we have chosen a passage for particular attention the first step to a proper understanding is a grasp of the way the talk unfolds. This step-by-step approach is painstaking but absolutely necessary.

Before reading Extract 4.4, study the points in Box 4.5, some of which will be at least vaguely familiar if you worked through the similar four steps in analysis in Level 1. Then, when you are ready, work through the list, providing a response to each of the questions. Finally, compare your findings with mine, which are provided immediately after the passage itself.

Box 4.5 Developing an analysis (A)

1. First read through the passage a number of times until you have a clear sense of what's happening. When you've done this you should be able to offer a brief description of the talk in response to the question, 'What's going on here?'

2. Now try to characterise the activity or activities that are taking place in the talk. For example, is this an example of 'a teacher-fronted question and answer session' or perhaps 'setting up an activity'?

3. Now work very carefully through the passage line by line, seeing how each turn builds on the one before and sets up what follows.

4. If the talk takes place in an institutional setting, look for evidence of ways in which the participants are orienting to their institutional identities, e.g. as teacher or student? How does this affect the ongoing exchanges?

(Continues on p. 195)

Extract 4.4   Arrival

```
01        ((door opens))
02    T:  Hello Ivan
03   S1:  Hello
04    T:  Welcome back,
05        ((S1 sits))
06    T:  right we'll do this- we can do that conversation again but
07        seeing's Ivan's just arrived I'll do it with Ivan. Ivan, ask me
08        those questions.
09   S1:  ((reading from OHP screen)) Hello,
10        where are you from?
```

My comments

1. If I were to describe this I'd say that it's an extract from a lesson already in progress, where a student enters during an activity. The teacher greets the student, welcomes him back and then immediately involves him in an activity, asking him to read some questions from an OHP. The student begins to do this.

2. There are lots of ways of labelling this, but I'd probably go for 'Dealing with an interruption [to an activity by a student arriving late]' or perhaps 'Involving a latecomer in an ongoing activity' or even just 'Dealing with a late arrival'. Perhaps you chose something different such as 'Maintaining focus on an activity'.

3. Here's a purely descriptive line-by-line analysis:

    1. This initiates the sequence and the entry of the student serves as a prompt for the greeting that follows (normally when someone comes into a room for the first time their arrival is acknowledged).
    2. The teacher greets Ivan, the new arrival. This is in response to his arrival and it requires a response from him. (The structural significance of this Greeting–Greeting exchange was first identified by Sacks (1992: Vol. 1 pp. 96–9). It is an example of an adjacency pair, a two-part sequence where the first part is designed to elicit the second part and where the second part is in response to the first part. If the second part is not forthcoming, this is significant and it's very likely that it will be accounted for in some way in the talk. A Question–Answer adjacency pair would be another example.)
    3. Ivan responds with a greeting, as expected.
    4. The arrival of a student in the middle of an activity is an unusual event and therefore invites some sort of comment, which is

what the teacher provides here. We don't know whether this student has left the room for some entirely legitimate purpose and is now returning, but the initial greeting and the way in which attention is drawn to his entrance here suggests that the arrival is in some way exceptional. It is either a distinctly late entry or the student has been away longer than expected.

5. The continuing contour at the end of l.4 indicates that the teacher wishes to keep the turn, so no verbal response is forthcoming. The student sits down.

6. The turn begins with 'right', which serves to direct attention away from the topic of Ivan's return and back to the topic which was the focus before he entered. (Sinclair and Coulthard, 1975, refer to this move as a Frame/Focus. The 'Frame' is 'right' and this is followed by a Focus on the relevant activity, 'we'll do this-we can do that conversation'. If you study classrooms, you'll probably find lots of examples of these, though 'right' might be replaced by other words such as 'okay'.)

7. The teacher then goes on to explain to the class what she has decided to do and why. This serves to focus their attention on the relevant activity and account for her actions.

8. Having announced her intention, she now executes the promised action. Her attention is directed from the class to Ivan and she instructs him to do something (another example of the first part of an adjacency pair).

9. In direct response to the teacher's instructions, Ivan reads out a question.

4. We can see various ways in which relevant institutional identities are invoked in the talk. First of all, we notice that only the teacher greets Ivan as he enters. It would be inappropriate for any other person present to greet him publicly, though there might be private acknowledgements. This is an example of the way in which the teacher has control of the floor, deciding who speaks and when in lessons. We also see how the teacher determines the activity and is free to make decisions about the way that activity is conducted, even changing in mid-flow if necessary ('but seeing's Ivan's just arrived I'll ... '). The teacher also initiates the talk and nominates the recipient, giving instructions as to the nature of the response required (ll. 7–8). Ivan, as a student, is expected to respond to the prompt directly and without comment, and this is what he does (he had already signalled his presence as a student non-verbally in l.5 by going to one of the seats in the student area of the classroom).

Looking for patterns

At this point we already have a reasonable picture of the extract as it stands, but we also need to connect this passage with its wider context and one way of doing this is to explore patterns within it (see Box 4.6). Let us first complete the analysis of this particular passage before moving on to consider how patterns might help us to extend our understanding. The procedure is the same as that above and Extract 4.4 is repeated below for your convenience:

Extract 4.4   Arrival

```
01          ((door opens))
02   T:  Hello Ivan
03   S1:  Hello
04   T:  Welcome back,
05          ((S1 sits))
06   T:  right we'll do this- we can do that conversation again but
07          seeing's Ivan's just arrived I'll do it with Ivan. Ivan, ask
08          me those questions.
09   S1:  ((reading from OHP screen)) Hello,
10          where are you from?
```

Box 4.6   Developing an analysis (B)

5. Try to identify any patterns in the talk. Some of them might be very brief and obvious, others more subtle, but try to describe them. Are they typical of the sort of talk you associate with that setting or do they differ in some way?

6. Identify any particular features in the talk that recur or that you find interesting in the light of the institutional setting and the activity that is taking place. What purpose(s) do these serve? Do they seem to have a particular function?

7. If you think there is anything interesting or unusual in the extract, try to identify how the participants deal with this. Can you account for its occurrence?

8. Finally, and most importantly, ask yourself what you can learn from the passage, in terms of the activities involved and/or process of analysis. What would you like to look out for in other extracts if you wanted to collect more data in order explore this further? Is there anything that still puzzles you, and how would you go about finding an explanation for this?

My comments

5. The main pattern we see here is the two-part pattern where the teacher initiates and the student responds. We see this in the exchange of greetings (ll.2–3) and the instruction – response pairing that closes the extract. There are no other patterns in the extract, but if we look at other parts of the lesson we might expect to find more examples of the teacher directing attention to particular activities (ll.6–8).

6. This two-part pattern is interesting because it relates to the broader issue of control: in both cases the teacher initiates and the student responds. The teacher's management of the lesson depends in part on her ability to manage the floor successfully, as here. She takes the initiative as soon as the student appears and, without making an issue of it, indicates by saying 'Welcome back' that this behaviour does not correspond to the norm. She also minimises the impact of the disruption by managing the transition back to the activity very smoothly, actually involving the student directly in the activity.

7. This method of managing the transition by involving the student is interesting because it seems to be an example of a teacher thinking on her feet and turning a potentially disruptive situation to her advantage. The attention of the class will inevitably be drawn to the newcomer, and she does not resist this. Instead, she acknowledges the interruption and exploits it to underline her control. At the end of the passage the attention of both class and student has been directed to the activity, and although she has not disciplined the student, the teacher has put him on the spot and, we might argue, in so doing sent out a subtle message to the class that latecomers may not be allowed the luxury of an easy re-entry into the class.

8. The response to this point will always be to some extent personal. What I see here is a good example of how it is possible to make quite subtle but quite powerful points without disrupting the flow of the lesson. I think it is also probably very important to make sure that the class knows exactly what is going on, and this teacher also manages that very effectively. If I wanted to look into this in more detail, I might listen to my recording(s) to identify more examples of the ways in which teachers respond to potentially disruptive occurrences, or I might prefer to look at ways in which they make explicit their decision-making and the situations in which this tends to happen.

A final comment

Don't worry if your findings were slightly different from mine: no response is definitive. My aim in this section was to develop important analytical skills and to give you an idea of how deep into the business of teaching this can actually take us. When you read other people's analyses, they can often seem quite impressive just because they're different, but all that really matters is that if you want to say something you ought to be able to point to the evidence in your data that supports your interpretation. In the end, there is no substitute for what you discover about yourself and your own teaching through the process of analysis.

Finding patterns

Some years ago a particular sort of picture was immensely popular in the UK. It consisted of an apparently random collection of colours and shapes which, when looked at from the correct distance and – most importantly – in the correct way, would yield a three-dimensional image. I believe that part of the reason for the popularity of these pictures, available eventually in a host of different books, was that not everybody could see these patterns, so those who could were entertained by the spectacle of others contorting their faces as they frantically sought the wonderful image that they had been promised was hidden in the picture. Sooner or later most people seemed to make something of at least some of the pictures, often not without considerable time and effort, but once they had mastered the art of seeing it was easy to repeat the experience.

Finding patterns in data is very similar to this. At first there seems to be nothing to see, but by living with the data, by returning to it again and again and looking at it from all sorts of different angles and perspectives, we will eventually begin to see patterns in it and a picture will emerge. There is no short cut to this and not even a convenient formula to guide us to the areas in which we should be looking, although studying the patterns that others have found can help us to develop a nose for them. In the end, though, it's a long and tiring business, and insights often emerge when we're least expecting them, seeming, like the hidden pictures, so obvious and so prominent that we wonder how we could ever have missed them. The best research is often that which finds things that people immediately recognise as being so obvious they could have found it themselves (if only they'd known how to look).

The initiation, response and follow-up (IRF) pattern

In Extract 4.4 we found a two-part question and answer pattern that is common in all talk. If we study talk closely we will find other examples of these 'adjacency pairs', such as request–response, invitation-acceptance/ refusal, and greeting–greeting, but a closer look at the classroom reveals that the dominant pattern in teacher-fronted exchanges is somewhat different. Question–answer exchanges are very common, but pedagogically the sequence is not complete: the teacher's confirmation of the answer is also part of the exchange. Sinclair and Coulthard (1975), building on the work of Bellack, highlighted this important three-part sequence and called it 'IRF': Initiation, Response and Follow-up (for an excellent brief discussion, see van Lier 1996:148–56). The opening of Extract 4.1, above, illustrates it very clearly:

- *Initiation*   But the writing is on 'weekends' which tells you::
- *Response*   When
- *Follow-up*   Whe::n. Ye:::s.

You will probably have noticed that the third turn in the sequence in 4.1 has two parts and that the second part is another Initiation: 'So would you like to give me the question again'. If you examine classroom talk, you may also notice that the third part is often an Evaluation, which is why the sequence IRE has also been proposed, though 'Follow-up' allows for other options. This pattern is so pervasive in teacher-fronted talk that it has come in for a great deal of attention, not all of it favourable. At one time the advice to teachers seemed to be that it was best to avoid this sort of pattern because of its unduly restrictive nature, but recently a more balanced view has developed (for example, Seedhouse 1996) and researchers have revealed that it has considerable pedagogic potential (for example, Jarvis and Robinson 1997, Nassaji and Wells 2000, Cullen 2002). The pedagogic advantages or drawbacks of the pattern are not our concern here; the mere fact that it has been the basis of so much lively debate is testament to its power.

Producing an adequate transcription

If you move on to more detailed analysis, you may find that you need to think carefully about transcription. The basic system outlined in Level 1 treated transcription as essentially unproblematic and for beginning researchers this is an entirely reasonable position, but more advanced inquiry demands a greater sensitivity to the factors involved in decision-making. The relationship between tape and transcript, which Ashmore and Reed (2000) argue is that between 'realist' and 'constructivist' objects, is an important one. Green *et al.* (1997:172) are not alone in believing that transcription 'reflects a discipline's conventions as well as a researcher's conceptualization of a phenomenon, purposes for the research, theories guiding data collection and analysis, and programmatic goals', so there is much to consider. Ultimately, though, what matters is that you should be able to defend your transcription decisions, and in this section I propose three criteria that are relevant to this: fitness for purpose, adequacy and accuracy.

Fitness for purpose

Transcription is not a mechanical process, even though it can seem that way at times. From the time we select specific conversations or extracts for transcription, we are making decisions that bear on interpretation. The standard advice is to make sure that we do not transcribe with any specific research question or hypothesis in mind, but this is easier said than done, and at least one researcher (Ochs 1979:44) takes the opposite position. It is easy enough to push such questions to the back of the mind when transcribing, but this is not to say that they might not exercise a subtle influence on our work. Perhaps, then, we should deliberately set out to bring them to the fore when we think we have a working transcript, if only to allow us the chance to look for potential bias in our work. Somewhere between a completely open mind and the perceptual constraints accompanying hypothesis-testing lies the territory most qualitative researchers occupy, a land where easy decisions are as rare as hen's teeth.

Fortunately, the decision we make will be realised in the transcription system we use, so it is open to immediate inspection. There is no method appropriate to all studies of discourse and the analyst must decide on an approach that will best serve research needs. Inevitably such choices are not neutral, so we can begin by asking what sort of information we hope to derive from our transcription. This is not the same thing as prejudging its outcomes – although it will inevitably serve to focus attention on the sorts of thing we might be looking for – and should offer a useful basis for sketching out a system. This done, the system can be tested through a process of piloting, in which a number of short transcriptions are made and subjected to a preliminary analysis in order to determine the degree of delicacy necessary. For example, if we transcribe interviews in the same detail as ordinary conversation, this may impede our reading of them and distract attention from the features that are important. For example, 'Well, >getting the: money< is (0.5) no:w really important (.) in a re(.)earch scientist's (.) job.' takes longer to transcribe, is more difficult to read, and is therefore potentially less revealing than 'Well, getting the money is (0.5) now really important in a research scientist's job'.

Adequacy

Anyone working within the CA tradition will be expected to meet the demanding standards of transcription associated with that approach, but the situation is less clear cut when we are collecting spoken data in the context of a broader qualitative study also featuring interview and observation data. The tendency here is, naturally enough, to keep things very simple: it makes for quick transcription and easy reading. However, if we simplify too much we risk losing important details of the talk and may be in danger of coming to mistaken conclusions.

To illustrate this, consider what interpretation you might put on the brief exchange in Extract 4.5. Speaker A, a teacher who is also acting as the school's social organiser, has drawn attention to poor student attendance at a recent social event and has suggested that the response might have been better had it been advertised with notices around the school (the 'one' in his turn refers to these).

Extract 4.5 Transcription A

```
01  A:  Should have put one up somewhere shouldn't we really?
02      We need a social organiser.
03  B:  Yes you should. Oh, is that your responsibility?
```

This seems to be a fairly straightforward exchange built around B's response to a question from A. A's contribution is clear enough, though B's position is harder to read. It seems that in saying 'Yes you should', she is placing the responsibility squarely on A's shoulders. Her second statement then seems to qualify that rather categorical position by checking whether this is indeed A's responsibility. In terms of the behaviour of the teacher concerned, this rush to judgement and readiness to assign responsibilities to others would have represented an interesting piece of discrepant data. Analytically, it would certainly have stood out and represented something of a challenge.

In fact, the inclusion of a 'grammatical' question mark and the period after 'should' are part of a 'tidied up' transcript that is easy to read but a travesty of what actually occurred. Extract 4.6 shows the transcript in its original form.

Extract 4.6 Transcription B

```
01  A:  Should have put one up somewhere shouldn't we really.
02      We need a sowcial ⌈owganisah
03  B:                   ⌊Yeah you should- (.) Oh is that your
04      responsibility? ((Spoken while laughing.))
```

In fact, A's first utterance is not a question at all but a statement setting up an ironic comment on his own position as social organiser, and B's initial response is cut off short when she realises that A *is* the social organiser. She then responds to the joke. Part of the misunderstanding arises because B has interrupted before A has completed the ironic comment on his first utterance. We have no way of knowing what she might have gone on to say in her unfinished sentence, but it is unlikely to have been as personally judgemental as the injunction that appeared in the first version. In any case, much more significant than this is the fact that she quickly re-orients to the joke and shows her appreciation of A's irony.

Tidying up a transcript, I would argue, is methodologically indefensible, but this still leaves the problem of how much detail to include. After all, conversation analysts have shown that even a micropause can be interactionally significant, and Jefferson's paper on the transcription of laughter (1985) reveals how delicacy of transcription can be essential if interactional realities are to be exposed. There is no easy solution, but the existence of a fairly common set of transcription symbols offers a sound starting point. Ochs' point that it may be difficult for readers to follow a transcript that is too complicated is true, but editing out symbols for the sake of clarity is a dangerous exercise.

The answer to these conundrums is not necessarily to be found in more detailed transcriptions; what matters is that we think carefully about our transcription. Take, for example, the representation of spoken words in a form that seeks to capture their sound without resorting to phonetic script, an approach that Stubbs (1983) has called folk transcription and Roberts (1997) eye dialect. One obvious problem is deciding where to draw the line. In Text B, 'sowcial owganisah' is clearly an example of eye dialect, but what about 'Yeah'? This is not a trivial point, because the 'Yes' in Text A looks much more formal, perhaps more of a challenge than an agreement; and, in fact, speaker B usually uses 'yes' rather than 'yeah' so the latter may be important here.

Roberts (1997:170) advises the use of standard orthography, 'even when the speaker is using nonstandard varieties to avoid stigmatisation and to evoke the naturalness of their speech, and never use eye dialect'. However, there may be situations where this approach reinforces the very stigmatisation Roberts is anxious to avoid. She seems to be suggesting that when I say to my brother (as I well might), 'He'd've bought it with him if he'd've known. Now I've gorragerrit', this representation would be more embarrassing to me than, 'He would have bought it with him if he had have known. Now I've got to get it'. In fact, the nonstandard 'bought' and 'had have' represented in standard orthography would be much more likely to make my toes curl than 'gorragerrit' – simply because I think they look as daft as raising a little finger while drinking a pint of beer.

But there's a more important issue than this. Suppose we follow Roberts' rule never to use eye dialect and write 'social organiser' in Text B. Where, then, is the joke that was so deliberately signalled in the pronunciation? The laughter from B now begins to look like embarrassment and a sign of an interactional trouble, instead of an example of alignment with A. This example does not amount to a case for eye dialect throughout the text, but it is a reminder that our efforts are merely 'theorised representations' (Atkinson 1988:454) and not unimpeachable representations of the talk itself. Coates and Thornborrow (1999:595) point out that any deviation from conventional spelling serves to mark the relevant words in some way and make the sensible suggestion that, unless such markedness is relevant to our analytic focus, 'little is to be gained by deviating from standard orthography'. Ultimately, then, the only way to come to terms with these issues is to deal with them in the context of your own research and in the spirit of reflective exploration.

Accuracy

Seen from this perspective, the search for accuracy is ultimately a doomed enterprise, and a number of writers have pointed out that the notion of a 'correct' transcription is an illusion: the same data will be transcribed in different ways by different people, and even by the same person at different times. We should therefore accept at the outset that the task of transcription as intrinsically incomplete; all we can do is seek to establish the most honest representation possible, given the resources at our disposal. We can never entirely remove the possibility that we may be subject to auditory hallucination, but we can minimise its effects by returning the same recording a number of times. I have found that it also helps if more than one machine can be used in the repeated listenings, since this changes the auditory representation. Ultimately, though, we have to rely on our own judgement. For example, in Text B above, I could detect no falling intonation in 'owganisah', so I have omitted a period – another transcriber might disagree.

Experience attunes the ear, and repeated listenings offer a degree of assurance that the final version is at least a reasonable representation of the talk, but researchers new to transcription can find it difficult to arrive at a satisfactory text. I am grateful to Marinus Lanbroek and

Daniel Waller for allowing me to use their first attempts at transcription as an illustration of just how much versions can differ (Extract 4.7). Having decided to record the same meeting, they set about the process of transcribing quite independently and submitted two similar but by no means identical texts. You might find it instructive to compare the two versions, identifying the differences between them and reflecting on the potential consequences of the differences.

Extract 4.7 Two transcripts of the same talk

	Version A	Version B
01	T1: I mean I think, the, yes the	T1: I mean, I think, yes, the,
02	idea of this (?not sure) for	the, the idea of this list
03	me is, the only way I can	for me, the only way
04	see the validity of it is erm,	I can see the validity of it
05	for teachers, and, the	is, er for the teachers, and
06	teachers can use it as a	their . . . the teachers are
07	resource.	going to use it as a
		resource.
08		T2: [It's great. I have no
		objection.]
09	T1: And I think I agree I don't	T1: but I think I agree, I don't
10	want to give this to the	want to give this list to the
11	students.	students.
12	T3: I mean for the teacher to	T3: I mean, yeah, for the
13	to know which meaning	teachers, you know,
14	of the word is being taught	which meaning of the
		word is being taught
15		[(Inaudible)]
16	T1: Yeah, that's what we're	T1: [Yeah, what we're sup-
17	supposed to be	posed to be teaching]
	teaching . . .	
18	T3: **If** it's sometimes you just	T3: **Because** sometimes you've
19	got the word you're not	only got the word, you're
20	sure yourself	not sure yourself but, the
21	but . . . students don't need	students don't need it. 'Cos
22	it. 'Cause they need to DO	they need to do something.
	something.	

23 24	T1:	They're not going to do anything with this.	T1:	They're not going to do anything with this list,
25 26 27 28 29	T3:	... **unless** you give them a blank piece of paper, which has got the word and maybe you can give them the word, the part of speech	T1:	unless you give them a blank piece of paper which has got only the word and maybe you can give them the word – the part of speech.
30			T3:	[The word] The word group
31 32 33	T3:	and then they have to fill in the chart, I mean that's another alternative.	T1:	And then they have to fill in the chart. I mean that's another alternative perhaps.
34 35 36 37 38 39	T4:	Maybe you're right, maybe we thought... we were getting too much into it, trying to be comprehens- ive, maybe you're right, I don't know....	T4:	Maybe you're right. Maybe we thought, we were too, we were getting to much into it, and trying to be comprehensive, maybe you're right, I don't know. Yeah, yeah
40 41	T3:	**because** what is there left for the students to put in?	T3:	**Because** what is there left for the students to put in [(Inaudible)]
42	T4:	No you're right, that is true.		
43 44 45	T3:	**and** they're not going to learn just by looking at this.	T3:	[There's nothing] and they're not going to learn just by looking at this.
46 47	T1:	by reading it, yeah	T1:	By reading it, yeah, right. That's right

Before showing how the differences between these two might influence the researcher's interpretive stance, I'd like to underline the fact that there is no 'correct' version of these exchanges so it would be a serious mistake to assume that one of them is better than the other. What matters is the difference between them and the effect that this might have.

To explore this, I should like to assume that the researcher has other data available and is particularly interested in the way in which T3 fits into this group of teachers, all of whom work at the same institution. It seems to the researcher that T3 adopts an overtly collaborative stance, usually taking her cue from colleagues. What evidence, if any, is there for this in the data? If we take Version B there is some evidence but it is not particularly conclusive. On a couple of occasions we see T3 building her turns on those of the previous speaker, but we also see evidence of this in T1's talk (arguably, l.9 and l.31). However, the evidence of Version A is overwhelming: in all but her first turn, T3 builds her turns syntactically on the previous speaker's contribution. The different speaker identifications in l.25 and l.43 produce two very different pictures.

In a nutshell, four out of five of T3's turns in Version A are explicitly collaborative (in the limited sense in which we are using it here) and only two out of five in Version B (the relevant links are highlighted in bold in the transcript). In fact, if we ignore T3's first turn, all of her contributions in A are collaborative and only half in B. However we choose to represent it, there is a difference. Of course, we can't build much of an argument on a short extract like this, but if we extrapolate these differences over a much more extensive database of talk then the picture changes and it is easy to imagine how interpretations might be affected by the accumulation of 'evidence' in one version that is missing in the other. If nothing else, this should serve as a spur to developing as accurate and complete a transcription as possible.

Case 4.2: questions and answers

Perhaps nothing is more pervasive in the TESOL classroom than question and answer exchanges, usually between the teacher and students. You can't study classroom interaction without sooner or later coming up against this aspect of our work, and the closer you look at it, the more interesting it gets. This case shows how a fairly short extract can reveal to teachers something of profound developmental significance to their teaching.

Extract 4.8 is taken from a lesson in which there were quite a few interesting 'trouble-spots' of a similar kind. If you'd like to attempt an analysis for yourself you can either plunge straight in or read my comments in the box (Box 4.7) that follows, which should help to focus your analysis. If, on the other hand, you'd simply like to read on, I've provided a discussion of what seem to me to be the most interesting aspects of this particular extract. My aim here is not to guide you through the process of analysis but to offer an example of the sort of things that might emerge from such an analysis. If you examine my response closely, you will see that it is based on the procedures recommended in Boxes 4.4 and 4.5, but this time I have organised my response less programmatically, focusing from the outset on pedagogic issues.

Extract 4.8   The same or not the same?

```
01   T:  Now, I'm going to write two sentences on the board and
02       please tell me what they mean
03       ((Teacher writes on board; students whisper
04       what they see.))
05   T:  Now do they mean the same thing?
06   S1:  Er (..) no
07   S2:  Yes
08   S1:  Not the ⌈same
09    T:       ⌊Paulo ((S3? S4?)). Not the same.
10       You think the same or not the same?
11       ((Student enters the classroom))
12       Hello! Come in. Stop to fill in- up the car. Stop filling up
13       the car. Do they mean the same
14       or do ⌈they mean something-?
15   S2:       ⌊Yes not ⌈same
16   S1:             ⌊Not same. Not same=
17    T:  =Not the same=
18   S1:  =Not same=
19    T:  =What do you think? ⌈D'you think the same?
20   S2:                    ⌊Not same. Not same.
21   S3:  Not the same=
22    T:  =Not the same=
23   S2:  =No
```

Box 4.7   Pointers to analysis

1. Have a look at what happens to S1. How does his contribution change through the extract? My analysis will boil down to an explanation for this.

2. Look closely at the teacher's response to the answers provided by S1 and S2 (ll.6–8). Does anything strike you as unusual about this?

3. How might this account for any subsequent confusion?

4. If you were this teacher, what might you learn from an analysis of this extract? Is there any aspect of your teaching that you might want to change as a result?

Before getting down the crux of my analysis, I think it's interesting to pick out aspects of this extract that relate to points we have already considered. The first thing to note is that the questioning here is pretty much in line with that of White and Lightbown (1984) in their Canadian study discussed in the previous chapter. The number of questions exceed the average identified in their study: if we begin from the point where the teacher stops writing on the board we find five questions (treating l.19 as comprising two questions) in the space of less than a minute. In fact, the question 'Do they mean the same thing?' is repeated three more times with slight variations in form and one of those repetitions (l.10) receives no audible reply.

My second point links back to Extract 4.4. In this passage, too, we have a late arrival, and as in 4.4 the teacher acknowledges this and greets the student (l.12). But this time the acknowledgement is a very brief interpolation between two formulations of the same question, contributing to the sense that a lot is happening quickly here, with events unfolding at a much more rapid pace than in the previous extract. The consequences of this are unfortunate.

What I find particularly interesting is that S1 moves from a correct form in l.8 ('Not the same') to an incorrect form in l.16 ('Not same'), repeated in l.18 despite the teacher's correction in the previous turn. One of our aims in language teaching is to help students become more accurate in their use of language, and when things move in the opposite direction this is sufficient incentive to discover the reason. So why has S1 abandoned the correct form? To answer this we need to look at the teacher's response to his original answer. She has asked whether 'stop to fill up' and 'stop filling up' mean the same thing and he has correctly answered 'no' (l.6), restating this as 'not the same' in his next turn (l.8). At this point we would normally expect feedback from the teacher indicating whether this answer is correct or incorrect, and we do indeed get a response, but it is a re-initiation addressed to a different student in which the teacher repeats S1's response and then asks the question again. What is S1 to make of this?

In order to answer this question we need to reflect on the norms of the classroom, and in matters of responding to students' answers these are very clear: a correct answer is acknowledged as such, perhaps with 'Yes' or an evaluation along the lines of 'Good' or 'Well done'. The teacher has a number of options if the answer is not correct, one popular response being the repetition of the question, perhaps reformulated or with emphasis on a specific element. In the light of this, S1 will interpret the lack of a positive response, coupled with a repeat of S1's answer and then the question addressed to another student, as a signal that his answer is in some way unacceptable. (Even if we accept that sometimes the teacher may allow a number of responses from the class before choosing to comment, this makes no difference to the rules for interpreting the teacher's response when it comes.)

The scene is already set for a certain amount of confusion, and the teacher's turn between l.9 and l.14 does nothing to change this. The question is repeated, slightly reformulated in polar form, then attention shifts briefly to the new arrival before returning to the language focus. Unfortunately, it's hard to hear the difference between 'fill in- up' and 'filling up', so this does nothing to clarify the situation or help any students who may already be confused. When the teacher begins to repeat the question (ll.13–14), S1 and S2 leap in to answer before her turn is complete. S1 copies S2's incorrect form, omitting the definite article he had included in l.8. We can't know what prompts this switch, but it is fair to assume that he might have decided that something was wrong with the form of his earlier response. Whatever the case, the teacher's correction (l.17) of his and S2's response falls on deaf ears. Again she repeats the question and again S2 leaps in, followed by S3, the teacher again and then S2 – a flurry of exchanges at the end of which it is difficult to see what progress has been made.

If you were this teacher, what might you learn from an analysis of this extract? Again, the response will vary from individual to individual, but for me the main thing to be learned is the importance of giving clear feedback so that students know whether or not their contributions are acceptable. Tied in with this are issues of pacing, direction and question formulation, so the picture is a complex one. In any case, because teaching is to some extent a matter of personal style, we must always beware of leaping to categorical conclusions. I chose the extract not to provide me with a basis for making claims about good or bad teaching but to show how the close examination of classroom interaction might provide teachers with insights into their practice.

Level 3: different approaches to analysis

Introduction

So far we have explored the analytical dimension from the perspective of particular interactions, leaving aside the broader issue of the relationship between these interactions and wider social structures. However, if we seek to use our analysis to make claims about anything beyond the immediate encounters in our study, we are forced to confront this relationship between the micro-world of the individual engaged in a specific interaction and the macro-world of social context in which that interaction is set. Its pervasive presence has been well noted:

> Probably the most basic dualism inherent in individual and institution is micro and macro. (Stubbs 1992:198)

> Social interaction is at the nexus of microissues and macroissues. (Ellis 1999:33)

Any attempt to explore this relationship must recognise, with Schegloff (1987:208), 'the utter relativity and likely hopelessness of these terms', but they nevertheless represent something to which anyone working with discourse in QI must respond. Represented at its crudest, the issue boils down to whether the analyst should draw on recognised aspects of social structure in order to explain features of the interaction, or whether any relevant features of social organisation will be recoverable from the talk. The former position is criticised because invoking 'classical dimensions of social organization' brings 'risks of underspecification of the interactional phenomena' (Schegloff 1987:217), while its defenders argue that the risks of the alternative are that important interpretive opportunities may be missed and that aspects of structure may be 'foregrounded without verbalization' (Ellis 1999:38). This level will return to this issue, but it begins with examples of three different approaches to analysis: conversation analysis, interactional sociolinguistics and critical discourse analysis. Space constraints mean that my analyses are necessarily highly selective in their focus, but they are designed to highlight the differences and – just as importantly – the similarities in these approaches.

Case 4.3: introducing a complaint

Extract 4.9 is taken from a pre-course staff meeting at the Pen, a small language school. Four teachers and Jenny, the principal, are involved and I am present as an observer. These meetings take place immediately before the start of a new course but after students have been assessed in order to determine their level. Various grading and placement issues are discussed and at one point mention is made of a new group that is being sent from the same British Council office as a previous group. Ed, a temporary teacher who began work at the same time as this earlier group, then brings up an issue relating to feedback from one of them. The extract starts as he raises this issue. You might like to begin by working up your own analysis of this from the perspective of whatever tradition(s) you are familiar with, so that you can compare your own notes with my comments as they develop through the remainder of this level.

Extract 4.9 The complaint

```
01      Ed:  Does Alan know that- you know that (.) you know (like)
02           Anne Grest (.) did they know that >they were
03           kind of< coming (.) to a general English type course.
04   Jenny:  °Uhuh°
05      Ed:  Uhuh
06   Jenny:  As far as I know. That's the information they should
07           have been given.
08           (1.0)
09   Jenny:  Why: (.) did you get the impression ⌈the other te-
10      Ed:                                        ⌊Well Thomas
11           seemed to give the impression that he (.) wasn't (.) he
12           didn't get quite what he was expecting.
13   Jenny:  Did he?
14      Ed:  Yeah.
15           (1.0)
16   Jenny:  O::h. This could be a fault at the British Council end
17           I suppose. What did he think (.) he was going to get.
18      Ed:  Well I mean he- (.) he just said on- on the Friday >he
19           said< 'I don't- I don't kno:w (.) how much I (.)
20           improved,' >he said< 'partly because I'm (.) slightly
21           out of my depth,' (.) he's-
22   Jenny:  Mm
23      Ed:  'and- and ⌈partly because (.)    ⌉because some of=
24   Jenny:             ⌊(I understand that.)⌋
25      Ed:  =the:' (.)>you know< 'materials w-' (0.5) some of
26           the things about (xxxxxxx) to him. Which was fair
27           enough (0.5) I suppose but I ⌈mean (.) anyway (.)=
28   Jenny:                               ⌊Mmm
29      Ed:  = the kind of course they're coming on
30           (0.5)
31   Jenny:  It's probably worth a (.) a note back to (.) the British
32           Council to make sure this gets conveyed.
```

```
33   Ed:     Mmm
34   Jenny:  Er (.) I don't know how well liaison goes on at that
35           end, (0.5) I know some of the (.) mistakes they've
36           made in getting accommodation information through
37           are not that (kind of job but)
38   Ed:     °Mm°
39   Jenny:  But yes it's probably worth finding out to make sure.
40           (0.5)
41   Jenny:  But apparently he went with great (.) thanks and (.)
42   Ed:     Yeah.
43   Jenny:  praise and everything.
44   Paul:   Who
45   Jenny:  Despite (.) Thomas
46   Paul:   Thomas. ⌈Yeah.⌉ Considering he went (.) extremely lazy
47   Jenny:          ⌊Mm  ⌋
48           (0.5)
49   Jenny:  °Mmm°
50   Paul:   Er I- I mean i- it could have been: (.) real problems
51           about loss of face, it could have been that.
52   Jenny:  Mmm. I felt
53   Paul:   E:m
54   Jenny:  he was worried about his status ⌈(xxxxxxx)
55   Paul:                                    ⌊But he- he: he
56           he- he didn't work well within the
57           group ⌈after- ⌉ you'd bear me out on this.
58   Jenny:        ⌊Mmm⌋
59   Paul:   He ⌈he was ⌉ I felt sorry for anybody working=
60   Ed:        ⌊Yeah he⌋
61   Paul:   =with ⌈him
62   Jenny:        ⌊Mm
63   Ed:     I think he felt a bit like
64           ((Tape snarled))
65   Ed:     I mean he's the president of the Chamber of
66           Commerce ° · hh heh ·hh hh° and ⌈er George was=
67   Jenny:                                   ⌊Mm
68   Ed:     =the director of the Chamber of Commerce, and I
69           just think generally ⌈that
70   Paul:                         ⌊George (.) seemed very
71           appreciative.
```

Extract 4.9   (Continued)

```
72     Ed:    Mmm =
73     Jenny:  = Mmm =
74     Paul:   = (Some.) Again this is (xxxxxxx) ⌈to reason.
75     Jenny:                                  ⌊Mmm
76     Jenny:  Yes George ⌈was incredibly nice to me =
77     Paul:               ⌊Er
78     Jenny:  = when I (xxxxxxxx) farewell to
79             him. ⌈(xxxx) with him he was very⌉ good. =
80     Paul:        ⌊And I had a chat with him.   ⌋
81     Jenny:  = (Gallant), °and°
82     Paul:   And he ⌈said ⌉ he he (.) he's really got a lot =
83     Jenny:          ⌊(xxx)⌋
84     Paul:   = from the course. =
85     Jenny:  = Yes.
86     Paul:   Because I asked him and ⌈he's- (.) he was =
87     Jenny:                           ⌊Mm
88     Paul:   = very (.) very (.) clear about it, =
89     Jenny:  = Mm =
90     Paul:   = and >kind of< (.)>you know< (.) ⌈sort of (just) (.) =
91     Jenny:                                    ⌊Mm
92     Paul:   = just (xxxx) by a stra:nge person. =
93     Jenny:  = Mmm. I think yes they (   ).
94     Paul:   It ⌈was ⌉ strange rather than: sort of =
95     Jenny:     ⌊(xxx)⌋
96     Paul:   = em (.) aggressive I felt.
```

Conversation analysis

Because this tradition has already been summarised in Chapter 1, I begin with the analysis itself and the assumption that the analyst is particularly interested in the way that external criticism of participants in the talk is handled. In this respect, what is particularly interesting about the opening of this extract is that Ed does not introduce his criticism immediately: it emerges only after a more general question and in response to a question by Jenny. Ed's first question is a general one, asking whether the students knew they were coming on a general course and it receives only a minimal response from Jenny: a quiet 'uhuh'. Ed's echo of this indicates that more is required and Jenny immediately provides this, but in a hedged form: 'As far as I know'. In going on to say that they should (emphasised) have been given this information, she distances herself from the responsibility for providing the information. In raising this general question as a new topic, the onus is on Ed to make its relevance clear, and now that Jenny has responded to his question the floor is open for him to do this. Instead we have a second's silence and Jenny explicitly raises the issue of relevance by asking 'Why'. Her continuation question is overlapped by Ed (l.10), who uses her formulation (getting/giving an impression) in order to present the criticism: Thomas didn't get what he was expecting. The presentation of criticism calls for a response, but this is not immediately forthcoming. First we have an *insertion sequence* (Schegloff 1972), a paired exchange inserted between the two parts of an adjacency pair (see Level 2). This consists of a slightly surprised 'Did he?' from Jenny and confirmation from Ed (ll.13–14), and it's followed by yet another silence of one second. Jenny's response, that it could be the fault of the British Council, is prefaced by 'O::h', an example of what Heritage (1984b) identified as a change-of-state token, indicating that the state of her knowledge has changed: this is news to her.

As even this brief description indicates, there is much that can be said about the way the presentation and receipt of this criticism are designed, but I'd like to draw attention to just one aspect. Sacks (1992: Vol. 2 p. 529) noticed that invitations are often prefaced by a more general question that enables the speaker to avoid a direct invitation that runs the risk of being declined. So, if I ask 'Are you doing anything tonight?' and you respond 'Not really', I can proceed pretty confidently with 'How about going for a drink'. We have here what looks like a preannouncement (an example of a pre-sequence), indicating that criticism is forthcoming and this enables the participants to structure the presentation of the criticism itself and the response to it in a very particular way. In lines 6 and 7, for example, Jenny is able to set up a response to the criticism that distances her from it *even before the criticism has been made* (what we might call *pre-emptive positioning*) and to invite the criticism in a way that invites a weak formulation of it, as an 'impression'. It may be that there are other examples of this in the data that will point to a particular way of dealing with this sort of interactional business, and the conversation analyst would be interested in exploring these.

Interactional sociolinguistics

Perhaps because of its particular focus on cross-cultural encounters, interactional sociolinguistics has not found itself embraced by other traditions in the way that CA has. It has 'diverse disciplinary origins' (Schiffrin 1994:7) in anthropology, sociology and linguistics, but in the form advocated by Schiffrin, which draws together the work Gumperz with that of Goffman, it offers interesting analytical possibilities. It is also relevant to the macro/micro relationship introduced as the theme of this level:

> In sum, the key to Gumperz's sociolinguistics of interpersonal com-
> munication is a view of language as a socially and culturally con-
> structed symbol system that is used in ways that reflect macro-level
> social meanings (e.g. group identity, status differences) and create
> micro-level social meanings (i.e. what one is saying and doing at
> a moment in time). (Schiffrin 1994:102)

Goffman was also 'primarily an observer of face-to-face interaction who possessed an extraordinary ability to appreciate the subtle importance of apparently insignificant aspects of everyday conduct' (Manning 1992:3), but his primary interest is in the interactive construction of social identities and relationships within the context of broader social organisation. Box 4.8 offers a brief summary of an interactional sociolinguistic perspective based on Schiffrin (1994, Chapter 4), but for a properly articulated analytic position the original is essential reading.

Analysis

For the purposes of analysis, I will concentrate on the way that Ed presents the criticism itself, for convenience presented here without Jenny's interpolations:

> Well I mean he- (.) he just said on- on the Friday >he said< 'I don't-
> I don't kno:w (.) how much I (.) improved,' >he said< 'partly because
> I'm (.) slightly out of my depth,' (.) he's - 'and- and partly because (.)
> because some of the:' (.)>you know< 'materials w-' (0.5) some of the
> things about (xxxxxxx) to him. Which was fair enough (0.5) I sup-
> pose but I mean (.) anyway (.) the kind of course they're coming on

Notice the subtle signals that Ed sends out at the beginning of this turn, in response to Jenny's question, 'What did he think he was going to get'. There are a number of initial markers that delay the response and, by signalling Ed's difficulty in formulating it, serve to distance him

---

Box 4.8 Key tenets of interactional sociolinguistics

- Language and cognition are affected by social and cultural forces (Gumperz).
- The self is a social construction, created and maintained through interaction (Goffman).
- 'What we perceive and retain in our mind is a function of our culturally determined predisposition to perceive and assimilate' (Gumperz 1982:12).
- Very small signals in talk relate what is said to the contextual knowledge relevant to its interpretation.
- This situated inference also depends on conversational involvement: 'understanding presupposes the ability to attract and sustain others' attention' (Gumperz 1982:4).
- Such involvements is socially situated and governed by the rules of social engagement.
- 'Goffman's focus on social interaction complements Gumperz's focus on situated inference' (Schiffrin 1994:105).

---

from it: 'Well', 'I mean' and 'just', as well as the much more subtle 'on the Friday'. Had he said 'on Friday' this would simply have located the utterance in time, but the addition of 'the' leaves open the possibility of alternatives and therefore, implicitly, other statements (expressions like this feature to establish differences in narratives, as in, 'We went to Warwick on the Friday and Stratford on the Saturday').

The distance suggested here is confirmed in the presentation of the criticism itself, and here Goffman's (1981) concept of the 'production format' provides a valuable analytic tool. He distinguishes between the *animator*, who produces the talk, the *author*, who creates the talk, and the *principal*, who is responsible for the talk. In this case Ed uses direct speech to represent Thomas's position, thus establishing Thomas as both author and principal, with Ed as merely the animator. Indirect speech would have transferred authorship to Ed, but by maintaining a minimal role he is able to place distance not only between himself and the complaint (for which the principal is responsible), but between himself and the complainant (who authors the complaint). In fact, Thomas's words trail off and the comment on materials is never completed – the criticism itself is left hanging.

Goffman said that a change in *footing* 'implies a change in the alignment we take up to ourselves and others present as expressed in the way we manage the production or reception of an utterance' (1981:128) and we see immediate evidence of such a shift. The evaluation of Thomas's claim, 'Which was fair enough', represents his comment on this *as a teacher*, as a member of the group to which the comment has been presented. Following a brief pause during which nobody offers a response to this, he hedges it ('I suppose') and begins a qualification ('but') to which Jenny responds ('Mmm'). In fact Ed's position is never clearly articulated beyond an indication that it has to do with the nature of the course, but this is unimportant: the 'but' aligns him with those who question the validity of the criticism. From this point on, Ed's primary interactional endeavour is that of alignment with his colleagues and therefore against Thomas. This grows in strength, from receipt tokens (33, 38), through explicit agreement (42, 60), to jointly constructed evaluation (63–72).

As a new teacher, Ed has to tread carefully if he is to meet his professional responsibility to Thomas by passing on his criticism while not setting himself up against his colleagues. As we have seen, he is able to achieve this by the use of very subtle signals in his talk and by the way he presents the criticism itself. This also allows him to bring about a shift in footing and begin the process of alignment with colleagues that will enable him to participate in the construction of a shared response and hence reinforce his identity as a member of this professional group. (Notice how this interpretation has drawn on aspects of Ed's social position relative to that of his colleagues in order to account for his behaviour, something that CA would not regard as a legitimate analytical resource.)

Critical discourse analysis

So far our starting point for analysis has been the interaction itself, and broader issues, although touched on, have been left unexplored. However, this is not an option with Critical Discourse Analysis (CDA):

> The starting point for CDA is social issues and problems...it does not begin with texts and interactions; it begins with the issues which preoccupy sociologists, or political scientists, or educationalists. (Fairclough 2001:229–30)

This is a relatively new approach to analysis, developing in the 1970s out of dissatisfaction with formal or descriptive approaches to linguistic analysis that ignored the power structures inherent in its social construction. For analysts working within this tradition, discourse is never neutral, and they set out to challenge the way that the powerful are able to use it in order to maintain their hegemony over those without access to mechanisms of control and influence. This position emerges not from moral imperatives as such but from principles of social justice most of which are derived from a broadly neo-Marxist orientation. It is contentious therefore in terms other than the merely linguistic and methodological. The analysis that follows, in line with an illustration of the approach provided by one of its leading figures (Fairclough 2001), will not explore this dimension, though it will identify possible lines of discussion. Because of the orientation of this chapter, I will also concentrate on the analysis of recorded data, but the approach allows for the use of other data collection methods and triangulation (for an excellent summary of different approaches, see Meyer 2001). Finally, of the two main approaches, associated particularly with the work of Wodak and of Fairclough (usefully summarised in Tischer *et al.* 2000), my approach will be closer to that of the latter but will reflect the main tenets of the approach summarised in Box 4.9.

Box 4.9   Key tenets of critical discourse analysis

- CDA focuses on the relationship between language and power.
- 'CDA aims to investigate critically social inequality as it is expressed, signalled, constituted, legitimized and so on by language use (or in discourse).' (Wodak 2001:2).
- It declares its interest in advance.
- It treats 'larger discursive unit of text' as 'the basic unit of communication' (ibid.).
- 'Discourses are diverse representations of social life which are inherently positioned.' (Fairclough 2001:235) They are essentially historical.
- Context is therefore very important. 'CDA refers to such extralinguistic factors as culture, society, and ideology' (Meyer 2001:15).
- The investigation of language in institutional settings is particularly important.

Analysis

The starting point of any CDA project might be represented as an interest in 'problems arising from ...' and in the case of the above extract two focuses immediately suggest themselves: the ways in which power is exercised by the core group of permanent teachers as a means of ensuring conformity to the dominant orthodoxies of the school, and the ways in which, within the context of a nominally empowering evaluation system, the views of students are marginalised. We have already seen Jenny's role in shaping the formulation of the criticism–response exchange and Ed's efforts to align with the other teachers, and this would certainly provide a basis for a response to the former problem. However, the relevant interactional issues have already been touched on and in order to do this topic justice it would be necessary to draw much more widely on the data set, which actually reveals a very interesting but complex nexus of issues. The following brief analysis will therefore address the second problem in the context of this particular passage.

A full discussion would need to develop a picture of the processes of student evaluation and feedback operating within the school, something which is beyond the scope of this analysis. However, there is a formal system of tutorials where feedback is encouraged, and it is worth noting that ratings from external inspections, which have an important influence in the vital area of student recruitment, will depend on the existence of such feedback mechanisms. It is therefore in the interests of the teachers to consider the views of students.

However, the way in which the production and reception of this particular criticism is constructed suggests that the discourse is designed to reinforce the teachers' current practices and to represent any challenges to these as directed to external agents or the product of 'deviant' (or otherwise compromised) individuals. We have already seen how the introduction of the criticism itself is designed to deflect responsibility for the problem from the school to the agency responsible for placing the students. Ed's presentation of the complaint also allows him to distance himself from the student responsible once he has offered a nominally sympathetic evaluation (ll.26–7).

At this point attention shifts from the complaint to Thomas, the complaining student, and is designed to undermine the legitimacy of his position. Jenny's immediate observation (which gains Ed's assent), that he left having thanked and praised them (ll.41–3), implies at best inconsistency and at worst duplicity. Paul now joins in, suggesting that Thomas 'went (.) extremely lazy', thus assigning the cause for his failure to improve to a failure in his own character. Paul and Jenny's tentative suggestions, that his loss of face and worry about status might also have been a factor, are followed by Paul's more confident assertion that he did not work well within the group and his appeal to colleagues to support this contention. Paul then expresses sympathy with other members of the group, thus subtly aligning the teacher's position with that of the rest of the students. All that remains is to call on a specific example, George, as representative of the rest of Thomas's group. George's position is represented unequivocally: he 'seemed very appreciative' (Paul: 70–1), 'was incredibly nice' to Jenny (l. 76), and was 'very (.) clear' that he 'really got a lot from the course' (Paul: 82–8). A final observation, that Thomas was a 'strange' person, confirms his deviancy and draws spurious professional legitimacy by its placement within a superficially balanced assessment recognising his lack of aggression.

A summary of the moves in this exchange demonstrates just how effectively this challenge to the professional competence of the Pen staff has been dismissed:

1. *Presentation*: a pre-sequence allows pre-emptive positioning before the criticism itself is formally requested and presented. The criticism is introduced in direct speech, allowing the speaker to distance himself from it and subsequently align with colleagues as they respond to the criticism.
2. *Deflection*: the pre-emptive positioning is taken up, as responsibility is explicitly shifted to an outside party.
3. *Typification*: the complainant is typified as a student who has problems or defects which set him apart from other students.
4. *Isolation*: the complainant is presented as someone who does not fit in with the rest of the group. Hence, implicitly, his views are dismissible as deviant.
5. *Contrast*: the contrast is made explicit by taking another member of the group and positioning him at the opposite extreme to the complainant.

By the end of this sequence the force of the complaint has been directed elsewhere and its validity undermined. The Pen staff have located the problem giving rise to the complaint outside the Pen and have effectively identified the source of the complaint itself (Thomas) as being 'outside' the main body of students. The analysis of critical feedback has served only to underline general satisfaction with the *status quo*.

The Pen teachers' own view of this is a factor that would be important in a full analysis. In fact, they welcomed my research precisely because they were extremely aware that, having worked together for a very long time, they were likely to have developed ways of preserving group identity and patterns of behaviour at the expense of a proper understanding. The maintenance of dominant power structures often depends on the construction of discourse in such a way as to ensure the compliance of all involved without bringing to the surface the means by which this is achieved. Its exposure is therefore not just something to be directed at others: our own consciousness is an issue.

The discourse palette

The analyses above provide at least a flavour of approaches to using discourse in QI, but they leave untouched broader issues of how this can be integrated into more extensive projects. The analytical process will be the subject of Chapter 6, but in the meantime I offer an overview of the relationships among the traditions introduced here in terms of their similarities and points of contention, concluding with a note on context. First, though, it is instructive to consider briefly a tradition that sets out explicitly to bring together the different data collection procedures that feature in this book.

The ethnography of communication (EC)

As its name suggests, this tradition has an integrative orientation, focusing on communicative aspects (verbal and non-verbal) of the ways in which groups are constructed, defined and maintained, and explicitly drawing together ethnographic data collection methods and interactional analysis:

> Drawing on social and cultural anthropology, linguistics, sociology, and education, EC brings together etic and emic analyses of discourse as well, to examine 'patterns and functions of communication, [and the] nature and definition of speech community', among other things (Saville-Troike 1989:11). (in Duff 2002:291)

There are a number of associated approaches, including micro-ethnography (for example, Erickson 1992, 1996) and interactional ethnography (for example, Green and Dixon 1993), all characterised by an overriding focus on interaction. In a profession such as TESOL, where issues of cross-cultural communication have particular salience, a tradition such as EC has considerable illuminative potential, and the only reason I have omitted it from the analytical samples in the last section is that to separate the analysis of a particular speech event from the broader context in which it is embedded would be to give a false impression of what is involved in this sort of analysis. In any case, an excellent recent example of EC applied to a TESOL classroom is readily available (Duff 2002), together with valuable discussions of this in the context of other approaches (Rampton *et al.* 2002; Green and Dixon 2002). The advice on data analysis in Chapter 6 will apply equally well to EC, where data triangulation is particularly important, and the comments that follow embrace this tradition as well as the others covered so far.

Points of agreement

Despite some obvious differences in emphasis and orientation, these analytical traditions overlap to a considerable extent and are agreed on the fundamental points summarised in Box 4.10. Analytically, the most fundamental of these is the last: the ethnographer, like the conversation analyst and the interactional sociolinguist, sets out to *discover* the ways in which social and interactional organisation is constituted, rather than identifying *a priori* particular linguistic (or social) categories and assigning discrete segments of talk (or action) to these. For example, there are strong and very productive analytical traditions within applied linguistics that draw on pre-determined functional categories (requesting, rejecting, and so on), but these need to be treated with considerable caution in the context of QI because, while they may provide the basis for interesting model-building (e.g. Wu 1998) or statistical claims (e.g. Nassaji and Wells 2000), they can easily distract attention from social and interactional *processes*. In this respect, my inclusion of CDA is slightly contentious, at least in so far as some of its practitioners draw on systemic functional linguistics (SFL) with its reliance on pre-set categories, as discussed below:

> Much of SFL analysis...relies on, and attends to, categories pre-coded in the analyst's grammatical model, and indeed the availability of a ready made coding system lends itself to quantitative and statistical validation, in which the particularity of specific acts is obscured. (Rampton *et al.* 2002:385–6)

Box 4.10   Interactional traditions: fundamental points of agreement

- 'Language, culture, and society are grounded in interaction: they stand in a reflexive relationship with the self, the other, and the self-other relationship, and it is out of these mutually constitutive relationships that discourse is created' (Schiffrin 1994:134).
- Interaction will show evidence of the participants' understanding and expression of meanings relevant to specific groups.
- Texts rather than single utterances are the units of analysis.
- Categories are not predetermined, but developed through analysis.

A final interesting point of similarity is the extent to which, with the exception of CA, these traditions recognise that they are drawing on a wide range of approaches. Meyer (2001:23), for example, admits that 'CDA does not constitute a well-defined empirical method but rather a cluster of approaches', while Duff (2002:292) draws on a 'composite of approaches I will refer to as EC' and Schiffrin (1994:97) considers that interactional sociolinguistics 'has the most diverse disciplinary origins'. While this may call for some careful analytical positioning, for the QI researcher in TESOL it holds out the prospect of considerable freedom to explore different perspectives and perhaps integrate these in our analysis (for an excellent example of this, see Rampton 1999, which draws on micro-ethnography, interactional sociolinguistics and CA).

That said, there are areas of contention. As we shall see, CA and ethnography have different views about the place of context, and the place of CA in applied linguistics has been challenged and defended (for example, Wagner 1996; Seedhouse 1998), but CDA is the tradition that has prompted most debate. Widdowson (1995, 1996, 2000) has challenged this as ideologically motivated and highly selective in its use of textual evidence, also drawing attention to links with SFL and its illegitimate treatment of text as 'a static patchwork' (2000:17). Despite Fairclough's defence (1996) of CDA on the basis of its explicit positioning and open-ended orientation, ideological neutrality – or the absence of it – remains a key point of contention and was the starting point for an interesting and in many ways productive debate between Billig and Schegloff (1999) that explores methodological aspects of CA and CDA. Anyone considering working within the CDA tradition should certainly consider very carefully the arguments developed in these key debates, but whatever our approach it is the issue of context that is likely to demand our most considered attention.

Context

As Goodwin and Duranti note (1992:2), a precise definition of context has so far eluded researchers. This may have something to do with the potentially infinite regress that faces anyone seeking a fully contextualised account: there is no *a priori* basis for saying that the limits of a particular context have been reached and explanatory resources are at an end. Goodwin and Duranti suggest that the notion of context involves the juxtaposition of a focal event and the field of action within which it is embedded, though they also recognise the 'dynamic mutability' of the concept itself (ibid., p. 5).

One way of thinking about context is to conceptualise it in terms of level or direction. Fetzer and Akman (2002), for example, identify three levels of context: linguistic, social and sociocultural, and categorisations such as these may help us to form a clearer picture of the connections we make in our analysis. Alternatively, we might be able to get a fix on our own position by making use of Meyer's suggestion (2001:19) that different approaches can be broadly divided into top-down, or those that work from structure to action, and bottom-up, or those working from action to structure. For the purposes of illustration, we might take ethnography as an example of the former (although this would be a gross simplification) and CA as an example of the latter.

It is the lack of precision in determining what can be invoked as legitimate context for explanatory purposes that accounts for CA's insistence on procedural relevancy, which means that it is not sufficient merely to show that the context is relevant for the parties, it is also necessary to demonstrate how the context is consequential to the parties' conduct in a specific context (Schegloff 1991). The conversation analyst argues that any *relevant* orientation to a specific context will be detectable in the talk itself as an accountable aspect of the participants' own construction of their shared understanding, thus rendering redundant and potentially misleading any attempt to import contextual detail from outside the talk itself.

From an ethnographer's perspective, this insistence on locating all relevant contextual detail in the talk itself excludes possible explanatory resources either not available to the participants or not actually manifested in their talk, even though these might offer insights into aspects of social structure. Although not seeking a 'complete' or 'final' specification, the analyst will try to develop explanations and accounts by going beyond specific events to the broader social and theoretical context in which they are embedded. While arguably broader in scope and potential than the CA approach, freedom is achieved at the expense of the latter's natural explanatory boundaries, opening up issues of inclusion and exclusion, something that Dilley, for example, has defined as 'process of power' (2002:453).

As with all aspects of QI, the role of context cannot be taken for granted and will demand of the researcher a considered response. In this chapter I have adopted an approach that leans heavily on CA, but this should not be taken as an argument for this particular tradition over others. In Chapter 6 I will outline a very different approach to analysis, but the considerations raised here should not be forgotten there. We do not need to be conversation analysts, in the strict sense of that term, to recognise the importance of attending to how talk is constructed or paying close attention to detail in our analysis of it. As Silverman (2000b) has shown, awareness of these dimensions can be of considerable value in sharpening analytical attention. In a field as demanding as QI, we need all the help we can get.

Transcription conventions

Basic transcription conventions are introduced in Level 1, but it's useful at the outset to have an idea of those which are typically used in the literature. Schiffrin (1994:422–33) summarises a number of approaches to transcription, but where the standard systems don't provide what you need, it is acceptable to include symbols of your own, provided that they are adequately glossed. (It's also worth noting that the use of Courier as a font should allow you to line up symbols or text without worrying about whether the alignment will disappear in the printing process.)

Skills development

All the tasks that follow (Tasks 4.1–4.3) assume that if you are recording interaction you will do so with the permission of those involved. The tasks are designed to develop important basic skills and are relevant at all levels.

Task 4.1 Comparing

One way of getting a sense of the real nature of spoken interaction is to compare transcribed extracts with other representations.

Setting up
1. Sit in on some ordinary conversations and try to capture the talk in writing as it is taking place. You won't be able to write down all of it, so go for extracts. At the same time, make a tape recording of the talk.
2. If possible, do this on a number of occasions.
3. Make sure that you label your notes and your tapes so that you can match them to one another.

Procedure
1. Have a look at your written record and choose something that seems to you to capture exactly what was said.
2. Now find this passage on the tape and transcribe it carefully.

---

3. Compare the two versions. Where are the main differences? Which omissions seem to you to be most serious? What do you learn about (a) the way ordinary conversations are constructed, and (b) the advantages or disadvantages of these two methods of collecting spoken data?

Development
1. When you have made a number of recordings, listen to the tapes and identify some of the everyday things that are going on (e.g. greetings, introductions, requests, disagreements, information-giving).
2. Identify where these occur on the tape.
3. Now see if you can find examples of these in coursebooks.
4. Compare the transcripts here with the ones you have made. Where are the differences? What are the implications for using these texts in your teaching? You might like to extend this and try using some of your own transcripts (simplified) with your classes.

Task 4.2   Transcribing

I suggested in the chapter that transcription is very important, but the best way of appreciating this is to explore it for yourself.

Setting up
The best setting for this is you own classroom, and if possible you should make both audio and video recordings, following the advice in the chapter.

Procedure
1. Select two segments for transcription: one where only one person is speaking at a time and the talk is very clear, and one where there is overlap in the talk and some of what is said is unclear. If possible, try to select recognisable pedagogic sequences; for example, where the teacher is pursuing a question or a series of questions with the class. These extracts needn't be long.
2. Transcribe each of the extracts as carefully as you can, first using the tape recorder and then using the audio track from the video recorder. Now compare these. How do they differ? How do you account for this? What do you learn from this in terms of data collection?
3. Set the transcripts aside for at least two weeks, then, without first looking at the transcripts, return to the talk and transcribe the extracts again.

Task 4.2   (Continued)

4. Compare your transcripts. Where are the differences and what do you learn from these? If possible, try a third transcription with a different tape recorder and see whether this produces something different. If you can involve someone else and compare their transcript with yours, so much the better. The aim here is to develop a sensitivity to your transcription technique.

Development

1. Choose one of your transcripts and identify the relevant passage on the videotape.
2. Study the non-verbal dimension revealed on the videotape very carefully and try to develop a description of this. Pay particular attention to changes in body position and orientation, and (if they are visible) shifts in gaze. The best way of noting this is to create space on your audio transcript by using at least double spacing and allowing a generous margin on the right. Add non-verbal transcription in different coloured ink or a different font.
3. Decide what the non-verbal details add to your understanding of the interaction. What are the implications of this for data collection and transcription?

Task 4.3   Analysing

Setting up

The best way of developing analytical skills is to work on passages that interest you, so begin by selecting a passage from the transcripts collected in the above tasks. It needn't be long, but it should stimulate your interest and curiosity.

Procedure

1. Analyse the passage using the techniques suggested in the chapter and set this aside for a couple of weeks.
2. Go back to the passage and analyse it again. Compare analyses and see whether there are any differences between them. If there are, try to account for these and reflect on their implications for your development as an analyst.
3. Try to identify a phenomenon (or phenomena) that interests you and go back through your transcripts to find other examples of this. Analyse these and see whether you can build up an under-

standing of what is happening in the passages you have selected
and how the phenomenon features in this.

Development
1. If you have identified something of interest, follow this up in the
   literature. Try to find out how other analysts have worked
   towards an understanding of the feature that interests you.
2. Return to your analysis in the light of this, perhaps adjusting
   your approach in the light of the tradition(s) you have encountered in the literature. If you find a particular approach helpful,
   use the recommendations for exploring the literature in Chapter
   5 to help you to understand it better.
3. In the light of your investigations here, you might wish to
   develop a larger-scale project to pursue your understanding further. Chapter 5 offers advice on how to do this.

The best way of ensuring that your skills continue to develop is to
transcribe and analyse short passages as often as you can. You will soon
build up quite a collection of transcribed passages, and you'll be surprised at how often you can go back to these and find new things – I still
enjoy revisiting passages that have been on my computer and in my filing
cabinet for well over a decade.

Reading guide

Level 1

You may be interested to explore what the investigation of classroom
interaction can reveal, in which case either of the following makes
revealing reading:

van Lier L. 1988. *The Classroom and the Language Learner.* London:
Longman.

Allwright, D. and Bailey, K.M. 1991. *Focus on the Language Classroom.*
Cambridge: Cambridge University Press.

Level 2

If you want to follow up the tradition that has informed the approach
adopted at this level, the following offers an excellent introduction and
analysis with useful activities:

Wooffitt, R. 2001. 'Researching Psychic Practitioners: Conversation Analysis', in M. Wetherell, S. Yates and S.J. Yates (eds) *Discourse as Data: a Guide for Analysis*, pp. 49–92. London/Milton Keynes: Sage in association with The Open University.

A valuable and extremely readable introduction to discourse analysis in general is to be found in the following:

McCarthy, M. 1991. *Discourse Analysis for Language Teachers*. Cambridge: Cambridge University Press.

Alternatively, you might be interested in the broader context of such research and the ways in which it links with educational issues and illuminates aspects of our pedagogic practice, in which case you can do no better than:

van Lier L. 1996. *Interaction in the Language Curriculum: Awareness, Autonomy and Authenticity*. London: Longman.

Level 3

The briefest overview I know of the fields covered here, albeit heavily weighted towards systemic functional linguistics is Chapter 2 of Eggins and Slade (1997), but for an introduction to various approaches to analysing discourse, covering everything except interactional sociolinguistics, Titscher *et al.* is probably the best starting point:

Titscher, S., Meyer, M., Wodak, R. and Vetter, E. 2000. *Methods of Text and Discourse Analysis*. London: Sage.

The main shortcoming of this is that it lacks worked examples, but the following pair offer excellent coverage of CA, CDA (albeit applied to written texts), interactional sociolinguistics and the ethnography of communication:

Schiffrin, D. 1994. *Approaches to Discourse*. Oxford: Basil Blackwell.

Wetherell, M., Yates, S. and Yates, S.J. (eds). 2001. *Discourse as Data: a Guide for Analysis*. London/Milton Keynes: Sage in association with The Open University.

Essential reading is the special issue of *Applied Linguistics*, where two of the three featured examples cover relevant areas (Duff 2002 and Mori 2002) and the papers by Rampton *et al.* (2002) and Green and Dixon (2002) also make valuable contributions:

> Zuengler, J. and Mori, J. (eds). 2002. *Applied Linguistics* 23(1) special issue: 'Microanalyses of Classroom Discourse: a Critical Consideration of Method'.

Finally, despite its relatively early date, Wittrock (1986) is still well worth reading if you want a wider perspective. More narrowly, the following are recommended as introductions to specific areas:

Conversation analysis

Seedhouse's forthcoming introduction to CA (2004) promises to be particularly valuable to ESOL professionals, but in the meantime ten Have (1999) offers an introduction that is exactly what it says it is: an excellent starting point for anyone who wants to get to grips with the basic conceptual and practical issues. He also has a paper in a wider-ranging collection that also covers CDA:

> McHoul, A. and Rapley, M. 2001. *How to Analyse Talk in Institutional Settings*. London: Continuum.

Interactional sociolinguistics

Two classic texts here repay careful study:

> Goffman, E. 1981. *Forms of Talk*. Oxford: Basil Blackwell.

> Gumperz, J.J. 1982. *Discourse Strategies*. Cambridge: Cambridge University Press.

Critical discourse analysis

Anyone interested in the two main approaches to this can follow them up in Chouliaraki and Fairclough (1999) and Wodak (1996), but the best starting point is the excellent collection edited by Wodak and Meyer:

> Wodak, R. and Meyer, M. (eds). 2001. *Methods of Critical Discourse Analysis*. London: Sage.

The ethnography of communication

Saville-Troike (1996) provides an excellent brief overview, but her earlier introduction is still a classic:

Saville-Troike, M. 1989. *The Ethnography of Communication* (2nd edn). Oxford: Basil Blackwell.

Ethnography and CA

Silverman (1993) is useful here, and the case presented in the following succinct paper is hard to better:

Silverman, D. 2002. 'Analyzing Talk and Text', in N.K. Denzin and Y.S. Lincoln (eds), *Handbook of Qualitative Research* (2nd edn). Thousand Oaks, CA: Sage, pp. 821–34.

5
Planning a Project

Preview

In Chapters 5 and 6 the focus shifts from developing the skills of data collection to identifying procedures that will enable you to plan, implement and write up a research project. At the core of each chapter is Level 2, which provides a range of easily accessible practical resources, while the other levels are briefer and more discursive in character. Level 1 follows the pattern of previous chapters and is introductory, though you will notice a difference in Level 3, where individual issues are selected for particular attention.

This chapter responds to questions about three important processes in project planning:

Thinking	How can we stimulate effective thinking? What kind of thinking is most appropriate at each stage?
Reading	What should we read? How should we approach reading?
Writing	When should we start writing? What forms of writing are most appropriate at each stage?

It follows the development of a plan from inception through to implementation:

Ideas	How can we generate ideas for suitable research projects?
↓	
Focus	Having decided what we'd like to find out about, how can we narrow down the focus so that the project is doable?
↓	
↓	
Approach	Which research approach is likely to provide the best means of answering our research question(s)?
↓	

↓

Design   How do we go about designing a successful project?

↓

Implementation   What do we need to bear in mind when we are
                     implementing our design?

These are realised as follows, with Level 3 providing comment on
issues arising at each stage (Table 5.1).

Table 5.1   An overview of the levels presented in Chapter 5

Element	Level 1	Level 2	Level 3
Ideas	Reflecting on practice	Fixing a topic	Responding to complexity
Focus	Formulating a question	From research topic to research question	Participatory dimensions
Approach	Deciding on a response	Working within a tradition [The literature]	Connecting with theory
Design	Making a plan	Design issues [Sampling. Triangulation]	Providing Leadership
Implementation	Making it happen	Forms of writing [The research proposal]	Providing Leadership

Level 1: the personal project

Reflecting on practice

If I had to choose a single reason for preferring 'inquiry' to 'research' as
a descriptive term it would be because the former is more strongly sug-
gestive of an approach that depends on thinking and questioning. This
matters a great deal because all good research rests on hard thinking
and lots of it. You can pile up interview transcripts or fieldnotes until
you're blue in the face, but unless you spend enough time thinking
about what you're up to, they're so much waste paper. A morning spent
thinking may produce little that is tangible, and in that sense will be
less satisfying than four or five pages of transcript, but it may well move
your research forward in a significant way.

Most ESOL teachers are natural researchers. We're used to working out
the needs of our students, evaluating the effects of particular approaches,
spotting things that work or don't work and adjusting our teaching
accordingly. Very few teachers approach their work mechanically and
nearly all of us reflect on what we do in the classroom. However, time is
usually pressing and many of the interesting reflections that occur to us
are lost in the welter of activity that passes for a normal teaching day.

Much has been written about reflective practice, but for most teachers it's a hidden part of their everyday world. In order to take the first steps towards a research project, what we have to do is bring it to the surface. Keep a small notebook or piece of paper handy and jot down anything that occurs to you as interesting about your teaching: questions, puzzles, insights, even moans and grumbles. Then make the decision to read through these and think about them when you have some free time at home. Ask yourself if there is anything particularly interesting or puzzling, or if there's a common theme connecting some of the comments. Try to identify an area that you would like to know more about in your work. For the purposes of illustration, I have chosen the classroom, but inquiry need not be confined to this; staff meetings, materials design, and so on, would make equally good areas.

Formulating a question

In all likelihood your first thoughts about an area of interest will be very general ones. Perhaps you're not happy with something about your questioning in class and you'd like to improve it. Because teacher questioning covers a very large area, you'll first of all need to decide what aspect of your technique you'd like to look at. There are two possible stages involved, as outlined below.

1. Focusing the mind: at this stage you need to reflect on the topic in order to identify areas that seem most pertinent to your interest. I like to sit with blank sheets of scrap paper and let doodling and jotting help me find a focus, but there are more structured approaches. Edge (2002:100–4) describes two very useful procedures for progressive focusing, one of which depends on circles and the other on branches. The first stage of the circle method involves writing the main topic in an inner circle and then noting relevant elements in segments of an outer circle, as shown below (Figure 5.1). Once the outside set of elements have been decided (and what appears here is entirely a matter of your interest rather than of any recognised 'list'), you choose the one that you find most interesting and make this the centre of the circle, repeating the process. Once again, you can make one of the outer elements the centre, and so on until you are happy with the precise focus you have established. The decisions along the way will be determined by reflections on your own teaching and may also be informed by stage 2 investigation.

2. Directing attention: it may be that what emerges from the focusing process is a very clear question that you would like to answer, in which

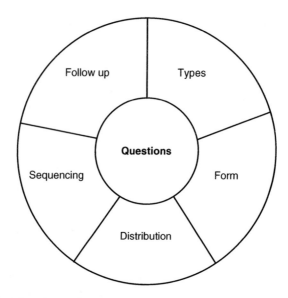

Figure 5.1   A focusing circle

case you should move on to deciding what form your response to this will take. However, the formulation of a precise question sometimes depends on finding out a bit more about the topic, in which case some preliminary investigation might be called for.

In order to do this, you can use any of the data gathering techniques dealt with in Chapters 2 to 4. For example, if might be helpful to observe the teaching of colleagues or to interview them about their approaches to the topic. Often, though, the best way forward is via an examination of your own teaching. The procedure described in Box 5.1 is relatively unobtrusive and usually very productive:

Box 5.1   A technique for exploring your own teaching

1. Decide on a class and tape some of your lessons. Ideally, you should get into the habit of taping every lesson as a matter of course, using the same tape over and over again until you come to a lesson which you feel would be worth looking at more closely. If you can't do this, just tape what you can, when you can.
2. Listen to the tape when you can: a bit here and there whenever you have the time will do. Eventually you'll come across a few

> passages which are good examples of the aspect of your teaching that you're interested in.
> 3. Concentrate on these and listen to them over and over again until you get a sense of what's going on. At first you may notice nothing at all, but eventually you'll find questions emerging. You don't need any special techniques for this – just the ears of a teacher.
> 4. If necessary, transcribe all or part of these extracts using the techniques described in Chapter 4. An examination of these should help you to understand how things are actually working.

Deciding on a response

If you have followed both stages described above, your understanding will already have deepened and you should now have a clear picture of what you would like to find out more about. There are two ways forward from this point, though it is possible to move from the first response to the second.

1. You can decide to deepen your understanding of this topic through further investigation. Having then decided just what it is you will be investigating, you should move on to the planning stage.
2. You may decide that the best way forward is by means of intervention in your own teaching. This will involve introducing a deliberate change to your teaching or some other aspect of your professional life, based on the understanding of your current practice that your preliminary investigation has revealed. You will then need to plan the nature of this intervention.

Making a plan

Whether your approach is to be descriptive (understanding more about some aspect of practice) or interventionist (exploring a change in practice), you will need to plan your research. What will the timescale be? How will you gather your data? How much data will you need? Who will be involved? What are the practical issues (permission, access, appointments, and so on)? How will you analyse the data? Take time to work out a timetable for the research reflecting your decisions on all these issues. When this is complete, stand back from it and ask yourself honestly whether it is doable. If it's not, go back and cut it down to size.

You need to bear in mind only one thing at this important stage: *small is beautiful.*

You'll be surprised how little data you actually need in order to improve your understanding. Always remember that you're not trying to change the whole world – just come to a better understanding of some small aspect of it. And an over-ambitious plan has little chance of being implemented. A few well-conducted interviews are worth a hundred superficial ones, and painstaking analysis of a single lesson can reveal more than casual descriptions of a whole term's worth.

Making it happen

If your plan is realistic, this stage should be quite straightforward. The key to success, though, is flexibility. The human dimension, in terms of which qualitative inquiry is defined, brings with it uncertainty, unpredictability and sometimes downright perversity. It is simply not susceptible to rigid predetermination, so treat your plan as a guide rather than a template. Try to keep your main research question in mind and be prepared to adjust your plan as much as necessary in order to respond to it. If you do this and bear in mind the tips listed in Box 5.2, you should find the research process stimulating and rewarding.

Box 5.2   Five tips for getting the best out of the inquiry process

Have faith	There will be discoveries, but not always early on.
Analyse early	It adds to the enjoyment and can provide useful insights.
Seize opportunities	Plans can always be revisited but sometimes there's no second bite of the cherry in the field.
Keep a diary	It aids reflection and charts progress.
Have fun	Your research will be the better for it, so if necessary amend your plan to include regular opportunities to do the tasks you enjoy most.

An action research project

The most powerful form of research for the beginning researcher in TESOL is action research (AR). It is powerful because, although it demands the same standards of inquiry as any other legitimate form of research, it goes beyond mere discovery and embeds the findings of the research in a process of professional self-discovery and development. The following definition captures its essential nature:

> Action research is used here to refer to ways of investigating professional experience which link practice and the analysis of practice into a single productive and continuously developing sequence, and which link researchers and research participants into a single community of interested colleagues. (Winter 1996:14)

The traditional structure of action research is very straightforward: plan, act, observe, reflect. Although this order is not a rigid one, I feel that it's essential to begin with reflection in order to understand the situation in which the research is to be embedded, and my own description of the research cycle (Box 5.3) reflects this.

Box 5.3	The Action Research cycle interpreted	
AR	*QI Cycle*	*Gloss*
Reflect	Reflect on practice	Understand the relevant professional situation.
Plan (1)	Formulate a question	Identify an aspect of practice (perhaps one which represents a particular challenge or puzzle) where intervention would be appropriate.
Plan (2)	Decide on a response	Decide in what ways your approach to this aspect might be changed.
Plan (3)	Make a plan	Design an intervention where this change in practice can be implemented and decide on how this can be observed.
Act	Make it happen	Put into practice the planned changes.
Observe	Make it happen	Observe the changes and their effects.
Reflect	Reflect on practice	Evaluate the outcomes of the change in terms of professional practice and development and, in the light of this, identify any further changes that might be made.

In terms of difference between the two approaches, only two things need to be noted. The first is that the AR process is best seen as part of a cycle: reflection on the outcomes of one intervention will often lead to the identification of further potential interventions. The second is that, because of the personal focus, data collection in AR typically involves the use of teacher journals, perhaps supported by recordings of lessons. However, seeking the views of students (on the intervention) or colleagues (on their views of the topic) and observation of colleagues' lessons (for a broader perspective) can add a valuable extra dimension to the research.

Extract 5.1   Summary of an action research project

I wasn't happy about my questioning in class: it seemed to me that I wasted opportunities and sometimes got in a bit of a mess [Reflect]. So I taped one of my lessons and spent some time examining aspects of my questioning [Observe]. One thing that emerged strongly was that I seemed to allow very little wait time and often waded in with the answer myself [Identify]. I therefore decided to concentrate on extending my wait time and varying it more deliberately according to circumstances [Respond]. I chose an intermediate class and planned first of all to tape all my lessons with them for a couple of weeks, then to spend the third week implementing the proposed change, keeping a journal based on notes made immediately after each lesson [Plan]. I implemented the plan and, although I found it difficult at first, as the week progressed I found that I was naturally giving attention to this aspect of my teaching [Implement]. When I read my journal and listened to my lessons on tape, I could detect a genuine sense of progress, as students found ways of saying things that before they had left to me. However, this didn't always happen and I think I need to work on my elicitation techniques to provide support where needed without actually closing down opportunities for students. This will be the subject of my next intervention [Reflect].

One of the beauties of the AR cycle is that it can be incorporated naturally into the normal routine of teaching, as Extract 5.1, demonstrates. If other colleagues or students can be involved in the process, so much the better, and this was a feature of one of my personal favourites among the many projects undertaken by students on the Masters programme with which I am involved. The researcher taught Business English at a French company and noticed something odd about the response to his corrections by the middle management clients who made up some of his classes. He decided to tape one of his classes in order to examine this feature in more detail and his analysis revealed that where his corrections were clearly grammatical the uptake was excellent, but where they were related in any way to business the students ignored them. He took some examples into one of his classes and asked the students whether this was deliberate. They insisted it was not and together teacher and students agreed procedures to improve this aspect of their interaction. A taped lesson a few weeks later confirmed that the changes had brought about an improvement in the students' efforts to incorporate correct forms into their talk, so the teacher adopted this new approach with all of his upper management classes. Straightforward research, a simple change, but everybody benefited.

Level 2: resources for project planning

Fixing a topic

Many years ago, at the end of my first year as a PhD supervisor, I went to a workshop held by a visiting academic on the subject of being an effective supervisor. 'Come with a problem' the advance literature said, so I did: after almost a whole year of supervision, my sole research student had *finally* pinned down *precisely* what she was going to do, so how could I ensure that future supervisees would avoid this fate? The workshop opened with an invitation to present our problems but another participant got in first – with my question. After over 20 years of supervision in the field of road engineering, he was no closer to solving this problem either and was seeking advice.

This unexpected contribution and the subsequent discussion made me feel a whole lot better, but more importantly it brought home to me the importance of beginning with a good topic. This first year hadn't been wasted at all; it had involved a necessary process of orientation that had enabled the researcher to get a better fix on her research question and the research process. All this was possible only because she had begun with a well-focused topic that served as an anchor for all the exploration that followed.

Because qualitative research is by its very nature exploratory, the line between aimless wandering and productive exploration needs to be carefully drawn. The latter is distinguished by its sense of purpose, its focus, and the careful preparation that lies behind it and, as Wolcott noted some twenty years ago, it is 'impossible to embark upon research without some idea of what one is looking for and foolish not to make that quest explicit' (1982:157). This section will help you to get a fix on a topic and point to some of the distractions that lie in wait.

Finding a topic

At first blush this would seem to be a simple matter of deciding on something you'd like to find out about. Unfortunately, there are plenty of things in TESOL that I'd like to find out about, but some of the questions are impossibly big, others demand research skills that I don't have, and one or two are personal hobby horses. Finding a topic is above all else a practical business, and three things really matter: (1) deciding on something that you want to do; (2) that you can do; and (3) that is worth doing.

Box 5.4 sums up the steps that lead to the formulation of a suitable topic. A good starting point is to think about what has given rise to your interest in the first place because this will help you get a better handle on exploring it from an outsider's perspective ('Choosing'). At this stage you should try to ask as many challenging questions as possible. Examining the topic from the point of view of its worth, practicality and connectivity should open it up to the sort of scrutiny that will test its mettle ('Checking'). Finally, you should be in a position to sum up in one sentence just where your interest lies, then to break this down into the sort of things you want to know ('Formulating').

Box 5.4   Choosing the topic

Choosing

Nature	Description	Response
Personal	Something you've always wanted to know about or that fires you with particular enthusiasm.	Explore the enthusiasm. Think *around* the topic, break it down.
Professional	A puzzle or problem or challenge in your teaching and/or in the teaching of colleagues or the work of your institution or in TESOL generally.	Have others tackled this one? If so how? Is this something that would be relevant to others?
Academic	A piece of research you've read about and that you'd like to take further.	How would your project differ (group? methods? focus?)?

Checking	
Why is it worth doing?	What difference will it make? Where will its contribution lie?
Can I do it?	What is the scale of the project? What sort of data might I be looking for? Is there anyone who can help me along the way? Do I need to get anyone onside?
Who will I talk to?	Where are the issues here? Who writes/ talks about them? If I do this research, where will my findings have most impact? On academics? Teachers? Administrators?

Formulating

1 What interests me is ....
2 I want to know how ....
　　　　why ....
　　in what ways .... etc.

You might also find it useful to consider in more detail how your topic connects to wider issues. It can be hard at this stage to predict just how your discoveries will contribute to the bigger picture, but you should at least be able to visualise where the contributions might lie. Agar's challenging demand of ethnographic research might be applied to qualitative inquiry generally and serves as a useful reminder of what might ultimately be expected:

> If a piece of research doesn't produce new concepts, concepts that take you closer to the world that is the object of research than previous understandings could have, then it isn't ethnographic. (Agar 1996:40)

Box 5.5 illustrates how connections might be sketched out for the topic of staffroom talk. At this stage they represent only possibilities (connections in brackets represent second-order ones) and not all of them will work out in practice, but the point about a diagram like this, however tentative, is that its formulation should at least be *possible* at this stage.

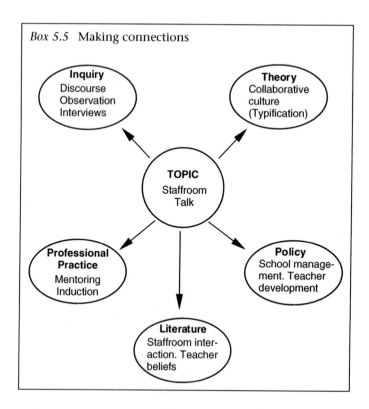

Box 5.5   Making connections

The above discussion has concentrated for the most part on academic aspects of the research project, but Bentz and Shapiro identify three further questions that seem to me to be very important, especially for TESOL practitioners whose work has direct relevance to their professional context (Bentz and Shapiro 1998:78):

- What good or harm may come from this project for myself or others?
- What changes in my life or the lives of others may occur as a result of this research?
- How will my skills as a scholar-practitioner be enhanced by this research?

From research topic to research question

If the procedures in the last section are followed, the process of carving a research question out of a topic should be straightforward. In Michelangelo's terms, if you choose the right piece of marble, the statue is there waiting to get out; all you have to do is chip away at the rock. The skill lies first of all in recognising what can be done with the raw materials and then knowing how to fashion them. The last section focused on recognition, but there is a rider to be added: how do we recognise the signs that a topic is losing its way? The process of deciding on a topic is quite exciting, and it's easy to lose a sense of perspective, so be on the lookout for the following dangers (summed up in Box 5.6):

1. The most common danger is that the project simply grows and grows until it's completely unmanageable. One question leads to another, and another, until you may as well solve all the problems of TESOL and the mysteries of the universe while you're at it.
2. The second danger leads to more or less the same situation but from a different direction. This time you get so wrapped up in the theory behind your topic that it becomes a matter of abstract concepts and philosophical speculation, perhaps seasoned by the merest suggestion of empirical data.
3. Alternatively, the prospect of empirical data and of what might be gathered becomes all-consuming, so that instead of thinking carefully about just what you want to discover and letting this inform decisions on data collection, you play it safe by aiming to assemble so much data that your eventual claims will be unassailable.
4. Research can be immensely exciting and lots of fun, but if it is to be genuinely worthwhile it has to contribute to the bigger picture. It is possible for novice researchers to forget this and become too wrapped up in the idea of the research process itself.

Box 5.6 Dangers to avoid

Balloon problems	1.	The project keeps getting bigger and bigger.
	2.	It's up there in the clouds.
Sandpit problems	3.	It's all evidence, no shape.
	4.	Lots of fun, but where's the bigger picture?

If you have managed to avoid the dangers outlined in Box 5.6, you should be in a position to fashion your general topic into something more specific. For the purposes of illustration, let's assume that you're interested in finding out more about tasks. I've chosen this topic partly because it has received considerable attention in TESOL and partly because in Johnson (2002) you can read an excellent example, focused on task design, of how qualitative research can provide important insights into our professional world. As your interest develops, you might consider a number of alternative projects, and it's very important to subject these to careful scrutiny. Box 5.7 illustrates the sort of questions you might usefully ask at this stage.

Box 5.7   Probing the topic

Possible topic	Probes
An examination of why tasks are motivating	This assumes that tasks *are* motivating, but I'd need to demonstrate this. (**Assumption**) Motivation is a psychological issue – would QI be the best approach? (**Approach**)
Successful strategies for setting up tasks in the classroom	What counts as success? How would I measure this? (**Measure**) Successful in what respects? From whose perspective? (**Perspective**) Will I limit this to teacher strategies or include strategies in the materials? (**Scope**) If I use the same materials but different teachers, on what basis do I select the latter? (**Sample**)
Teachers' views of authentic tasks	What do we mean by 'authentic' (**Definition**)? We already know that there's wide range of views so how would presenting them be useful? (**Contribution**)

To help us focus on this let's assume that you have overheard a number of conversations in your staffroom that revolve around the subject of task implementation. You've noticed that beginning teachers often describe the process of implementation in problematic terms, whereas more experienced teachers rarely if ever report any problems. You find this interesting and decide to explore further. Realising that this may simply be because established teachers are reluctant to make public their worries, you've established through informal conversations that their public position reflects their private view and that they find the position of new teachers rather puzzling. After further thought and careful consideration of possible lines of approach, you decide that you need to work towards an understanding of this complex problem and that a case study approach might be the most suitable.

If you've thought hard enough about the topic, you should be able to frame your eventual position in terms of a research question. As I indicated at the outset, sometimes the precise nature of this becomes clear only later in the research process, but the struggle to produce something preliminary is nevertheless worthwhile. Cresswell (1994) provides a useful framework for specification at this stage, along the following lines: 'The aim of this project is to (understand, explore, etc.) the (central concept) of (unit of analysis), using a (method), resulting in a (outcome)'. This is then followed by a general definition of the central concept. Using this model, you produce something along the following lines:

> The aim of this study is to compare the approaches to task implementation in the TESOL classroom of beginning and experienced teachers using a case study approach, resulting in a description of the strategies used and views of the teachers and students involved. At this stage task implementation is defined as the explicit introduction of coursebook tasks into the classroom and the subsequent activities to the conclusion of feedback, whether specified in the task description or not. 'Approaches' includes planning and classroom implementation.

Having got this far, you now need to explore the literature in order to get to know more about the topic.

Dealing with the literature: getting to know a tradition

If you are lucky enough to have someone guiding your research, they will be able to point you to key papers and towards useful literature in the relevant research tradition. However, many researchers begin their exploration alone, with only basic ideas of a topic they would like to know more about and just the literature for company. If this is your situation, you will need: (a) a way into the relevant literature; (b) a means of identifying the key papers; (c) effective methods for researching the literature; and (d) a good note-taking system. Figure 5.2 should help you to get a fix on the territory by exploring the literature in a principled way (the best approach is to follow both routes and compare your findings).

I have referred to journal papers here because they offer a bigger range of immediately accessible coverage and can be read relatively

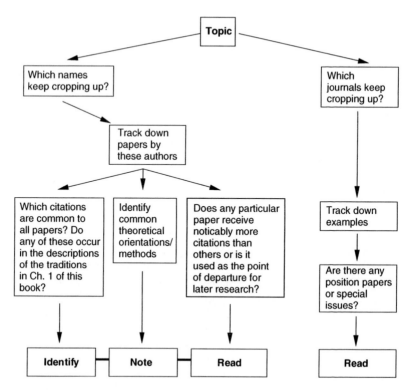

Figure 5.2   Orienting your research topic

quickly, but your search will often lead to key books. Your aim here should be to become familiar with the territory prior to digging deeper into the literature, so beware of balloon problems. Try to keep in mind that when you present your research findings, you'll have to take a stand somewhere, and this is a way of surveying the territory. The approach will not work for everyone – few, if any, approaches do – but it should give you a start and some ideas to work on. In the end, the process must be your own, along with the joys of discovery and the enriched understanding that results.

By the time you have a good picture of the lie of the land you will already have encountered some key texts, but these are just a beginning. The next stage involves a systematic exploration of the literature relating to your own project in order to situate your work in the context of earlier work, learning from this and building on it. Box 5.8 summarises methods for to doing this effectively.

Box 5.8	Some searching techniques
Databases	If you can, get to know library staff and seek their help. Failing this, try to find someone who has used this method. If all else fails, follow printed advice (Burton 2000 has a useful brief summary of database issues).
Libraries	Sniff around libraries. Get to know the relevant library codes and explore these (my current collection has lots of 301.072, 307.2 in it), together with contiguous sections. Dip into abstracting journals, skim books and bibliographies.
Contacts	Go to conferences if you can, talk to colleagues, join lists on the Internet, see what alerting services you can use (publishers are increasingly offering these as a free service). Explore the homepages of researchers.
Reading	Treat all your reading as an opportunity to identify further reading.

Finally, you will need to develop good reading and note-taking habits. This is largely an individual matter, but there are two golden rules: reading should always be strategic and notes must include all references (names, dates, page numbers for all quotes, and so on) in full.

As TESOL practitioners, we need to remind ourselves of the advice we give to our students about selecting appropriate reading strategies – something that seems to be all too often forgotten by novice researchers. If you approach reading as a matter of the mere accumulation of information, you will waste valuable time at the beginning of the project. I recommend a two-stage process:

1. *Read for worth*: identify which parts of a text (if any) will be useful to you. This produces a selection.
2. *Read for work*: undertake focused, careful, detailed reading of that selection in order to produce notes that can be used in your research.

The first of these is little more than skimming and should be used to inform the second. My own approach to a new book is to begin by folding a sheet of A4 into three and using this as a bookmark and note-pad on which I will identify paragraphs, pages or whole chapters with a few words indicating their value to my research. My aim is to skim any book in about an hour before returning to those parts of it (which occasionally means all of it) that need careful reading as a basis for my own notes. At first this process is pretty exhausting, but as you get to know the field your selections will be easier to identify, less extensive and probably more useful.

Box 5.9 is an example of some notes I took about five years ago when working on staffroom talk. I've chosen this example because it's brief and because it identifies all the aspects (in italics) that I include in my own notes. This is to some extent idiosyncratic and you will inevitably develop your own system (my own, for example, tends to rely heavily on direct quotations from the text as summaries of key points), but you should always include full references and page details for quotations.

Box 5.9   Example of notes on literature

Text	Smithson, J. and Díaz, F. 1996. Arguing for a collective voice: Collaborative strategies in problem-oriented conversation. *Text* 16(2):251–268.
Keywords	collaboration, argument, voice
Summary	Basic position is that most research is more concerned with individual differences between participants' positions, and conflicts arising from this, than with collective positions leading to consensus.
Theory	Argue for 'collective voice'. Develops this from Goffman's notion of footing.
Quote	'The way participants argue is dependent in part on the current state of the argument, and is not all predetermined by the opinions the participants originally brought to the argument.' (254)
Links to literature	Antaki (1994:139): 'ordinary talk is full of claims being made and defended, positions being put, evidence being adduced, and support being offered.'
Conclusion/ Contribution	Offer examples of completion (supportive and oppositional) and develop the case for two levels of identity: physical speaker and socially constructed 'voice'.
Methods	Reservation: The data are drawn from two laboratory activities rather than natural interaction.

Box 5.9	(Continued)
Comments	The biggest drawback seems to be that examples are taken from the problem-solving activity (translating from French) rather than the ethical debate (abortion).
References	Antaki, C. 1994. *Explaining and Arguing*. London: Sage.

Design issues

I explained in the Introduction why design issues would be deferred until this part of the book, and if by now you have developed an understanding of data collection issues you should be in an excellent position to make informed decisions about the design of your project. The process for this, which begins with your research focus and is informed by your reading, can be summed up in the following questions:

1. What sorts of things are you looking for?
2. Who will be involved?
3. How will you collect the data?

The first question can be answered in terms of the work you have already done on narrowing down the research question. What sort of information will be needed in order to achieve the aims of the research? It can help at this stage to ask yourself to what extent your research aims to describe, explain, evaluate or inform action. You should also think critically about the research designs you have encountered in your reading. It's essential at this stage to be selective and to bear in mind the following fundamental characteristic of qualitative inquiry: *qualitative inquiry aims at depth of understanding.*

With a clear picture of the sort of information required, sampling issues can be addressed. These have been categorised in various ways, but the approaches proposed by Miles and Huberman (1994:28) and Patton (1990:169–86) are particularly helpful. The former also offer a useful summary of the key features of qualitative sampling, which these authors say tends to focus on small samples of people and be purposeful rather than random. They also point out that it is often theory-driven and can evolve once fieldwork has begun.

Box 5.10 does not cover all the sampling strategies offered by the above writers but selects those of most potential value to the researcher in TESOL. I have also drawn a distinction between those relating to the process of actually finding the sample ('Process') and those informed by consideration of the information that will be obtained ('Case'). The former describe approaches where the researcher is guided by encounters in the field, making assessments and decisions as opportunities arise, while the latter are usually determined in advance, as the researcher decides what sort of sample will be most appropriate for the project they have in mind. Of course, it may be that a group has been identified on the basis of its composition (for example, its typicality), but when the researcher goes into the field a better prospect presents itself, so data collection shifts to another group (opportunistic sampling). This final sample is therefore arrived at by combining two different strategies.

Box 5.10   Some useful sampling strategies

1.   Process characteristic

Snowball (Chain)	Draws on the knowledge of informants, as one contact leads to another until a suitable case is identified.
Opportunistic	Follows leads or hunches, taking advantage of opportunities in order to identify best case.
Convenience	Settle for what is convenient because of advantages it offers or difficulty of using other samples.

2.   Case feature

Typical	Takes a very typical case and therefore one that is likely to be found fairly generally, so that any findings are likely to reflect what is normal.
Extreme (Deviant)	A very unusual situation, an understanding of which is likely to throw light on other contexts or on particular issues.
Maximum variation	Any patterns that can be found in a very heterogeneous sample may well be core features and relevant more generally.

Decisions on data collection methods can be informed by your experiences in developing the relevant skills as part of your response to Chapters 2 to 4, but you will need to consider how best to combine them. This decision should be informed by your research aims and your answer to the question of what sort of information you require. Box 5.11 offers a very brief and rather crude summary of the orientations of the three different data collection procedures introduced in this book and is designed as an *aide-mémoire* but no more than that.

Box 5.11	Contributions of different data collection methods	
Focus	*is collected through . . .*	*and shows . . .*
Behaviour	Observation	What people do and how behaviour is organised
Ideas/beliefs	Interviews	How people view/ understand the world and their own actions
Talk	Recording	What people say and how talk is organised

Note: The data are *not* the experience itself, so following the collection procedure we must deal, at one step further removed, with our representations of it.

These different data collection methods can be combined in a process known as between-method *triangulation*. Triangulation, as the name suggests, is based on the idea of getting a fix on a particular point by viewing it from different perspectives, thus minimising the danger of a one-sided representation. As well as methodological triangulation, Denzin (1970) identifies three other ways in which this might be achieved: data triangulation (from different time, space or person perspectives), investigator triangulation (more than one person in the same situation), and theory triangulation (from the point of view of alternative or competing theories).

The problem with triangulation is that it suggests a rather mechanical approach that can distract attention from more subtle data collection issues, which is why some researchers prefer other terms (for example, Burgess's multiple strategies, 1984b:146). Terminology here is much less important than a careful consideration of the contributions that different approaches can make to the project as a whole, and this is where the researcher's attention should be directed. If triangulation helps to direct attention to these, it serves its purpose, though it may have other contributions to make (Seale 1999a, 1999b:52–86).

Forms of writing

Many forms of writing can feature in the planning of a research project and Box 5.12 summarises the part these might play. However, the single most important written outcome is likely to be the Research Proposal, and at this level the PhD proposal. Box 5.13 provides a template for the production of such a proposal.

Box 5.12 Forms of writing at the planning stage	
Diagrams, doodles, sketches	Ideas generation, planning
Memos and personal notes	Reminders relating to ideas, connections, theory
Research diary	Thoughts, feelings, reflections, ideas, plans
Notes	Information (on literature etc.)
Proposal	A formal research proposal

Because a research proposal is designed to convince the reader that your research is worth supporting (in the form of supervision, grants, and so on), it should be designed to persuade. The length may vary according to any local guidelines that apply, but something in the region of around 3–5,000 words would be a reasonable expectation. However long it may be, the reader will have the following basic questions in mind when assessing the proposal:

- What does the research aim to do?
- Is it worth doing?
- Can it be done?
- Can the writer do it?

Notice that just because the research can be done, it does not follow that this *particular* writer can do it. The proposal should dispel any doubts on this score.

Box 5.13 A PhD research proposal		
Section	*Purpose*	*Comments*
Title	This should identify the precise topic (and possibly indicate the approach)	The aim here is to be as precise as possible. A colon can be used to add important extra information to pin down the main title further.

Introduction	This should: • pin down the topic precisely; • identify the relevant research space; • show why the research is worth doing; • indicate what the researcher hopes to achieve.	This is probably the most important part of the proposal, not least because a failure to cover these points briefly and succinctly suggests to the reader that the research proposal is woolly, inadequately researched or trivial.
Research aims	This expands on the first of the above topics. The section should set out clearly what the writer takes the aim of the research to be (it therefore represents an opportunity to develop the research question) and specify the intended outcomes of the research.	If the research topic is too broad, this will become apparent here. It should be possible to state the research question in one sentence, although elaboration of this and the intended outcomes of the research will take longer (specifying intended outcomes is, of course, not the same thing as predicting what will be discovered).
Contextualisation	This builds on the previous section, setting the work in the context of previous research and wider issues. The writer is expected to justify the research in the context of other studies, showing how it builds on and/ or orients to these. The section should	This section is often referred to as the literature review, but this is a misleading term because it suggests that a simple review of the literature is sufficient. What is actually needed is a properly developed justification of the project in terms of other contributions to the field. The reader should be

Box 5.13   (Continued)

	demonstrate an acquaintance with relevant research and the issues it raises.	able to follow a clear line of argument demonstrating the value of the research and the researcher's familiarity with the relevant field.
Methodology	This provides details of the research methodology and should include the following: • a statement of the tradition(s) (and possibly paradigm) within which the project is set; • a description of the data collection procedures to be used and a justification for these; • a consideration of practical issues (e.g. permissions, ethics), demonstrating that data collection is practicable; • the analytical approach that will be adopted.	This section is sometimes dismissed too lightly, with perhaps a general statement along the lines that the approach will be 'ethnographic' and data will be collected by interviews and observation. In fact it demands as much reading and preparation as the last section because it is on this that the successful outcome of the research will depend. The section should demonstrate a familiarity with relevant techniques and issues, and an ability to relate these to the aims of the research.
Timetable	This presents a realistic timetable for the research, corresponding to the time available for the project.	The timetable should be broken down into manageable segments, each with a realistic target.
References	All references should be presented consistently, in a standard format.	It's surprisingly easy to make mistakes (e.g. omit a reference or two) and this gives a bad impression to the reader.

Level 3: wider engagement

In the first two levels I was able to concentrate on the practicalities of project planning, identifying characteristics that will apply to any project. However, at this level the researcher is likely to follow paths that are less easy to predict, so in what follows I offer examples drawn from my own experiences and current concerns as illustrations of how project planning engages with wider research issues. The topics covered will relate to: (1) encountering new ideas; (2) the relationship between research and action; (3) leading a team; and (4) the status of theory. In each case, I indicate how these issues arose in the context of research projects and draw attention to practical issues relevant at this level.

Responding to complexity

About a fortnight before this was written I sat on a panel with someone qualitative researchers know well. He'd never done any research himself, but he had read about it and he knew that in drawing together the results of numerous research projects we were finally making a breakthrough (the same one we made in the heady days of large-scale classroom observation projects and will doubtless make again). We would soon be able to predict what teachers should do in order to guarantee successful language learning. Our exchanges followed what is probably a fairly standard pattern, but they did stimulate me to think about ways of accounting for the indeterminacy that I am happy to embrace and my fellow panellist was so keen to eliminate. That's what led me to find out more about Complexity Theory.

Complexity Theory is anything but simple. It predicts that nothing is entirely predictable, and that though the pattern of complex systems may exert a very powerful influence and be susceptible to identification, it is never *quite* clear and can never *quite* be pinned down. Complex systems are the outcome of local actions and perturbations interacting with other local systems in response to local rules and routines. There is a bigger pattern, but it's a messy one. Van Geert (1994:153, Knight 2002) captures the essential position delightfully: 'In nature, it seems the shortest line between the two points is the wiggle'.

Although this brief and brutal characterisation of a beautiful theory goes just about far enough for my purposes here, it also represents about the limit of my understanding. My next step will be to read

Byrne's (1998) book on the relationship between this theory and the social sciences in order to get a better grip on the issues, but in the meantime it seems clear that it lays down challenges not only to positivist interpretations of human behaviour, but also to the sort of research that interests me.

There is a danger, for example, that in setting applied research against 'pure' research we seek to justify the former in terms of benefits delivered, and complexity theory serves as a reminder of the limits to this. Intervention, the theory claims, is not predictable and we must learn to live with indeterminacy. Avoidance of crude theory-application discourse (Clarke 1994) should not commit us to similarly crude assumptions about determinable intervention; instead we need to recognise that the process of engagement is an ongoing and dynamic one.

Participatory dimensions

Not long before sitting down to write this I was at a wonderfully productive conference on applied linguistics when one of the participants, with sad resignation, mentioned that there were moves afoot in the USA to replace the term with something that did not include the term 'applied'. No explanation was necessary for those of us working in the UK: despite the many abominations that have been wrought in the name of purity, the term 'pure' in the academic world serves not only as an ideal to be pursued but apparently also as an incentive to belittle research that is intimately involved with practice – as if the challenge of living up to the responsibilities of that engagement were not daunting enough in itself.

My position is not a disinterested one, but neither is it embittered. Working for the most part on the cusp of descriptive and interventionist research has spared me the full force of the academic world's disdain for 'applied' research, but as a TESOL practitioner I have seen enough of this to recognise its force. It has particular relevance in our profession, where there is a well-established tradition of action research (for example, Nunan 1992; Edge and Richards 1993; Wallace 1998; Burns 1999; Edge 2001a), and in the broader field of education, where McTaggart (1996:249) points to sales of 10,000 (excluding translations) for his and Kemmis's book, *The Action Research Planner* (Kemmis and McTaggart 1988). But how are such researchers to respond in the face of a continuing assault on the status of their work?

Since many TESOL researchers at this level will be involved in some way in teacher development and this may create opportunities for participatory research with the experienced researcher playing a key role, I will focus here specifically on participatory action research (PAR). What distinguishes this from action research is that the latter can be undertaken by individuals, whereas the orientation of PAR is explicitly collaborative (see Greenwood and Levin, 1998:203–14, for a useful discussion of related terms). My discussion will be organised on the basis of four key themes from a collection on this tradition (McTaggart 1997): research, participation, reflection and communitarian politics.

Research: above all else, PAR must meet the criteria for acceptable research: if it falls short in this respect, it builds on inadequate foundations and reinforces the misconception that action research is not 'real' research. Although PAR usually involves novice researchers, it must be more than mere tinkering, awareness raising or information gathering, and the challenge facing the coordinator is to build research development into team development.

Participation: 'Engagement in PAR' says Smith (1997:6), 'is a journey of development, permitting people to rediscover the realities of their lives and their potential capabilities'. This places considerable responsibility in the hands of the researchers coordinating a PAR project. Winter (1996:17) points to four practical problems they might face, three of which are particularly relevant here:

- the necessity of formulating a method of work that is productive but economical enough for practitioners to take on alongside their normal workload;
- the need to develop research techniques for small-scale investigation that will yield practical insights and at the same time satisfy the criteria for research validity;
- the challenge of making these techniques available to practitioners through building on the competencies they already possess.

In planning a PAR project these are considerations that must bear heavily on the decision-making process, particularly in matters of methodology.

Reflection as collective critique: a further challenge facing the coordinator in PAR projects is that of integrating individual and shared reflection into the research and development process. This, and the participatory dimension, are discussed in more detail below.

Communitarian politics: this is perhaps the most contentious aspect of PAR, largely because of the problematic relationship between research and politics. By its very nature, PAR thrives in and works towards conditions where egalitarian rights and just process prevail, so there will be contexts in which it represents a threat to the established order, but this does not mean that it is politically motivated:

> Participatory research is political because it is about people changing themselves and their circumstances and about informing change as it happens, but it is no more political than any other kind of research. (McTaggart 1997:7)

For a sense of perspective it is only necessary to reflect on the promiscuous potential of 'pure' research that refuses to acknowledge a moral dimension.

Providing leadership

Recently I read a posting from someone on the subject of a large-scale project he is developing with an international team. In it this gentle and generally sensitive individual made a comment about 'lurkers' who had yet to participate and seemed to suggest that they were a drag on the project. Some might have found the message hurtful, but I firmly believe that the force of it was not apparent to him when he wrote it, and in reflecting on the potential effects of his action I was acutely aware of all the new and very different skills demanded of researchers who also lead projects. This has particular resonance in PAR, where the sense of shared ownership is especially strong:

> In PAR, the consultant/facilitator acts less as a disciplinary expert and more as a coach in team building and in seeing to it that as much of the relevant expertise as possible from all over the organization is mobilized. (Whyte *et al.* 1991:40)

There will, of course, be differences between heading a team of professional researchers and a group of novice researchers, but the skills of team-building are essential in both contexts. Success will depend on the extent to which the leader can negotiate a situation in which all participants are able to share in – and feel valued as part of – the development of the research project.

Management is a tricky business at the best of times and my own experiences (Richards 2002) have probably been as varied as most people's, but research represents particularly sticky territory. The problem is simple: the more significant the progress in research terms, the greater the temptation simply to assume that all is well. Research is an exciting process and researchers naturally respond to this, but the involvement and enthusiasm of others cannot be taken for granted; it has to be worked for. This might explain Huberman's surprising – and very sobering – discovery (1992:131) that the least happy careers tended to be those of teachers heavily involved in school- or district-wide research projects. If they felt no sense of ownership of these projects, success could have been as much a cause for resentment as celebration.

The project leader must therefore be more than just a good manager of time and resources, important though these are; ways must also be found of integrating team-building into the research process itself. In addition, therefore, to establishing the foundations for effective communications (Martin 2001 provides excellent practical advice here on working with large groups), a discourse of collaboration has to be developed. Edge (2002) describes an approach to development founded on just this premise and provides guidance on developing the necessary skills. If teams can be built around these principles, the research dynamic and the group dynamic become mutually supportive, driving discovery across all relevant dimensions.

Connecting with theory

'Theory', says Becker (1993:221), 'is a dangerous, greedy animal, and we need to be alert to keep it in its cage'. But we have to get it into the cage in the first place, and Becker's warning has something of the 'First catch your tiger...' about it. Theory resists easy definition: a set of concepts? an interpretive framework? a predictive explanation? It all depends how you use it, and I raise it as my final issue because it is a constant source of concern to me in my own research. For the purposes of this discussion I concentrate on the core research value of theory: its worth as an explanatory phenomenon. It has other functions (Henstrand 1993, for example, points to its value in helping her work through her rôles as a researcher), but if it fails in this respect, data analysis never rises above the level of local description.

My position is in fact slightly different from that of Becker, though I suspect we are both getting at the same thing. I think theory is more dangerous in its cage than out and that somehow we need to find a way of living with it out in the wild without getting our heads bitten off. This means integrating it into our work as soon as we can naturally do so, and it means that we should not tack it on to either the beginning or the end of our inquiry. If we embrace it too early, we invite it to dominate our thinking and close off opportunities for discovery at a vital stage in the research process. If we seek it out only when all other work has been done, it will have lost its power to illuminate and energise our inquiry.

Despite the best efforts of grounded theorists, there remains no formula for timing or managing engagement with theory, beyond looking always for connections between what we discover through data gathering, analysis, reading and thinking. A perspective that might encourage such natural development, especially amongst TESOL researchers, is one that recognises the intimate link between language and theory. Agar (1996) has pointed to the relationship between developing a theory and developing a language of explanation, and implicit references are to be found in the literature, as in Seale's reference to a 'theoretical language grounded in the data' (1999b:89). The development of emerging discourse in TESOL teacher education has already been highlighted by Freeman (1991, 1992), and as language professionals this is something to which we can easily sensitise ourselves. One use of a research diary might therefore be to note and reflect on this dimension, tracing through it the ways in which theory seeps naturally into our own discourse as researchers.

This perspective links naturally with the proposal for establishing the discourse of collaboration proposed above, as well as reflecting the organic nature of the research process and its essentially pragmatic orientation. I end this level almost where it began, with a view of theory from a PAR perspective that implicitly recognises the dynamic relationship between local and global on which complexity theory is based:

> [T]he underlying pragmatism of research attempts to derive theoretical insights from ongoing participation in social life and make those insights directly applicable. While broader or more objective explanatory frameworks may be derived from the macro-analyses of small-scale projects, the focus for socially responsive educational research lies in the micro-analysis of events at the local level. (Stringer 1993:160)

Reading guide

General

Marshall, C. and Rossman, G.B. 1999. *Designing Qualitative Research* (3rd edn). Thousand Oaks, CA: Sage.

Now in its third edition (1999), this is a very readable general introduction that would work at any of the three levels, and although it also includes chapters on data collection and management this is not where its main focus lies. One of its most attractive features is the large number of vignettes distributed through the text, many of which are drawn from research in educational contexts.

Freeman, D. 1998. *Doing Teacher Research: From Inquiry to Understanding.* Pacific Grove, CA: Heinle & Heinle.

Freeman's 1998 book on teacher research has the advantage of being based in our area and, although it covers the whole of the research process, it has particularly useful things to say about ideas generation and focusing. It would work well at either Level 1 or Level 2 even though it seems at first sight to be more appropriate to the former.

Specific topics

Dealing with the literature

There is probably no better text for this than Hart (1998). As its subtitle, 'Releasing the Social Science Research Imagination', suggests, it covers more than merely doing a literature review, even extending as far as the research proposal. If the process of researching the literature is an area where you wish to develop your skills, you could try the author's more recent book, *Doing a Literature Search* (2001).

Writing a research proposal

Punch (2000) provides a useful introduction to this, pitched very much at Level 2. Apart from its clarity and brevity, what's especially useful about this book is the excellent example of a PhD qualitative proposal and references to other examples in the literature.

Morse's observation (1994:226) that the 'first principle of grantsmanship is to recognize that a good proposal is an argument' is worth pinning to the front page of any draft and gives a good flavour of her position. Dreher's (1994) advice on why grant applications fail also deserves serious respect. Though written from a nursing perspective, it is nevertheless generally applicable and serves as a useful guide to reviewing a first draft.

Practical planning issues

Marshall and Rossman (1999) have a very useful chapter on planning time and resources, which includes tables illustrating how these can be presented in a proposal.

Action research

Apart from the references in the text, Bob Dick's web pages, responding to the question 'You want to do an action research thesis?', are well worth checking out, especially for Level 1 researchers:

(http://www.scu.edu.au/schools/gcm/ar/art/arthesis/html).

6
Analysis and Representation

Preview

This chapter moves attention from the collection of the data towards the representation of what the researcher has been able to discover from it. The core of the chapter is concerned with data analysis and is designed to highlight the important considerations and approaches in this vital phase of qualitative research. It should enable you to approach analysis with confidence and with an appreciation of the challenges that face you, but no attempt is made to summarise the full range of possible approaches since this is a task that would go far beyond the scope of a chapter such as this. Table 6.1 highlights the issues that it addresses.

As with the last chapter, the informational core is in Level 2, accessible from either of the two other levels, which are also designed to stand alone. Level 1 summarises the characteristics of sound QI, while Level 3

Table 6.1 An overview of the levels presented in Chapter 6

Focus	Level 1: Discovery	Level 2: Analysis	Level 3: Interpretation
Issues of evidence	What counts as evidence?	Data and analysis	Issues of reliability and validity
The specific and the general	General and particular	Categorisation and coding	Generalisation
Making wider connections	Resonance	Techniques for seeing and representing	Connecting with theory
Representation	Going public	Building a picture	Writing and representation
Evaluation	Evaluating contributions	Assessing claims	Judging QI

addresses issues that have received considerable attention from leading writers in the field.

Level 1: discovery

What counts as evidence?

Provided that the aims of the investigation are clear and that the methods used to obtain and analyse data relate appropriately to these, the most important relationship is that between the claims that are made and the evidence used to support them. Perhaps the greatest danger facing a novice researcher is the desire to claim too much in order to live up to an exaggerated idea of what research can achieve. In fact, nearly all research is very modest indeed, playing an infinitesimally small but nevertheless valuable part in the advancement of our understanding. The aim, then, should be to share insights rather than to change the world.

In order to establish a basis for making claims, the researcher needs to interrogate all aspects of the investigation in order to reveal weaknesses or bias. Box 6.1 summarises the sorts of questions that might be asked, but it is worth drawing attention to two aspects that have received particular attention: triangulation and member validation. I have represented the former as a matter of perspectives since it is concerned with the extent to which the researcher is able to get a 'fix' on the data by approaching that data from different perspectives (for example, using observation and interviews). I have described the second as feedback in order to underline the fact that it involves more than simply asking members to confirm what we have discovered about them: as participants in the research process, they have a wider call on our attention and it may be worthwhile to involve them in other ways. This is particularly important in action research, where their involvement in implementation contributes to the validation of the research.

Box 6.1   Questions to ask about the research process

Sample Why was this appropriate?
Data collection How did I approach this and why?
  Have I established different perspectives?
  Were my records made as close to the event as possible?
  Are my records full? Is anything missing?

Analysis	What methods did I use and why?
	Did I seek feedback from those involved?
Interpretation	Is there any negative evidence?
	Can I explain things in a different way?
	How does this connect with other research?
	Does it feel right?
Representation	Have I honestly represented the data?
	Have I fairly represented all relevant positions?
	Am I helping readers to see things for themselves?

There are many ways in which research might go astray and the desire to explain exerts a powerful and not always benign attraction. One way to counter this is to set out to see whether we can use the data to produce an entirely different account than the one we have, and in doing so we should pay particular attention to any negative or disconfirming evidence. If we have gone wrong, it may well be the result of settling for a single explanation where a more subtle and complex account is called for. The social world, like education generally and language teaching in particular, is never straightforward.

General and particular

There is nothing more natural than to want our findings to be relevant to as many people as possible, but this is not the same thing as insisting that they should be 'generalisable'. Although it makes sense to ask whether something is generally true, or generally true given certain circumstances, this still leaves open the possibility that it may not be true for *this* group in *this* situation. And there is no merit in chasing after the impossible, especially if it distracts attention from what really matters. If we want others to regard our findings as relevant to themselves and their own professional circumstances, we must make sure that we provide them with a sufficiently rich account. This means giving as much attention as possible to making the *particular* real rather than trying to shore up claims with appeals to what might be general. The general is only interesting when it takes the form of concrete connections to other contexts, findings, experience, and so on.

Resonance

Resonance is not a word that is used in QI, at least outside the action research tradition, but it offers a way of orienting to research outcomes that extends beyond the narrow ambit of 'results'. A piece of advice to which Wolcott has returned on a number of occasions is that it is usually better to err on the side of description rather than interpretation. This is not to say that description alone is sufficient, rather to emphasise the importance of how well the lived world is represented, whether through extended narrative, sharply realised pictures or carefully wrought interactional analysis. Adequate representation matters because the meaning that readers find in the research will depend to a large extent on whether they are able to authenticate it in terms of their own experience.

Writers in the field of QI have revisited traditional views of how research is to be evaluated and have recognised the importance of concepts such as credibility and plausibility. Reason and Rowan (1981:241) have suggested that 'valid knowledge is a matter of relationship', and the forging of a relationship of understanding between researcher and audience is as important as that between researcher and researched, for by embedding reflection and interpretation in the lived world the researcher is able to create the conditions under which insights can 'ring true' in the minds of those who encounter them. Provided that readers can find through their own experience a means of connecting with the research, they will be open to share in the researcher's understandings and find instantiations of them in their own professional experience.

Going public

In order to achieve this, the researcher must 'go public', and for some the prospect of this is more daunting than any other aspect of the whole process. And yet there is a sense in which we do this all the time in sharing our experiences with those around us. The difference is really one of scale and expectation: allowing an account to emerge in a conversation with a group of two or three colleagues is very different from standing up in front of a room full of people who have come for the express purpose of listening to you. Going public frightens people because their conception of it is too grand – like most things, you have to build up gradually.

The ideal place to start is with colleagues. If you can find a way of sharing your findings with them, perhaps as part of a staff meeting, or even for half an hour at the end of the day, you have begun a process that's much the same whatever the audience. Try to provide them with a picture to which they can respond, and learn from their feedback. On the basis of this, write up a short piece and ask them to respond to it. If you feel this has gone well, you can consider a small local teachers' conference, preferably one where some of your colleagues can support you.

But when you begin the presentation try to remember how quickly the time went by when you first entered the classroom as a teacher. The desire to fill this time with as much information as possible can leave the audience dazed by a barrage of detail but with no clear idea of what it all amounts to. It's not a bad idea to think of your presentation as a story with illustrations and a point, because this will orient you naturally towards engagement with your audience. The following considerations might also be helpful:

- Make it real – set the scene.
- Don't present data – share it with the audience.
- Allow plenty of time to paint a picture – but keep data in reserve.
- Base claims on the data shown – the audience can respond to this.

Many conferences provide the opportunity to write up presentations for publication in the proceedings, but if this is not possible you should consider other outlets for your work. A newsletter might provide a gentle introduction to publishing, but you should also consider the journals you yourself read (including those online): you'll be familiar with the style and as a reader will have a grasp of what's expected. Seek the advice of at least a couple of colleagues or fellow researchers on early drafts – if they both agree that something needs changing, it probably does.

Evaluating contributions

Whether we are representing or responding to research, we inevitably engage in evaluation of it and I conclude this level with a list of five characteristics that I consider fundamental to sound qualitative research. I frame them from the researcher's perspective because this is where the buck stops.

1. Openness: by this I mean that the researcher should remain open to possible lines of investigation and interpretation, respecting the complexity of the social world and its workings. There's no such thing as a completely open mind, but we can at least avoid the mistake of setting out having already decided what we want to find – if you set out to discover something, you *will* discover it. We also need to remain open to different layers and dimensions of explanation, and reflect on our own procedures in trying to uncover these.

2. Inquisitiveness: inquisitiveness is a quality that can be developed through practice. If we bear in mind that it is our responsibility to continue to ask questions, even when the 'truth' seems to be staring us in the face, this will foster the spirit of openness and receptivity that are so important in research.

3. Honesty: this is essential in all research, but particularly relevant in QI. The issue is not one of deliberate deception (elaborate and artfully crafted deceit is hard to detect in any research, and clumsier attempts are quickly apparent to the practised reader) but of more subtle forms of distortion. Even the most earnest efforts can be undermined by a failure to identify personal bias in perceptions of actions or processes, or in the selection and presentation of evidence. Because research is not neutral, it is essential to establish a reflexive relationship with the process itself, constantly calling into question the assumptions that underlie the decisions we make. Honesty in research cannot be taken for granted but must be pursued through a constant examination of method and motive.

4. Authenticity: this refers to a record of experience, perception and interpretation that recognises the legitimate voice of not only the researcher but of all those involved in the research. It therefore depends on making available an honest and representative selection of the records of the research process such as transcripts, logs and fieldnotes.

5. Legitimacy: this is 'the process according to which data is transformed by its organisation into evidence for (or against, or in addition to, or separate from) a reasoned argument or stance' (Edge and Richards 1998a:352). It represents the researcher's attempt to forge demonstrable links between evidence and claim.

6. Transparency: the honest presentation of an authentic account demands transparency. Transparency of motive, method, procedure and presentation offers the reader legitimate access to the research process, and in so doing it establishes the conditions under which resonance is possible.

Level 2: analysis

Data and analysis

Analysis is neither a distinct stage nor a discrete process; it is something that is happening, in one form or another, throughout the whole research process. The relationship between data and analysis is therefore an intimate one, and like most intimate relationships it is also very complex, so that getting to the heart of things is a difficult and messy business. Like many other researchers, Ely (1991:87) is perfectly frank about its elusive quality: 'Establishing categories from qualitative data', she says, 'seems rather like a simultaneous left-brain right-brain exercise'. Hardly surprising, then, that it is not reducible to any convenient protocol:

Analysis is not about adhering to any one correct approach or set of right techniques; it is imaginative, artful, flexible, and reflexive. It should also be methodical, scholarly, and intellectually rigorous. (Coffey and Atkinson 1996:10)

Coffey and Atkinson do not go on to gloss their excellent characterisation, but Box 6.2 indicates what such a gloss might look like. It should serve as an essential reminder of how much qualitative analysis demands of the analyst.

Box 6.2	Essential qualities of qualitative analysis
Artful	Successful analysis is founded on good technique, but this in itself is not enough and there is always more to be learnt.
Imaginative	Analysis is not mechanistic. In order to penetrate beneath the surface of things, the researcher must make time to stand back and find different ways of seeing the data.
Flexible	Where necessary, the researcher must be prepared to find alternative approaches to organisational and interpretive challenges, which means not adhering too rigidly to any one approach.
Reflexive	In order to make the best of opportunities to advance the process of discovery, the researcher should keep in review the continually evolving interrelationship between data, analysis and interpretation.
Methodical	Although feeling and instinct may play an important part in all of the above, the researcher must decide on appropriate analytical methods and continue to reflect on these as they are applied.
Scholarly	Analysis should take place in the context of a wider understanding of the relevant literature, whether relating to analytical or interpretive issues.

Box 6.2   (Continued)

Intellectually rigorous	The researcher must be prepared to make available the workings of the analytical process and take account of all available evidence, including discrepant cases. This also means that the researcher has to resist the temptation to reduce everything to a single explanation.

Although there are distinctly different approaches to analysis, some of them quite specific in terms of procedure, all successful analysis of the data must combine – in different proportions according to its particular orientation – categorisation and interpretation. Wolcott identifies the relevant elements as follow (original italics):

Description addresses the question, 'What is going on here?' Data consists of observations made by the researcher and/or reported to the researcher by others.

Analysis addresses the identification of essential features and the systematic description of interrelationships among them – in short, how things work. In terms of stated objectives, analysis also may be employed evaluatively to address questions of why a system is not working or how it might be made to work 'better'.

Interpretation addresses processual questions of meanings and contexts: 'How does it all mean?' 'What is to be made of it all?' (Wolcott 1994:12)

Although the terminology might differ (Dey 1993:53, for example, describes an 'iterative spiral' of describing, classifying and connecting that enables the researcher to work from data to an account), other descriptions are in line with Wolcott's description. All draw attention to the importance of breaking down and recombining the data in an effort to build a picture that will respond to the aims of the research. Such an approach inevitably involves an element of categorisation and it is perhaps tempting to think that the systematic identification and application of appropriate categories to an adequate data set will, when linked to relevant concepts, establish the basis for interpretive claims. However, a sausage-machine approach of this sort does not reflect the analytic qualities identified in Box 6.2, nor does it capture the essentially explora-

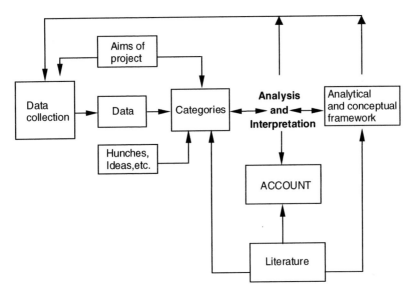

Figure 6.1   Aspects of analysis

tory nature of analysis. A much better way of understanding the process is as a means of sense-making in which the three elements identified by Wolcott interact.

Figure 6.1 represents one way of capturing the different elements in the process of analysis and their interactive relationship, although in truth the process is not susceptible to neat summary. The diagram reflects the centrality of categorisation as a link between interpretive positioning and data collection, suggesting a degree of interconnectivity that undermines any notion of analysis as a linear process that can be instantiated in a series of clearly specifiable steps.

A simpler way of seeing this is as an open process of breaking down the data set and exploring different ways of arranging it in order to promote a better understanding of what it represents. The principles of rearrangement will be derived from a variety of sources, including theoretical and conceptual links, analytic notes and ongoing analysis, while the ways in which data are displayed may themselves prompt further insights. Miles and Huberman's apothegm (1994:91) pays due respect to the importance of representation: 'You know what you display'.

It is with these considerations in mind that the operations in Box 6.3 should be approached. The elements here are not steps in analysis but activities that will involve the researcher in the search for clearer perception and better understanding. There is a strong case, argued persuasively by Silverman (e.g. 2000a), that analysis should begin as soon as possible. Early engagement with the data provides an excellent opportunity for the researcher to test out early decisions about, for example, the tradition within which they are working or the concepts they have brought into play. It also encourages valuable practice in writing analytic notes and allows the literature to be approached from the perspective of someone with analytical insights that need to be chewed over. More immediately, it exposes the researcher to the mechanics of coding and categorising that are so important in the analytic process.

Box 6.3   Aspects of analysis

Collect	Collect data
Think	Think about the data, the aims of the project, other research, etc. in order to inform categorisation
Categorise	Code the data in order to assign it to categories
Reflect	Add notes, comments, insights, etc.
Organise	Arrange the categories in different ways in order to see the data from different perspectives, looking for connections, relationships, patterns, themes, etc.
Connect	Link discoveries generated by these procedures to concepts and theories, seeking explanation and understanding
Collect	In the light of insights gained, collect further data

---

A note on research diaries

The case for a research diary was made earlier, but it deserves an extra mention in this context, not least because it can help to establish a critical distance from the process of analysis and perhaps reveal distortions that have crept in. One of the most pervasive of these arises from the need for signs of visible progress. In analysis, the most valuable investment to be made is in thinking time, where the researcher wrestles with complex lines of connection and interpretation or seizes on the creative insight that moves the research to a new plane of understanding. But all this is invisible – you can sit at a desk for hours and have nothing more to show for it than a full wastebasket and a headache. The fact that tomorrow's insight is built on today's apparent failure is a hard one to pin down, whereas a pile of transcripts or a collection of notes represent success, visible and undeniable. A diary can help bring otherwise hidden progress to light and provide a means of resisting the temptation to make what might be called 'paper progress' at the expense of genuine analytical development.

Categorisation and coding

Analysis depends on identifying key features and relationships in the data, something that is difficult if not impossible unless some degree of order is imposed. Categorisation tends to occupy a more central position in realist approaches than it does in more interpretive positions, but in one way or another it will feature in the development of a final account. The emphasis in what follows is therefore on procedures for developing effective categories.

Initial coding

In a sense, categorisation has already begun when the aims of the research are formulated because implicit in their selection is an element of conceptual identification. However, the categories here will be broad ones – something more refined must be developed. In practical terms the best starting point for this involves getting stuck into the data itself, coding it freely.

The advantage of such an approach is immediate engagement with the data, though it is also an excellent prescription for avoiding premature commitment to particular categories, always more likely when they are theoretically derived. This initial coding can be applied to a selection from the data set and continued for as long as it seems productive. The aim here is not to produce a set of categories but to generate a set of labels from which categories can be derived. Therefore, while it is possible to approach the task by coding paragraphs or even larger sections of data, the most productive approach is probably to work on a line-by-line basis, leaving any winnowing and sorting until later. Box 6.4 illustrates what such an open approach might produce. The labels here suggest possible lines of organisation, but they have not been assigned with this in mind: decisions about categorisation must wait until later.

Box 6.4   An example of initial detailed coding

We were much more into the	*teaching philosophy*
student as autonomous learner and their	*- student autonomy*
own, (sic) setting their own learning	*- learning styles*
styles, which was a thing that had been	

Box 6.4 (Continued)

laughed at, or <u>were</u> laughed at as concepts over there. So we just felt that was terrific that <u>nobody</u> was going to hold us back on the teaching side. We could let all our ideas free and we could just experiment for a bit. We didn't even have to decide on a style that we went along with, we just had all the freedom in the world.

team
- prior negative experience
- shared feelings
- T freedom in CR important
teaching
- open ideas
- experimentation
- individual freedom
- no agreed style

Category types

A rough initial coding along these lines will generate a number of possible categories, but the process of developing categories that will be employed to analytical effect involves standing back and assessing ways in which the data might be organised. Purpose is important. 'We split categories in a search for greater resolution and detail', says Dey (1993:139), 'and splice them a search for greater integration and scope'. At an early stage, then, emphasis is likely to fall on ensuring adequate and precise coverage, leaving issues of organisation largely in the background, but the coding itself will suggest a number of relevant categories and, in all likelihood, ways in which these might be grouped, thus moving the process naturally into its next phase. Although the data themselves provide the main resource for categorisation, this might also be informed by a range of other sources including memos, notes, observations, the theoretical context, and ideas from reading. Careful analysis and reflection, perhaps interspersed with wilder and freer bursts of ideas generation, will move the researcher towards a position where more systematic organisation can be attempted.

There are various techniques that can be used for the purposes of organisation. Filing cards, scissors, glue and coloured pens have provided the traditional approach to coding and categorising, offering the opportunity for separating, sorting and recombining, but I know of at least one researcher whose walls were decorated from floor to ceiling with a moving jigsaw of cards and bits of paper. My own preference is for pages from a reporter's notebook (I always feel more reluctant to tear up file cards), highlighters, a huge packet of coloured fine markers and carpet space. What matters most is not so much the niceties of technique as finding a method that will allow relationships to be noticed and alternative arrangements to be tried and assessed.

An alternative to these physical approaches is the use of a computer programme, and the design of such programmes has become increasingly sophisticated. The advantages and disadvantages of using these have been widely discussed and the Reading Guide at the end of this chapter includes advice on brief introductions to the programmes available. The only criterion that really matters, however, is whether the individual researcher finds that they offer the best way of seeing and working the data. It may be, for example, that the sorting procedures already available on standard word processing packages will be adequate when combined with one of the above approaches using printed out text. It all depends on how well you feel that you are *connecting* with the data, and that's pretty much a matter of feeling. With this in mind, Wolcott's emphasis on the physicality of the process is worth noting:

> I grew accustomed to putting data on 5×8 papers easily typed or handwritten, easily stored, and easily sorted. My stacks of cards or papes may seem archaic in this computer age, but I describe them to help you visualize processes partly hidden by technology. I encourage students engaging in fieldwork exercises to do the same thing, manually manipulating actual bits rather than electronic bytes to get a physical feel for what they are trying to accomplish. (Wolcott 2001:43)

Some attention also needs to be given to the specification of categories and the criteria that will determine what is excluded and what excluded. Figure 6.2 summarises the features of an effective category and also points to connections with the bigger project. Asking questions about particular categories may raise larger questions about the conceptual dimensions of the analysis and may also draw attention to different category types, for example those which are descriptive, such as *teacher* and *lesson* and those which are conceptual, such as *conflict* and *involvement* (Mason 1994). Developing analysis, evolving theory and further data collection will all bear on the process of categorisation as it develops through the interpretive and representational journey.

Two approaches to analysis

Perhaps the best known approach to analysis is offered by *grounded theory*, an analytical tradition that draws strength from its willingness to specify in detail how the process of coding and analysis can be managed. The fact that its originators, Glaser and Strauss, eventually disagreed

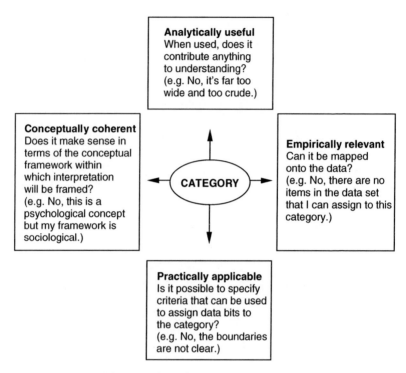

Figure 6.2   Essential features of an adequate category

about the extent to which this process can be pinned down to a specific set of procedures should not obscure the important contribution it has made to the field of QI, especially through its exploration of the relationship between data gathering and theory generation.

Strauss and Corbin (1998:101) accept an element of artificiality in their approach but justify it in practical terms: 'Breaking the analytic process down is an artificial but necessary task because analysts must understand the logic that lies behind analysis'. The process involves at its core three distinct types of coding, designed to open up inquiry and move it towards interpretation:

- *Open coding*   This is the process of breaking down the data for the purpose of categorising, conceptualising and comparing.
- *Axial coding*   This concentrates on organising the data, based on the 'axis' of a category. It involves relating categories to subcategories and making connections between categories.

- *Selective coding*   At this stage a central category (or explanatory concept) is identified, in terms of which other categories can be refined and integrated.

The relationship between coding, analysis and data collection can be understood in terms of the key concept of theoretical sampling:

> Theoretical sampling is the process of data collection for generating theory whereby the analyst jointly collects, codes and analyzes his data and decides what data to collect next and where to find them, in order to develop his theory as it emerges. The process of data collection is controlled by the emerging theory. (Glaser and Strauss 1967:45)

It's useful to compare the development of explanations characteristic of this approach with one that begins with an explanation which is then tested. *Analytic induction* starts with a definition of a phenomenon to be explained and the formulation of a hypothesis which is then checked against the data. If any negative (deviant) cases are found, either the phenomenon is redefined in order to exclude the case or the hypothesis is reformulated and checked once more against the data. The aim is to repeat these steps until the researcher identifies a hypothesis that accounts for all cases. The process is a rigorous one and more constrained in terms of procedure than the broadly integrated approach recommended here, but it does have an important contribution to make in the procedures for assessing analysis considered below.

Techniques for seeing and representing

Most of us have had the experience of struggling almost to the point of despair to grasp something, then someone else breezes into the room and lights on a solution as though it were the most obvious thing in the world. The nature of qualitative data analysis, with its emphasis on immersion in the data (Borkan 1999), means that this sort of situation is very likely to arise – but usually without the prospect of a helpful outsider. This puts the onus on the researcher to create situations that make outsider perspectives possible.

One way of shifting perspective is simply to stand back and look for different things in the data. The most obvious approach is to look for patterns and follow threads, trying to get a sense of an emerging picture, but individual features can also prompt interesting discoveries. For example, if anything stands out, lines of connection can be explored in order to account for this and relate it to other data; and the same applies to striking contrasts and contradictions. A particularly rewarding exercise is to look for stories in the data. How do actors construct these? What resources do they draw on? Are there common narrative threads or themes in different stories and what do these reveal about shared or contrasting beliefs or assumptions? This might be particularly fruitful in TESOL, a profession that brings together people from different educational and cultural backgrounds.

In addition to these core methods, a variety of other techniques can be used. For example, thinking metaphorically can shift perceptions quite radically or suggest new ways of thinking about the data. An example of how metaphorical thinking might suggest new ways of looking at the data is provided in Box 6.5, which also indicates ways in which diagrams might be exploited.

Box 6.5   Two approaches to working the data

1. Metaphors for analysis

- Do the jigsaw puzzle (Dey 1993:40)
- Follow the threads
- Rearrange the boxes
- Find the nuggets
- Trace the tree

2. Some uses for diagrams

- Family connections/relationships
- Chronological patterns
- Causal links
- Processes
- Conceptual frames

As coding and categorising develops, it's useful to build in analytical notes or memos, drawing attention to points that might be relevant to the analysis. These might range from a word or two noting an idea, connection or possible category, to an extended elaboration of an interpretive position. Box 6.6 illustrates how coding (the areas in bold) can be combined with memos linking this text to others, to the literature and to the developing analysis. If analytic memos of this sort are typed up and kept on a computer, searching for links can be very straightforward.

Box 6.6   Example of notes on transcripts

Transcript	Memos
I suppose I was a bit nervous but I think I always felt that it **wasn't quite the same as going**	*EFL v Mainstream teaching* *This is emerging as a significant category.* *Explore links with*

into an <u>English</u> classroom and teaching English, or anything, because you always hold the trump card. Maybe this still holds true today. **You walk into a classroom and it's <u>your</u> language, it's not <u>their</u>** language...So you're actually not laying yourself on the <u>line</u> to the same extent....Looking back on it now, I think I had no <u>idea</u> what I was doing....It was a major revelation to me when I discovered that they didn't have much idea about **what I now <u>know</u> are called phrasal verbs or multi-word verbs.** I actually thought they were prepositions at the time. I seem to remember, 'This is a preposition problem.' And I started typing out lists from my head of what I thought were common. If I look back at them now I'd probably realise that it was actually quite a mish-mash and they weren't all the same thing at <u>all</u>...But in a sense that didn't matter.'... That's **one of the satisfactions is working out problems and a way of teaching.**

---

discipline / interaction / knowledge issues.

Views of language
Huberman leitmotif of career entry: 'survival and discovery' – 'continuous trial and error,
preoccupation with oneself and one's adequacy...' (1989:349). C.f. Louise's search for a style (4.3).

Linguistic knowledge
Thought: No evidence so far of Britzman's second cultural myth, that teachers are 'born' into the profession and that social factors and institutional context are relatively unimportant (1986:451).

Approaches to teaching
'working things out' still a key characteristic of H's style (4.6).

Building a picture

As category development moves forward through a process of conceptual, analytical and theoretical refinement, an explanatory picture begins to emerge. This is a difficult process to capture, but grounded theory proposes two terms that illuminate the nature of the progress involved. The first is *constant comparison*, representing the process by which connections between data and conceptualisation are maintained, leading

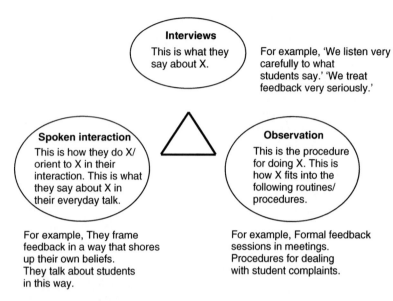

Figure 6.3   Bringing together different data sources

to the emergence of theoretical elaboration. The second, *theoretical saturation*, captures the point that is eventually reached where any new data added to a particular category throws no new light on the relevant concepts (Glaser and Strauss 1967).

Provided that enough care has been expended on this process of development, the building blocks of an adequate account – core concepts informing a sufficiently extensive, well-organised data set – will already be in place, although it may also be necessary to frame these in terms of broader (sometimes called *formal* or *grand*) theory. When developing the account, it may also be useful to go back to the original research design to consider how the products of different methods might be most effectively brought together. Figure 6.3 illustrates this in terms of the three data sources featured in this book.

TESOL professionals will probably find the act of writing itself less challenging than most, though establishing a solid relationship between evidence and claims is always demanding. The organisation of the text will follow a pattern not dissimilar to that of the proposal outlined in the previous chapter, at least as far as the early chapters (introduction, contextualisation/literature review, methodology) are concerned, but careful consideration will need to be given to the way that the analysis and discussion are developed. In some cases description and interpretation might effectively be separated, while in other texts organisation along thematic lines might be more appropriate. Much depends on finding a form of organisation and display that brings out the relationship between the conceptual framework and the descriptive foundations of the study. The textual achievement of this will depend in part on the inclusion of features typical of the genre of QI theses or books. Box 6.7 provides examples of these.

Box 6.7 Some features of the written account

In addition to the information and argument developed through the text itself, there will also be other elements that can contribute to the account as a whole. These may take the following forms:

Claims	Apart from the claims embedded in the unfolding argument, it can also be useful to summarise claims or key observations and place these strategically as a means of orienting the reader to the overall structure or themes of the account.
Quotations	These may be from fieldnotes, interviews, transcripts, research diary, the literature, etc. It's helpful if different sources can be distinguished by format.
Analysis/Commentary	Transcripts usually need to be accompanied by specific analysis, while other data sources can often benefit from interpretive commentary
Vignettes/Narratives	Even though the account may not be based on narratives, short narrative vignettes or, in some cases, longer narrative exposition can help the reader get a fix on important aspects of the setting.
Photographs/Documents	Carefully selected photographs or copies of documents can often convey more than extended text, especially if they are accompanied by interpretive comment.

Box 6.7 (Continued)	
Tables, figures, etc.	These can represent the most efficient means of summarising information or relationships. Remember, too, that qualitative research can include some quantification.
Other	Depending on circumstances, other elements may be included, such as video or audio tapes, poems, or (dramatic) dialogue.

Assessing claims

There are no guarantees that an analysis will hold water, but there are checks that can be made for major flaws in construction. In this section, in order to highlight where attention should fall when assessing claims, I identify three areas where weaknesses might emerge.

Human

So much in QI depends on the human dimension that it seems inappropriate to single this out as a category in itself, but we must always be on the lookout for researcher effects. There are also specific weaknesses to which we might be prone, of which the following are typical.

The inclination to tidy up: a clear-cut case is superficially very attractive, but if it depends on ignoring or smoothing over tiny pieces of evidence that do not fit, the really interesting connections and insights may have been missed. Life is rarely neat and tidy, so resist the temptation to package it up too tightly.

The desire to explain everything: the desire to understand and explain is what drives researchers, but this does not mean that everything can be explained. It is sometimes necessary to acknowledge the inexplicable and it is always necessary to recognise that where explanation is possible it is rarely simple.

Susceptibility to first impressions: initial impressions are usually powerful ones, while those that emerge tentatively from long hours of struggle and frustration can seem grey and tired. However, in assessing their relative importance, any feelings arising from the context of discovery must be set aside.

Evidentiary

Our claims will be judged on the extent to which we are able to support them with adequate evidence that is fairly representative of our data set. This means that we need to ensure that there is sufficient evidence and sufficient *kinds* of evidence. It also means that the link between the evidence we present and the interpretations we derive from that evidence must be robust. Erickson (1986:140) identifies five types of flaw we should be on the look-out for:

1. Inadequate amounts of evidence.
2. Inadequate variety in kinds of evidence.
3. Faulty interpretive status of evidence.
4. Inadequate disconfirming evidence.
5. Inadequate discrepant case analysis.

Negative evidence presents a particular challenge. It is never legitimate to sweep this under the carpet, but it may be acceptable to recognise it and perhaps even speculate explicitly as to why it appears. First, though, it should be given due respect in the analytical process. Figure 6.4 represents an approach characteristic of analytic induction (though the emphasis here would be on cases), but one that usefully directs attention to the interpretive context.

Peräkyla (1997), applying the work of Clayman and Maynard (1994) to the analysis of conversation, discusses three possible responses to deviant cases: examples where participants orient to the unusualness of the instance, in which case they offer further support for the analyst's position; those that cannot be discounted and therefore require modification

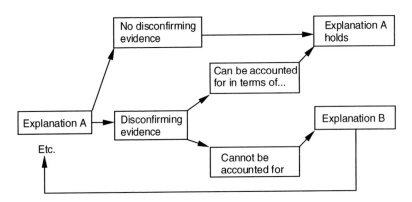

Figure 6.4 An approach to disconfirming evidence

of the analyst's position; cases that are demonstrably exceptional and can be accepted as such. Seale (1999a:73–86) also provides a useful general discussion of the issue of negative instances.

Explanatory

Since Occam first wielded his Razor, the explanation that can account for most, with the least multiplication of parts, has had the strongest claim on our attention. If we can explain a great deal with simplicity and elegance, so much the better, but in QI we need to subject our explanations to the same close attention as we lavish on our data – which means we sometimes have to settle for complexity and awkwardness.

As with all aspects of QI, there are no easy rules that can be used to operationalise assessment; so much depends on the sensitivity, application, attention and fundamental integrity of the assessor. And where we find something that does not fit, we should remember Miller and Crabtree's (1999:142) recommendation: 'Celebrate anomalies. They are the windows to insight'.

Level 3: interpretation

Reliability and validity

When it comes to assessing the value of QI, there is nothing more fundamental than what these two terms represent. Kirk and Miller capture their flavour as traditionally understood:

> A thermometer that shows the same reading of 82 degrees each time it is plunged into boiling water gives a reliable measurement. A second thermometer might give readings over a series of measurements that vary from around 100 degrees. The second thermometer would be unreliable but relatively valid, whereas the first would be invalid but perfectly reliable. (1986:19)

Unfortunately, as with so much else in QI, the waters are muddied by the confluence of positivist concepts and naturalistic concerns. Between outright rejection of such terms as products of an inappropriate paradigm (for example, Lincoln and Guba 1985; Wolcott 1990) and their appropriation in order to claim evidential parity with the natural sciences (for example, Hammersley 1990; Morse 1999) lies a range of fecund alternatives generating connections that reach into all aspects of QI. In this section I sandwich a handful of representative positions between a brief gloss on Kirk and Miller's example and a list of recommendations for tackling the important issue of validity.

Validity might be summed up, in Kirk and Miller's terms, as a matter of making sure our reading is in line with the way things are. From a QI perspective we might ask how we can be sure that our representations correspond to the phenomena we have encountered. Or, more practically, what we have missed in our analysis/interpretation. These are matters of *interpretation*.

Kirk and Miller's example highlights the fact that reliability is a matter of being able to depend on getting the same reading if we follow the same procedures. We will want to know, in QI, how we can be sure that our representations of the data are consistent. How tough are our procedures for collecting and categorising the data? These are fundamentally matters of *procedure*.

A common misconception about QI is that it's a fairly sloppy business involving little more than taking up a position and supplying a few well-chosen examples to to lend it support. Silverman suggests (1993:153) that some published qualitative research does reflect such 'anecdotalism', so it is vitally important that concerns of validity and reliability are not swept aside.

Developing the model

The traditional model of reliability and validity has been glossed along realist lines (see, for example, Le Compte and Goetz 1992), but validity in particular has been developed in various ways. Meadows and Morse (2001), for example, recast its primary concerns along the lines of a movement from verification (relating to strategies of inquiry), through validation (evaluation within the project in terms of auditing and so on) to validity (outcomes, externally judged). However, one of the most illuminating categorisations is offered by Maxwell (1992), who proposes five aspects, three of which seem particularly helpful (the gloss is mine):

- *Descriptive validity*: are descriptions accurate, complete, etc.?
- *Interpretive validity*: are interpretations adequately grounded in participants' perspectives?
- *Theoretical validity*: are concepts coherent and legitimately applied to the phenomena and do the relationships among the concepts hold water?

Maxwell also includes generalisability (the possibility of extension to other settings – this is considered as a separate issue in the next section) and evaluative validity (judgements of the value of participants' actions), which are less central and more contentious, but the three core elements provide a useful framework for developing claims in QI.

Alternative formulations

Other approaches have rejected realist terminology altogether and developed instead alternative formulations based on the central concerns of QI. Perhaps the best-known position is that developed by Lincoln and Guba, who emphasise the importance of trustworthiness (1985:290): 'How can an inquirer persuade his or her audiences (including self) that the findings of an inquiry are worth paying attention to, worth taking account of?' They develop a set of relevant naturalistic criteria, relating these to the conceptual foundations of their rationalist alternatives (289–331). These criteria can be glossed along similar lines to Maxwell's (the rationalist equivalent appears in square brackets):

- *Credibility* [internal validity] depends on evidence of long-term exposure to the context being studied and the adequacy of data collected (use of different methods, etc.).
- *Transferability* [external validity] depends on a richness of description and interpretation that makes a particular case interesting and relevant to those in other situations.
- *Dependability* [reliability] and *confirmability* [objectivity] are to be assessed in terms of the documentation of research design, data, analysis, reflection, and so on, so that the researcher's decisions are open to others.

Edge and Richards (1998a) discuss these issues in the context of research in TESOL, developing a description of what constitutes adequate warrant for claims in QI. They suggest that responses must address three core issues: *position*, referring to where the researcher locates themself in terms of paradigm and tradition, *voice*, or the extent to which 'the research allow[s] people among whom it is taking place to speak their own thoughts in terms meaningful to themselves' (1998:340), and *representation*, which relates to the forms of discourse used by the researcher. They argue that in responding to these, researchers may extend established traditions, adopt alternative stances within them, or develop their own position. For the authors, authentication and legitimation have particular salience, embracing in their different dimensions the considerations that will allow corroboration and endorsement by peers.

Validity checks

There are no agreed procedures for validity checks, though three techniques (summarised in Box 6.8) feature in most approaches. Grounded Theory and Analytic Induction make odd bedfellows, but each makes a contribution: the constant comparative method of the former informs an approach that draws attention to the need constantly to review and if necessary revise previous categorisations in the light of new ones, while the search for negative evidence is characteristic of the latter. Member validation, which Lincoln and Guba consider to be a core check, is unlikely to be adequate on its own (some writers have challenged the assumption that members' views are more reliable than those of researchers), but it provides an invaluable extra perspective.

Box 6.8 Three key validity checks	
Member validation	Seek views of members on accuracy of data gathered, descriptions, or even interpretations
Constant comparison	Keep comparing codings with other codings and classifications, looking for new relationships, properties, etc.
Negative evidence	Seek out negative evidence/cases and assess their relevance to interpretations

In addition to these core methods, there is a variety of additional checks that might be employed. For example, Silverman (2000a) advocates a 'refutability principle' where the data are used in an attempt to refute original assumptions, while Lincoln and Guba (1985) recommend using peer debriefing for additional critical purchase. In fact, any method that challenges or checks the robustness of the data or the process of analysis and interpretation in new ways is worthy of consideration. As ever, what matters most is the researcher's commitment to producing an account that will bear close and critical scrutiny.

Generalisability

External validity in the form of generalisability has attracted the attention of a number of qualitative researchers. Between the extremes of denying that generalisation is possible (for example, Lincoln and Guba 1985) and claiming that it as 'necessary and inevitable' (Williams 2002:138) lies a middle ground that argues for its significance in terms of the claims we might make (for example, Gomm *et al.* 2000b) or the ways in which we might regard it (for example, Schofield 1990). In this section I briefly review some of the responses that have been made to this issue and draw attention to important practical considerations, beginning with a distinction that is sometimes drawn between idiographic and nomothetic approaches (Box 6.9). This seems to me to be a useful means of highlighting two very different positions (see Johnson 1997 for further discussion).

Box 6.9 Idiographic and nomothetic			
	Focus	Orientation	Concern
Idiographic	Particular	Meaning	Representation
Nomothetic	General	Explanation	Representativeness

There is no debate about the fact that, if it is to be worth its salt, research must have relevance to others outside the setting(s) with which it is concerned; the issue at stake is the extent to which it makes sense to think of this in terms generalisation. For some this concept, derived from the natural sciences, should be set aside and replaced with an alternative approach reflecting the richly contextualised nature of QI. Lincoln and Guba, for example, propose *transferability* as a more appropriate term. Others disagree, arguing that in practice generalisation is very common and not as restrictive as its opponents suggest. They may not deny that some cases have intrinsic relevance (for example, Gomm *et al.* 2000b), but claim that these are a small minority and that in most research the typicality or otherwise of the situation is a key issue.

One response to the problem lies in seeking to qualify the nature of generalisation in some way (Box 6.10 identifies three responses to this), but so far none of the proposed alternatives has won general acceptance and many have been criticised on practical (Gomm *et al.* 2000b) or conceptual (for example, Hammersley 2001) grounds. Cruder attempts to sidestep the issue, for example by claiming that QI offers 'insights' rather than generalisations, fail to avoid the question of how generally relevant these insights might be (Heap 1995).

Box 6.10 Proposed generalisation types for QI		
Type	Proponent	Characterisation
Naturalistic	Stake 1995	'conclusions arrived at through personal engagement in life's affairs or by vicarious experience so well

		constructed that the person feels as if it happened to themselves' (p. 85)
Fuzzy	Bassey 1999, 2001	'the kind of statement which makes no absolute claim to knowledge, but hedges its claim with uncertainties' (1999:120)
Moderatum	Williams 2002	'aspects of a situation can be seen to be instances of a broader recognizable set of features' (p. 131)

An alternative approach, avoiding the problems associated with such formulations, is to emphasise the importance of the particular, to claim, for example, that '[t]he real business of case study is particularization, not generalization' (Stake 1995:8), or to argue the case for 'the ethnography of the particular' where the focus is on the individual rather than the group (Abu-Lughod 1991:154). This is a route that at least some researchers in TESOL have taken (for example, Clarke 1995). Lincoln and Guba (1985) have suggested that here the burden of responsibility is on the user of the research, an exaggeration perhaps, but an interesting one. The success of such research will certainly depend on the extent to which it allows readers to *engage* with the situation described and interpretations offered in terms of their own contextualised experience and its power is more likely to be *transformative* than merely persuasive.

The danger, I think, of worrying too much about how generalisable a particular case might be is that it is all too easy to take our eye off the ball: in seeking the reassurance of the general, we miss the eloquence of the particular. Much depends on the nature of the project, but I believe that it is possible to learn from both positions and therefore end by proposing three rules that we should observe whatever our orientation (Box 6.11).

Box 6.11   Before thinking about generalising

Think about the sample	Is this situation typical and if so how? Is it exceptional and if so why?
Aim for thick description	Is the description sufficiently detailed and richly articulated to allow readers to respond to it in terms of their own experience?

Box 6.11 (Continued)	
Look for connections	Are there connections with other research, other situations, other cases, that we can usefully point to?

Connecting with theory

The relationship between the development of categories and the emergence of theory was discussed in the previous chapter, so I will not dwell on it here, but as Walford (2001:147) suggests, '[t]here is far too much mystique about theory'. Some clarity is called for. My own research suggests that teachers frequently make connections with theory but avoid doing so explicitly, opting instead for public scepticism (Richards 1999a), and while it would be foolish to deny the importance of connecting with theory in QI, I admit that to a certain extent I share their suspicion. Much of the problem, I think, has to do with a tendency to see theory in terms of *grand theory* and to demand of it a level and range of explanatory power far beyond what it will bear. For that reason, I recommend Walford's proposal of *middle-range theory* as the most appropriate for work in QI.

Walford (2001:148) identifies *grand theory* as a way of interpreting the world (Marxism would be a good example) and *micro-theory* as 'testable propositions that attempt to attribute causality to particular phenomenon (*sic*)'. Between these two lies *middle-range theory*, 'where a set of concepts is used to define, describe and suggest possible explanations for some phenomenon or activities' (ibid.). Such theories can stand alone but may also connect to the other two levels and are linked to model building. Models, Walford argues, are ways of simplifying and representing complex phenomena, human constructs that aid understanding.

This straightforward view of theory fits in well with the approach of grounded theory, where theories are developed from concepts arising out of the data as the process of categorisation and constant comparison develops. A recognition of this intimate connection between concepts and theory does not commit us to the analytical canons of grounded theory but it does reflect an important relationship: as researchers we bring our need to explain, connect and understand to our treatment of the data and it is through the interaction of thought and evidence that concepts emerge, models are constructed and theories discovered or developed. 'Theorising', as Woods (1996:70) observes, 'begins from the very first day of fieldwork with the identification of possibly significant events or words'. Theory, then, is not something that stands apart from the data or the process of analysis, it represents a level of explanation that allows us to make important connections among elements in the data and between our findings and others in the field.

Writing and representation

The representation of QI is no less contentious than issues of reliability and validity, reflecting significant changes over the past quarter of a century. As with all processes of change, the sources and confluences resist easy mapping, but particularly significant was the rejection of the researcher as 'knower' and the impact of postmodern views of textuality. The problematising of the privileged authorial voice and a blurring of genres led eventually to what Denzin and Lincoln (1994b) describe as a crisis of representation, in the wake of which the representational options for qualitative researchers continue to multiply. The inexperienced researcher can easily become disorientated by the contiguity of traditional textual forms and experimental genres within the same journal, so the aim of this section will be to introduce two very different positions, identify the qualities that characterise sound textual practice in QI, and indicate where overviews of the alternatives are to be found.

The most convenient way of sampling the debate is to be found in Bryman (2001b), where papers by Tyler (1986/2001) and Hammersley (1993/2001) represent opposing viewpoints. For Tyler, postmodern ethnographies are dialogic, fragmentary productions, collaboratively evolved between reader and writer. Their effect is therapeutic, the outcome of 'a journey apart into strange lands with occult practices – into the heart of darkness' (ibid., p. 315). Hammersley regards this anti-realist stance, which replaces validity as a criteria for assessment with 'aesthetic and/or instrumental criteria' (2001:330), as deceptive because of the way it 'hides' the presence of the researcher and potentially destructive because, if no position is privileged, any position has claims on acceptability. Hammersley accepts that texts are rhetorically constructed, but nevertheless insists that they can reasonably claim to represent reality, provided that they explicitly recognise their status as fallible constructions of this reality.

Conceptually, these two positions are antithetic and will have different views of the truth value of any ethnographic text. However, Hammersley's stance does not rule out what he describes as 'experimental' rhetoric, while the conventional construction of Tyler's own text implicitly recognises this as a valid form, at least in writing *about* ethnography. While rapprochement is unlikely, all writers seem to agree that good ethnography depends on good, involving writing, whatever form it might take – and the same might be said of QI in general. Research texts are not literary texts precisely because of the particularity of their reference: a specified experiential world the means of access to which has been the subject of all the chapters leading up to this point. Ultimately, there is more at stake than intertextual authority or creative integrity, and the representation of QI must struggle with the best means of establishing productive engagement with the lived world. Writing, as Richardson points out, is 'a method of inquiry . . . a research practice through which we can investigate how we construct the world, ourselves, and others' (2000:924). A tall order, and rightly so.

In all writing we grow through our own struggles and in the light of the work of others. How we explore the intimacy of reading and writing is an individual matter, but we should at least acquaint ourselves with the range of what is possible. For example, Richardson's (2000) listing of the species of CAP ('Creative Analytic Practices') ethnography is eloquent in itself and encourages exploration, while Tedlock's narrower focus (2000) allows her to capture the flavour of a more defined selection. As an example of open-mindedness, this extract from a review of a paper submitted for publication shows appreciation of something written within a genre different from the one with which the reviewer is familiar:

> It is a product of the 'literary turn', reflective, poetic, exploring feel-ings and relationships, and modes of representation. The strength is in the expression. . . . Some may consider the paper a self-indulgence, and in a way it is. But the point is, does it have relevance for others, and does it deal with a worthy subject? I would say incontrovertibly 'yes'. . . . (Woods 1999:127)

Judging qualitative inquiry

The different positions that have featured in the discussion so far at this level find their most vehement, and often most intractable, expression in the field of criteriology:

> The word criteria itself is a term that separates modernists from post-modernists, foundationalists from antifoundationalists, empiricists from interpretivists, and scientists from artists. It is not that one side thinks judgments have to be made and the other side does not. Both agree that inevitably they make choices about what is good, what is useful, and what is not. The difference is that one side believes that 'objective' methods and procedures can be applied to determine the

choices we make, whereas the other side believes that these choices are ultimately and inextricably tied to our values and our subjectivities. (Bochner 2000:266)

It's not necessary to look far to find lists of relevant criteria and attempts to make the contents commensurate with those in other lists as part of a 'constant search' (Garratt and Hodkinson 1998:515) for inclusivity. 'The urge to generate criteria for judging good quality studies', observes Seale (1999a:467), 'seems irrepressible'. It would be pointless, then, to offer yet another table of equivalences, especially since the key issues have already been touched in the above sections. However, the following four perspectives provide a summary of relevant practical considerations.

1. Aspects: there are three aspects that evaluation of QI must embrace: process, product and position. *Process* aspects are those that relate to the collection and analysis of the data, and hence address issues of validity or credibility. *Product* is concerned with the presentation of the research: not just the quality of the writing as an act (see Lincoln and Guba 1990 for proposals of relevant criteria) and an adequate representation of the inquiry, but also its contribution to understanding. This addresses issues of representation and generalisability/transferability. Finally, *position* embraces matters relating to the standpoint of the writer, including the moral dimension. Particularly complex in this respect are issues of reflexivity (for a recent discussion, see Finlay 2002) and authenticity (for an accessible overview of relevant dimensions, see Manning 1997).

2. General criteria: the selection of any single set of criteria from the many available must be to some extent subjective, but the five general standards for educational research proposed by Howe and Eisenhart (1990) seem to me to be sufficiently broad to accommodate most if not all positions and yet precise enough to serve as a practical framework for judgement. They can be summarised very briefly as follows:

1. data collection and analysis techniques must be appropriate to and driven by the research question;
2. these techniques must be competently applied;
3. 'studies must be judged against a background of existent knowledge' (1990:7) and aspects of the researcher's subjectivity must be made explicit;
4. overall warrant for any claims must be established and will include consideration of disconfirming evidence and justification for the theoretical position; and

5. the researcher must be able to demonstrate internal and external
    value. The former relates to research ethics and the latter to the
    relevance of the research to educational practice as well as its acces-
    sibility to actors in the relevant setting and to other researchers.

3. The TESOL context: in a very useful discussion of evaluative criteria
proposed for qualitative research in our field, Lazaraton (2001) identified four easily accessible guides: one referring to QI in general
(Johnson 1992), one from a CA perspective (Markee 2000), and two
from relevant journals (*TESOL Quarterly* 2000, 34(4):805–6) and
Language Learning and Technology (http://llt.msu.edu/resguide.html).
To this I would add Brumfit and Mitchell's 1989 criteria for compe-
tent classroom research, which, although not focused specifically on QI,
is certainly relevant. A more general context for evaluating QI in TESOL is
provided by Edge and Richards (1998a), discussed briefly above.

4. A reviewer's perspective: there is a sense in which no research project is
truly complete unless its outcomes have been made public, so the evaluation of our own writings can benefit from a consideration of the perspective of those who are in a position to judge them. Perhaps the most
valuable approach is via the examination of reviewers' reports, and
Woods' examples (1999) provide a very useful sample. Box 6.12 summarises some of the typical weaknesses to be found in draft papers,
accompanied by (slightly amended) extracts from my own reviews of
failed submissions.

Box 6.12   Some areas of weakness in draft papers

Knowledge of field	The author is not well-informed about recent and current work in ...
Definition of terms	There are weaknesses in the definition of [X] as used here ...
Familiarity with relevant research tradition	There is evidence that the author is not properly acquainted with the tradition within which he claims to work ...
Research design	There are serious weaknesses in the research design, specifically in terms of the sample and ...
Evidence for claims	Some of the claims here are not supported by the evidence provided ...

Good research, like good writing, cannot be pinned down by any list of criteria or captured in guidelines, however general. It is accomplished through involved practical engagement, and demands as much of its judges:

> In the end, the task of distinguishing knowledge from opinion and good from bad research is an eminently practical and moral task – not an epistemological one whose rationality is directed by more or less determinate rules or standards. (Smith 1993:163)

The screen of 'objectivity' is not available to shield the qualitative researcher and indifference is not a mark of achievement but an abrogation of responsibility.

Reading guide

Analysis

Most books mentioned here are located within a particular tradition, in which case they are best explored in the context of your own reading in that tradition. However, there is one book that provides a very readable general introduction that covers a broad range while remaining eminently practical. It is accessible at all three levels:

> Coffey, A. and Atkinson, P. 1996. *Making Sense of Qualitative Data.* Thousand Oaks, CA: Sage.

Quality

Seale provides an intelligent discussion of the main areas of debate, though he does argue strongly for his own position on these:

> Seale, C. 1999b. *The Quality of Qualitative Research.* London: Sage.

The papers in Morse *et al.* (2001) adopt a more practical perspective, and although the focus is on research in medical contexts some of the papers make useful points.

Writing

For coverage and depth, the best practical resource here is probably Woods:

> Woods, P. 1999. *Successful Writing for Qualitative Researchers.* London: Routledge.

For anyone aiming eventually for publication, this is definitely the book to have to hand, though it is probably more suited to researchers at Level 3. Holliday (2002) offers an introduction that would work at this level and at Level 2, and the author has a TESOL background. However, a book that manages to combine readability, huge experience, sound advice and accessibility at all three levels is Wolcott (2001). It's also the only one that can be read more or less at a single sitting.

Computers

Because of the speed of developments in this area, any recommendation is likely to date extremely quickly. I have therefore chosen texts focusing on important general issues (especially those relating to decision-making) that are likely to be relevant for some time, as well as recommending a current website that provides a good gateway to further exploration.

Chapter 7 of Coffey and Atkinson (1996) is a very readable introduction to the issues in computer-aided analysis, and even if you're not tempted to make use of one of the software packages on the market it would still be worth reading this.

Seale (2000) offers a useful brief overview of the pros and cons of computer-assisted analysis of qualitative data (CAQDAS). The paper includes very short summaries (a paragraph or two for each) of ETHNO-GRAPH, NUD • IST and ATLAS. Fielding (2002b) also provides an excellent discussion of research issues bearing on the use of CAQDAS. This would make an ideal starting point for anyone wishing to develop a perspective on the subject.

Getting to know a software package is very much a hands-on affair and written descriptions usually make for hard reading. However, Stroh (2000) provides an accessible 'lesson' in using NUD • IST. An added advantage is that his 'to use or not to use' paper on CAQDAS is available in the same collection. These can be read along with Barry's very useful online paper comparing ATLAS and NUD • IST (1998). Even though the programmes themselves may eventually be superseded, there's much to be learnt from the approach adopted by these authors.

For an updated resource list including books, articles and websites for relevant packages, go to the CAQDAS project website as Surrey University (UK) (http://www.soc.surrey.ac.uk/caqdas).

Epilogue: Qualitative Inquiry and Teaching

> Educational researchers are practitioners in an engaged social science and it isn't an easy ride.
>
> Edwards 2002:158

In this epilogue I return briefly to the relationship between teaching and research touched upon in the Introduction. This time, though, I explore common perspectives by considering what I take to be two fundamental responsibilities that hold them in the same moral orbit: recognition of complexity and respect for difference.

Recognition of complexity

The common struggle of all teachers and all qualitative researchers lies not in simply accepting that life is complicated but in recognising and finding ways of representing its complexity: in matters of research and education, resistance to dogma is both a professional imperative and a moral duty.

Both QI and education have tried to find the best way of representing their essential characteristics, exploring their activities from the perspectives of science, craft and art (see, for example, Eisner 2002), but even where this leads to conclusions they are at best tentative or incomplete. The addendum to Woods' confident pronouncement (1996:31) is fairly typical: 'Clearly, teaching is both a science and an art – and more besides'. As well as being rational, informed, planned and considered, teaching and research are also intuitive, original, improvised and instinctive. Different teachers or researchers might load the sides of the balance differently, but success depends on continual movement about the pivot: stasis is never an option.

In this continually shifting world, knowing and feeling co-exist in creative tension. It is part of the evolutionary imperative that we should seek knowledge, but some things, says Eisner (2002:381), 'you can understand only through your ability to feel'. Angela, an experienced teacher of business English, reads academic and professional journals in pursuit of insights into her teaching and ideas for the classroom, but when she encounters an idea or proposal she insists that it 'has to feel right. I can't do anything if it doesn't feel right' (Richards 2001). And because teachers and researchers are both engaged in committed activity, the balance that must be struck may extend into to moral and aesthetic as well as conceptual and social dimensions, challenging those who seek to understand the nature of decision-making. Williams and May (2002:5), for example, have pointed to a tension 'between enquiry and commitment running throughout the social sciences', while Edge (1996) has explored the ethical challenges inherent in TESOL's cross-cultural nature.

In a professional world as involved as this one, the search for best practice is a dangerous distraction from our struggle towards the good (Edge and Richards 1998b), and any research that offers simple recipes for effective teaching must be regarded with suspicion. Because QI engages directly with the complexity of our professional world, it can help us find ways of understanding that will inform action without confining it in the straitjacket of mere procedure: we need it not because it has answers but because it understands what questions are important.

Respect for difference

In the global community that is TESOL, difference is a way of life. Any local community of teachers is likely to include representatives of very different groups: inhabitants who have grown up in the country and know its educational and cultural systems as insiders; travellers from a different cultural and educational background who have lived in the country for a short time; and residents who have grown up in a different country but have been so long settled in the host country that they have absorbed many of its ways and understandings. Teaching has long been regarded as an essentially individual activity, taking place in what Lortie (1975) described as the 'egg-crate' structure of schools, but in the culturally complex world of TESOL understanding cannot be taken for granted – it must be worked for.

The international professional organisations in TESOL are a testament to those who engage in this work and seek understanding across cultural boundaries, and the contribution of research in this enterprise should not be underestimated: what brings teachers together are the teachers' groups, conferences, workshops and journals through which they share their insights and discoveries. TESOL, it would seem, has already responded to Edwards' (2002) call, in her presidential address to the British Educational Research Association, for educational researchers to think globally. However, if we are to nurture the sort of research that will do justice to the 'tangled up' nature of schools and teaching (Nespor 1997; Eisenhart 2001), we will need to ensure that respect for difference in research is also nurtured. Four areas seem to me to be particularly important:

1. In other educational subjects the translation of good practice from one educational culture to another is a cause for celebration (for example, Crockett 2002), but it is something that we might easily take for granted. We should resist this by encouraging the global exchange of locally focused research, pursuing inquiry that respects and explores the 'polyphony of views' (Holliday 1996:234) that makes up our international community.
2. We should recognise the importance of appropriate inquiry and not confuse scale with quality. What is possible for a professional researcher with time, knowledge, experience and craft skills at their disposal is not within immediate reach of the classroom teacher; to suggest otherwise is to demean research and place impossible demands on an already overworked teaching profession. It takes time to develop research skills, but all teachers can be encouraged to find modest ways of investigating their own practice and sharing their findings with others. When this is done well, it should be respected as a legitimate contribution to professional understanding.
3. We need to listen to minority voices calling for change (for example, Canagarajah 1996) and try to understand the perspectives from which they speak.
4. We should resist the arrogance of certainty and promote the sharing of understanding, which means presenting our research in a way that does not establish an agonistic relationship with other researchers: 'making a choice does not mean turning those who make a different choice into our enemies or rivals' (Bochner 2001:154).

'We are', says Schwandt (1996b:158), 'part of a moment in human inquiry when many songs of experience are being heard' and the road ahead in QI, as in TESOL, is unpredictable. It will be determined in part by the positions we take up now, and our concerns must lie not just in the mode of our knowing but the manner of our sharing.

References

Abrams, M.H. 1988. *A Glossary of Literary Terms* (5th edn). New York: Holt, Rinehart and Winston.

Abu-Lughod, L. 1991. 'Writing Against Culture', in R.G. Fox (ed.), *Recapturing Anthropology: Working in the Present*. Santa Fe, NM: School of American Research Press, pp. 137–62.

Adams, R.S. 1972. 'Observational Studies of Teacher Role', *International Review of Education*, 18, 4, 440–59. (Special Number: N. Flanders and G. Nuthall (eds), *The Classroom Behavior of Teachers*).

Adler, P.A. and Adler P. 1994. 'Observational Techniques', in N. Denzin and Y. Lincoln (eds) *Handbook of Qualitative Research*. Thousand Oaks, CA: Sage, pp. 377–90.

Agar, M.H. 1996. *The Professional Stranger*. San Diego: Academic Press.

Allwright, D. 1988. *Observation in the Language Classroom*. London: Longman.

Allwright, D. and Bailey, K.M. 1991. *Focus on the Language Classroom*. Cambridge: Cambridge University Press.

Angrosino, M.V. 1997. 'Among the Savage Anthros: Reflections on the SAS Oral History Project', *Southern Anthropologist*, 24, 25–32.

Angrosino, M.V. and de Pérez, K.A. Mays. 2000. 'Rethinking Observation: From Method to Context', in N.K. Denzin and Y.S. Lincoln (eds) op. cit., pp. 673–702.

Antaki, C. 1994. *Explaining and Arguing*. London: Sage.

Arksey, H. and Knight, P. 1999. *Interviewing for Social Scientists*. London: Sage.

Ashmore, M. and Reed, D. 2000. 'Innocence and Nostalgia in Conversation Analysis: the Dynamic Relations of Tape and Transcript' [45 paragraphs]. *Forum Qualitative Sozialforschung/Forum: Qualitative Social Research* [Online Journal], 1(3) December. Available at: http://qualitative-research.net/fqs/fqs-eng.htm [Accessed 8/6/01].

Atkinson, J.M. and Heritage, J. (eds). 1984a. *Structures of Social Action*. Cambridge: Cambridge University Press.

Atkinson, J.M. and Heritage, J. 1984b. Introduction, in J.M. Atkinson and J. Heritage (eds), Cambridge: Cambridge University Press, pp. 1–15.

Atkinson, P. 1988. 'Ethnomethodology: a Critical Review', *Annual Review of Sociology*, 14, 441–65.

Atkinson, P. 1992a. *Understanding Ethnographic Texts*. Newbury Park, CA: Sage.

Atkinson, P., Coffey, A., Delamont, S., *et al.* (eds). 2001. *Handbook of Ethnography*. London: Sage.

Atkinson, P. and Silverman, D. 1997. 'Kundera's *Immortality*: the Interview Society and the Invention of the Self', *Qualitative Inquiry*, 3, 304–25.

Bakeman, R. and Gottman, J.M. 1997. *Observing Interaction: an Introduction to Sequential Analysis* (2nd edn), Cambridge: Cambridge University Press.

Baker, C. 1997. 'Membership Categorization and Interview Accounts', in O. Silverman (ed.), op. cit., pp. 130–43.

Baker, C.D. 2002. 'Ethnomethodological Analyses of Interviews', in J.F. Gubrium and J.A. Holstein (eds), pp. 777–95.

Banks, M. 2001. *Visual Methods in Social Research*. London: Sage.

Barry, C.A. 1998. 'Choosing Qualitative Data Analysis Software: Atlas/ti and Nudist compared', *Sociological Research Online*, 3/3 (http://www.socresonline.org.uk/socresonline/3/3/4.html).

Bassey, M. 1999. *Case Study Research in Educational Settings*. Buckingham: Open University Press.

Bassey, M. 2001. 'A Solution to the Problem of Generalization in Educational Research: Empirical Findings and Fuzzy Predictions', *Oxford Review of Education*, 27, 1, 5–22.

Becker, H.S. 1993. 'Theory: the Necessary Evil', in Flinders and Mills (eds), pp. 218–29.

Benney, M. and Hughes, E.C. 1956. 'Of Sociology and the Interview', *American Journal of Sociology*, 62, 137–42.

Bentz, V.M. and Shapiro, J.M. 1998. *Mindful Inquiry in Social Research*. London: Sage.

Beretta, A., Crookes, G., Gregg, K. and Long, M. 1994. 'Comment on van Lier 1994', *Applied Linguistics*, 15, 3, 347.

Berg, B.L. 1998. *Qualitative Research Methods for the Social Sciences*. Boston, MA: Allyn and Bacon.

Billig, M. and Schegloff, E.A. 1999. 'Critical Discourse Analysis and Conversation Analysis: an Exchange between Michael Billig and Emanuel A. Schegloff', *Discourse and Society*, 10, 4, 543–82.

Block, D. 2000. 'Research Issues: Problematizing Interview Data: Voices in the Mind's Machine?', *TESOL Quarterly*, 34, 4, 757–63.

Bloor, M., Frankland, J., Thomas, M. and Robson, K. 2001. *Focus Groups in Social Research*. London: Sage.

Bochner, A.P. 2000. 'Criteria Against Ourselves', *Qualitative Inquiry*, 6, 2, 266–72.

Bochner, A.P. 2001. 'Narrative's Virtues', *Qualitative Inquiry*, 7, 2, 131–57.

Borkan, J. 1999. 'Immersion/Crystallization', in B.F. Crabtree and W.L. Miller (eds), op. cit., pp. 179–94.

Brown, G. and Yule, G. 1983. *Discourse Analysis*. Cambridge: Cambridge University Press.

Brumfit, C. and Mitchell, R. 1989. 'The Language Classroom as a Focus for Research', in C. Brumfit and R. Mitchell (eds), *Research in the Language Classroom*, London: Modern English Publications and the British Council, pp. 3–15.

Bryman, A. 2001a. *Social Research Methods*. Oxford: Oxford University Press.

Bryman, A. (ed.). 2001b. *Ethnography Vol. 4*. London: Sage.

Burgess, R.G. 1984a. 'Autobiographical Accounts and Research Experience', in R.G. Burgess (ed.), *The Research Process in Educational Settings: Ten Case Studies*, Lewes: The Falmer Press, pp. 251–70.

Burgess, R.G. 1984b. *In the Field*. London: Allen and Unwin.

Burgess, R.G. 1991. 'Sponsors, Gatekeepers, Members and Friends: Access in Educational Settings', in W.B. Shaffir and R.A. Stebbins (eds), op. cit., pp. 43–52.

Burgess, R.G. 1992. Introduction, in R.G. Burgess (ed.), *Studies in Qualitative Methodology, Vol. 3: Learning about Fieldwork*, London: JAI Press, pp. ix–xiv.

Burns, A. 1999. *Collaborative Action Research for English Language Teachers*. Cambridge: Cambridge University Press.

Burton, D. (ed.) 2000. *Research Training for Social Scientists*. London: Sage.

Byrne, D. 1998. *Complexity Theory and the Social Sciences: An Introduction*. London: Routledge.

Cameron, D. 2001. *Working with Spoken Discourse*. London: Sage.

Canagarajah, A.S. 1993. 'Critical Ethnography of a Sri Lanka Classroom: Ambiguities in Student Opposition through ESOL', *TESOL Quarterly*, 27, 4, 601–26.

Canagarajah, A.S. 1996. 'From Critical Research Practice to Critical Research Reporting', *TESOL Quarterly*, 30, 2, 321–30.

Carr, W. and Kemmis, S. 1986. *Becoming Critical: Education, Knowledge and Action Research*. Lewes: The Falmer Press.

Cazden, C.B. 1986. 'Classroom Discourse', in M.C. Wittrock (ed.), op. cit., pp. 432–63.

Chouliaraki, K. and Fairclough, N. 1999. *Discourse in Late Modernity: Rethinking Critical Discourse Analysis*. Edinburgh: Edinburgh University Press.

Christenson, M., Slutsky, R., Bendau, S., *et al.* 2001. 'The Rocky Road of Teachers Becoming Action Researchers', *Teaching and Teacher Education*, 18, 3, 259–72.

Clarke, M.A. 1994. 'The Dysfunctions of the Theory/Practice Discourse', *TESOL Quarterly*, 28, 1, 9–26.

Clarke, M.A. 1995. 'The Importance of Particularisability', Paper presented at the 1995 TESOL Convention, Long Beach, California.

Clayman, S.E. and Maynard, D.W. 1994. 'Criteria for Assessing Interpretive Validity in Qualitative Research', in P. ten Have and G. Psathas (eds), *Situated Order: Studies in The Social Organization of Talk and Embodied Activities*. Washington DC: University Press of America, pp. 1–30.

Coates, J. and Thornborrow, J. 1999. 'Myths, Lies and Videotapes: some thoughts on Data Transcripts', *Discourse & Society*, 10, 4, 594–7.

Coffey, A. and Atkinson, P. 1996. *Making Sense of Qualitative Data*. Thousand Oaks, CA: Sage.

Cohen, J. 1960. 'A Coefficient of Agreement for Nominal Scales', *Educational and Psychological Measurement*, 20, 37–46.

Crabtree, B.F. and Miller W.L. (eds). 1999. *Doing Qualitative Research* (2nd edn). Thousand Oaks, CA: Sage.

Cresswell, J.W. 1994. *Research Design: Qualitative and Quantitative Approaches*. Thousand Oaks, CA: Sage.

Cresswell, J.W. 1998. *Qualitative Inquiry and Research Design: Choosing Among Five Traditions*. Thousand Oaks, CA: Sage.

Crockett, M.D. 2002. 'Inquiry as Professional Development: Creating Dilemmas through Teachers' Work', *Teaching and Teacher Education*, 18, 609–24.

Crotty, M. 1998. *The Foundations of Social Research*. London: Sage.

Cullen, R. 2002. 'Supportive Teacher Talk: the Importance of the F-move', *ELT Journal*, 56, 2, 117–27.

Davis, K.A. 1995. 'Qualitative Theory and Methods in Applied Linguistics Research', *TESOL Quarterly*, 29, 3, 427–53.

de Laine, M. 2000. *Fieldwork, Participation and Practice*. London: Sage.

Delamont, S. 2002. *Fieldwork in Educational Settings*. London: Routledge.

Denzin, N.K. 1970. *The Research Act*. Chicago, IL: Aldine.

Denzin, N.K. 1997. *Interpretive Ethnography: Ethnographic Practices for the 21st Century*. London: Sage.

Denzin, N.K. 2000. 'Aesthetics and the Practices of Qualitative Inquiry', *Qualitative Inquiry*, 6, 2, 256–65.

Denzin, N.K. and Lincoln, Y.S. (eds). 1994a. *Handbook of Qualitative Research*. Thousand Oaks, CA: Sage.

Denzin, N.K. and Lincoln, Y.S. 1994b. 'Entering the Field of Qualitative Research', in N.K. Denzin and Y.S. Lincoln (eds), Ibid., pp. 1–17.

Denzin, N.K. and Lincoln, Y.S. (eds). 2000. *Handbook of Qualitative Research* (2nd edn). Thousand Oaks, CA: Sage.

DeVault, M.L. and McCoy, L. 2002. 'Institutional Ethnography', in J.F. Gubrium and J.A. Holstein (eds), pp. 751–75.

Dey, I. 1993. *Qualitative Data Analysis: a User-Friendly Guide for Social Scientists.* London: Routledge.

Dey, I. 1999. *Grounding Grounded Theory.* San Diego, CA: Academic Press.

Dilley, R.M. 2002. 'The Problem of Context in Social and Cultural Anthropology', *Language and Communication*, 22, 437–56.

Dingwall, R. 1980. 'Ethics and Ethnography', *Sociological Review*, 28, 4, 871–91.

Dreher, M. 1994. 'Qualitative Research Methods from the Reviewer's Perspective', in J.M. Morse (ed.), *Critical Issues in Qualitative Research Methods.* Thousand Oaks, CA: Sage, pp. 281–97.

Drew, P. and Heritage, J. 1992. Introduction, in P. Drew and J. Heritage (eds), *Talk at Work*, Cambridge: Cambridge University Press, pp. 3–65.

Duff, P.A. 2002. 'The Discursive Co-construction of Knowledge, Identity, and Difference: an Ethnography of Communication in the High School Mainstream', *Applied Linguistics*, 23, 3, 289–322.

Edge, J. 1996. 'Cross-Cultural Paradoxes in a Profession of Values', *TESOL Quarterly*, 31, 1, 9–30.

Edge, J. (ed.). 2001a. *Action Research.* Alexandria, VA: TESOL Inc.

Edge, J. 2001b. 'Attitude and Access: Building a New Teaching/Learning Community in TESOL', in J. Edge (ed.), op. cit., pp. 1–11.

Edge, J. 2002. *Continuing Professional Development: A Discourse Framework for Individuals as Colleagues.* Ann Arbor, MI: The University of Michigan Press.

Edge, J. and Richards, K. (eds). 1993. *Teachers Develop Teachers Research.* London: Heinemann.

Edge, J. and Richards, K. 1998a. '"May I See your Warrant, Please?" Justifying Outcomes in Qualitative Research', *Applied Linguistics*, 19, 3, 334–56.

Edge, J. and Richards, K. 1998b. 'Why Best Practice isn't Good Enough. *TESOL Quarterly*, 32, 4, 569–76.

Edwards, A. 2002. 'Responsible Research: Ways of Being a Researcher', *British Educational Research Journal*, 28, 2, 157–68.

Eggins, S. and Slade, D. 1997. *Analysing Casual Conversation.* London: Cassell.

Eisenhart, M. 2001. 'Educational Ethnography Past, Present, and Future: Ideas to Think with', *Educational Researcher*, 30, 8, 16–27.

Eisner, E.W. 2001. 'Concerns and Aspirations for Qualitative Research in the new Millennium', *Qualitative Research*, 1, 2, 135–45.

Eisner, E.W. 2002. 'From Episteme to Phronesis to Artistry in the Study and Improvement of Teaching', *Teaching and Teacher Education*, 18, 375–85.

Elbaz, F. 1983. *Teacher Thinking: a Study of Practical Knowledge.* Beckenham: Croom Helm.

Ellis, D.G. 1999. 'Research on Social Interaction and the Micro–Macro Issue', *Research on Language and Social Interaction*, 32, 1&2, 31–40.

Ellis, C., Kiesinger, C.E. and Tillman-Healy, L.M. 1997. 'Interactive Interviewing: Talking about Emotional Experience', in R. Hertz (ed.), *Reflexivity and Voice*, pp. 119–49. Thousand Oaks: Sage.

Ely, M., with Anzul, M., Friedman, T., Garner D. and Steinmetz, A.M. 1991. *Doing Qualitative Research:/Circles within Circles*. London: Falmer Press.

Emerson, R.M., Fretz, R.I. and Shaw, L.L. 1995. *Writing Ethnographic Fieldnotes*. Chicago: University of Chicago Press.

Emerson, R.M., Fretz, R.I. and Shaw, L.L. 2001. 'Participant Observation and Fieldnotes', in Atkinson *et al.* (eds), op. cit., pp. 352–68.

Erickson, F. 1986. 'Qualitative Methods in Research on Teaching', in M.C. Wittrock (ed.), op. cit., pp. 119–61.

Erickson F. 1992. 'Ethnographic Microanalysis of Interaction', in M.D. LeCompte, W. Millroy and J. Preissle (eds), *The Handbook of Qualitative Research in Education*, pp. 201–25. New York: Academic Press.

Erickson F. 1996. 'Ethnographic Microanalysis', in S.L. McKay and N.H. Hornberger (eds), *Sociolinguistics and Language Teaching*, pp. 283–306. Cambridge: Cambridge University Press.

Erickson, K.T. 1967. 'A Comment on Disguised Observation in Sociology', *Social Problems*, 14, 366–73.

Evertson, C.M and Green, J.L. 1986. 'Observation as Inquiry and Method', in M.C. Wittrock (ed.), op. cit., pp. 162–213.

Faiclough, N. 1996. 'A reply to Henry Widdowson's Discourse Analysis: a Critical View', *Language and Literature*, 5, 1, 1–8.

Fairclough, N. 2001. 'The Discourse of New Labour: Critical Discourse Analysis', in M. Wetherell, S. Yates and S.J. Yates (eds), op. cit., pp. 229–66.

Fetterman, D.M. 1991. 'A Walk through the Wilderness: Learning to Find your Way', in W.B. Shaffir and R.A. Stebbins (eds), op. cit., pp. 87–96.

Fetzer, A. and Akman, V. 2002. 'Contexts of Social Action: Guest Editors' Introduction', *Language and Communication*, 22, 391–402.

Fielding, N.G. (ed.). 2002a. *Interviewing* (4 vols). London: Sage.

Fielding, N.G. 2002b. 'Automating the ineffable: Qualitative Software and the Meaning of Qualitative Research', in T. May (ed.), op. cit., pp. 161–78.

Finlay, L. 2002. 'Negotiating the Swamp: the Operation and Challenge of Reflexivity in Research Practice', *Qualitative Research*, 2, 2, 209–30.

Flanders, N.A. 1970. *Analysing Teaching Behavior*. Reading, MA: Addison-Wesley.

Flick, U. 2002. *An Introduction to Qualitative Research* (2nd edn). London: Sage.

Freeman, D. 1991 'To Make the Tacit Explicit: Teacher Education, Emerging Discourse, and Conceptions of Teaching', *Teaching and Teacher Education*, 7, 5/6, 439–54.

Freeman, D. 1992. 'Language Teacher Education, Emerging Discourse, and Change in Classroom Practice', in J. Flowerdew, M. Brock and S. Hsia (eds), *Perspectives in Second Language Teacher Education*, pp. 1–21. Hong Kong: City Polytechnic of Hong Kong.

Freeman, D. 1998. *Doing Teacher Research: From Inquiry to Understanding*. Pacific Grove, CA: Heinle & Heinle.

Frey, J.H. 1989. *Survey Research by Telephone* (2nd edn). Newbury Park: Sage.

Gardner, G. 2001. 'Unreliable Memories and other Contingencies: Problems with Biographical Knowledge', *Qualitative Research*, 1, 2, 185–204.

Garfinkel H. 1984. *Studies in Ethnomethodology*. Cambridge: Polity Press.

Garratt, D. and Hodkinson, P. 1998. 'Can there Be Criteria from Selecting Research Criteria? A Hermeneutical Analysis of an Inescapable Dilemma', *Qualitative Inquiry*, 4, 4, 515–39.

Geer, B. 1964/1999. 'First Days in the Field', in P.E. Hammond (ed.), *Sociologists at Work*. New York: Basic Books. Reprinted in A. Bryman and R.G. Burgess (eds), 1999, *Qualitative Research, Vol. III*, pp. 33–52. London: Sage.

Glaser, B.G. (ed.). 1993. *Examples of Grounded Theory: a Reader*. Mill Valley, CA: Sociology Press.

Glaser, B.G. and Strauss, A.L. 1967. *The Discovery of Grounded Theory: Strategies for Qualitative Research*. New York: Aldine.

Goffman, E. 1981. *Forms of Talk*. Oxford: Basil Blackwell.

Gold, R.L. 1958. 'Roles in Sociological Field Observations', *Social Forces*, 36, 217–23.

Gomm, R., Hammersley, M. and Foster, P. (eds). 2000a. *Case Study Method*. London: Sage.

Gomm, R., Hammersley, M. and Foster, P. 2000b. 'Case Study and Generalization', in Gomm *et al.* (eds), pp. 98–115.

González, K.P. 2001. 'Inquiry as a Process of Learning about the Other and the Self', *Qualitative Studies in Education*, 14, 4, 543–62.

Goodall, H.L. Jr. 2000. *Writing the New Ethnography*. Walnut Creek, CA: AltaMira Press.

Goodson, I.F. 1992. 'Studying Teachers' Lives: an Emergent Field of Inquiry', in I.F. Goodson (ed.), *Studying Teachers' Lives*, pp. 1–17. London: Routledge.

Goodwin, C. and Duranti, 'A. 1992. Rethinking Context: an Introduction', in A. Duranti and C. Goodwin (eds), *Rethinking Context: Language as an Interactive Phenomenon*, pp. 1–42. Cambridge: Cambridge University Press.

Grbich, C. 1999. *Qualitative Research in Health*. London: Sage.

Green, J.L. and Dixon, C.N. 1993. 'Talking Knowledge into Being: Discursive Practices in Classrooms', *Linguistics and Education*, 5, 231–39.

Green, J.L. and Dixon, C.N. 2002. 'Exploring Differences in Perspectives on Microanalysis of Classroom Discourse: Contributions and Concerns', *Applied Linguistics*, 23, 3, 393–406.

Green, J., Franquiz, M. and Dixon, C. 1977. 'The Myth of the Objective Transcript: Transcribing as a Situated Act', *TESOL Quarterly*, 31, 1, 172–76.

Greenwood, D.J. and Levin, M. 1998. *Introduction to Action Research*. Thousand Oaks, CA: Sage.

Guba, E.G. (ed.). 1990. *The Paradigm Dialog*. Newbury Park: Sage.

Guba, E.G. and Lincoln, Y.S. 1994. 'Competing Paradigms in Qualitative Research', in Denzin and Lincoln (eds), pp. 105–17.

Gubrium, J.F. and Holstein, J.A. (eds). 2002a. *Handbook of Interview Research: Context and Method*. Thousand Oaks, CA: Sage.

Gubrium, J.F. and Holstein, J.A. 2002b. 'From the Individual Interview to the Interview Society', in Gubrium and Holstein (eds), pp. 3–32.

Gumperz, J.J. 1982. *Discourse Strategies*. Cambridge: Cambridge University Press.

Hammersley, M. 1980. 'A Peculiar World? Teaching and Learning in an Inner-city School', Unpublished doctoral thesis, Faculty of Economic and Social Studies, University of Manchester.

Hammersley, M. 1981. 'Ideology in the Staffroom? A Critique of False Consciousness', in L. Barton and S. Walker (eds), *Schools Teachers and Teaching*, pp. 331–42. Lewes: Falmer Press.

Hammersley, M. 1984a. 'Staffroom News', in A. Hargreaves and P. Woods (eds), *Classrooms and Staffrooms: the Sociology of Teachers and Teaching*, pp. 203–14. Milton Keynes: Open University Press.

Hammersley, M. 1984b. 'The Researcher Exposed: a Natural History', in R.G. Burgess (ed.), *In the Field: An Introduction to Field Research*, pp. 39–68. London: George Allen & Unwin.

Hammersley, M. 1990. *Reading Ethnographic Research: A Critical Guide*. London: Longman.

Hammersley, M. 1992. *What's Wrong with Ethnography?* London: Routledge.

Hammersley, M. 1993/2001. 'The Rhetorical Turn in Ethnography', *Social Science Information*, 32, 23–37. Reprinted in Bryman 2001b (ed.), pp. 329–40.

Hammersley, M. 2001. 'On Michael Bassey's Concept of the Fuzzy Generalisation', *Oxford Review of Education*, 27, 2, 219–25.

Hammersley, M. and Atkinson, P. 1995. *Ethnography* (2nd edn). London: Routledge.

Hart, C. 1998. *Doing a Literature Review: Releasing the Social Science Research Imagination*. London: Sage.

Hart, C. 2001. *Doing a Literature Search*. London: Sage.

Heap, J.L. 1995. 'The status of Claims in 'Qualitative' Educational Research', *Curriculum Inquiry*, 25, 3, 271–92.

Henstrand, J.L. 1993. 'Theory as Research Guide: a Qualitative Look at Qualitative Inquiry', in D.J. Flinders and G.E. Mills (eds), pp. 83–102.

Heritage, J. 1984a. *Garfinkel and Ethnomethodology*. Cambridge: Polity.

Heritage, J. 1984b. A change-of-state Token and Aspects of its Sequential Placement, in Atkinson and Heritage (eds), pp. 299–435.

Heritage, J. and Sorjonen, M.L. 1994. 'Constituting and Maintaining Activities across Sequences: *And*-prefacing as a Feature of Questioning Design', *Language in Society*, 23, 1–29.

Heshusius, L. and Ballard, K. (eds). 1996. *From Positivism to Interpretivism and Beyond: Tales of Transformation in Educational and Social Research*. New York: Teachers College Press.

Hester, S. and Eglin, P. (eds). 1997. *Culture in Action: Studies in Membership Categorization Analysis*. Washington, DC: University Press of America.

Heyl, B.S. 2001. 'Ethnographic Interviewing', in Atkinson *et al.* (eds), op. cit., pp. 369–83.

Hoffman, J.E. 1980. 'Problems of Access in the Study of Social Elites and Boards of Directors', in W.B. Shaffir, R.A. Stebbins and A. Turowetz (eds), op. cit., pp. 45–56.

Holliday, A. 1996. 'Developing a Sociological Imagination: Expanding ethnography in International English Language Education', *Applied Linguistics*, 17, 2, 234–55.

Holliday, A. 2002. *Doing and Writing Qualitative Research*. London: Sage.

Holstein, J.A. and Gubrium, J.F. 1995. *The Active Interview*. Thousand Oaks, CA: Sage.

Howe, K. and Eisenhart, M. 1990. 'Standards for Qualitative (and Quantitative) Research: a Prolegomenon', *Educational Researcher*, 19, 4, 2–9.

Huberman, M. 1989. 'The Professional Life Cycle of Teachers', *Teachers College Record*, 91, 1, 31–57.

Huberman, M. 1992. 'Teacher Development and Instructional Mastery', in A. Hargreaves and M.G. Fullan (eds), *Understanding Teacher Development*, pp. 122–42. London: Cassell.

Huberman, M. 1993. *The Lives of Teachers*. London: Cassell.

Hutchby, I. and Wooffitt, R. 1998. *Conversation Analysis*. Cambridge: Polity Press.

Jackson, J.E. 1990. '"I Am a Fieldnote": Fieldnotes as a Symbol of Professional Identity', in R. Sanjek (ed.), *Fieldnotes: The Making of Anthropology*, pp. 3–33. Ithaca, NY: Cornell University Press.

Janesick, V.J. 1998. '*Stretching' Exercises for Qualitative Researchers*. Thousand Oaks: Sage.

Jarvis, J. and Robinson, M. 1997. 'Analysing Educational Discourse: an Exploratory Study of Teacher Response and Support to Pupils' Learning', *Applied Linguistics*, 18, 2, 212–28.

Jefferson, G. 1984. 'On Stepwise Transition from Talk about a Trouble to Inappropriately Next-positioned Matters', in Atkinson and Heritage (eds), pp. 191–222.

Jefferson G. 1985. 'An Exercise in the Transcription and Analysis of Laughter', in T. van Dijk (ed.), *Handbook of Discourse Analysis Vol. 3: Discourse and Dialogue*, pp. 25–34. London: Academic Press.

Johnson, D.M. 1992. *Approaches to Research in Second Language Learning*. New York: Longman.

Johnson, J.C. and Weller, S.C. 2002. 'Elicitation Techniques for Interviewing', In J.F. Gubrium and J.A. Holstein (eds), *Handbook of Interview Research: Context and Method*, pp. 491–514. Thousand Oaks, CA: Sage.

Johnson, J.L. 1997. 'Generalizability in Qualitative Research: Excavating the Discourse', in J. M. Morse (ed.), *Completing a Qualitative Project*, pp. 191–208. Thousand Oaks, CA: Sage.

Johnson, K. 2002. *Designing Language Teaching Tasks*. London: Palgrave Macmillan.

Jones, J. 1985a. 'Depth Interviewing', in R. Walker (ed.), *Applied Qualitative Research*, pp. 45–55. Brookfield, VT: Gower.

Jones, S. 1985b. 'The Analysis of Depth Interviews', in R. Walker (ed.), *Applied Qualitative Research*, pp. 56–70. Brookfield, VT: Gower.

Karp, D.A. 1980. 'Observing Behavior in Public Places: Problems and Strategies', in W.B. Shaffir, R.A. Stebbins and A. Turowetz (eds), op. cit., pp. 82–97.

Kemmis, S. and McTaggart, R. (eds). 1988. *The Action Research Planner* (3rd edn). Geelong: Deakin University Press.

Kincheloe, J. and McLaren, P. 2000. 'Rethinking Critical Theory and Qualitative Research', in Denzin and Lincoln (eds), op. cit., pp. 138–67.

Kirk, J. and Miller, M. 1986. *Reliability and Validity in Qualitative Research*. London: Sage.

Kuhn, T.S. 1962. *The Structure of Scientific Revolutions*. Chicago, IL: University of Chicago Press.

Kumaravadivelu, B. 1993. 'Maximising Learning Potential in the Communicative Classroom', *ELT Journal*, 47, 1, 12–21.

Kvale, S. 1996. *InterViews: An Introduction to Qualitative Research Interviewing*. Thousand Oaks, CA: Sage.

Kvale, S. 1999. The Psychoanalytic Interview as Qualitative Research', *Qualitative Inquiry*, 5, 1, 87–113.

Lazaraton, A. 1995. 'Qualitative Research in Applied Linguistics: a Progress Report', *TESOL Quarterly*, 29, 3, 455–72.

Lazaraton, A. 2001. 'Standards in Qualitative Research: Whose Standards? And Whose Research?', Paper presented at the American Association of Applied Linguistics annual conference, 26 February 2001.

LeCompte, M.D. and Goetz, J.P. 1982/2001. 'Problems of Reliability and Validity in Ethnographic Research', *Review of Educational Research*, 52, 1, 31–60. Reprinted in A. Bryman (ed.), 2001, *Ethnography Vol. 3*, pp. 100–32, London: Sage.

Lerner, D. 1957. 'The "Hard-headed" Frenchman: On se défend, toujours', *Encounter*, 8, 27–32.

Lincoln, Y.S. and Guba, E.G. 1985. *Naturalistic Inquiry*. Beverly Hills, CA: Sage.
Lincoln, Y.S. and Guba, E.G. 1990. 'Judging the Quality of Case Study Reports', *Qualitative Studies in Education*, 3, 1, 53–9.
Lofland, J. and Lofland, L.H. 1984. *Analyzing Social Settings* (2nd edn). Belmonst, CA: Wadsworth.
Lofland, J. and Lofland, L.H. 1995. *Analyzing Social Settings: A Guide to Qualitative Observation and Analysis* (3rd edn). Belmont, CA: Wadsworth.
Lortie, D.C. 1975. *Schoolteacher: a Sociological Study*. Chicago: The University of Chicago Press.
McCarthy, M. 1991. *Discourse Analysis for Language Teachers*. Cambridge: Cambridge University Press.
McHoul, A. and Rapley, M. 2001. *How to Analyse Talk in Institutional Settings*. London: Continuum.
MacLure, M. 1993. 'Mundane Autobiography: some Thoughts on Self-talk in Research Contexts', *British Journal of Sociology of Education*, 14, 4, 373–84.
McTaggart, R. 1996. 'Issues for Participatory Action Researchers', in O. Zuber-Skerritt (ed.), pp. 243–55.
McTaggart, R. 1997. 'Reading the Collection', in R. McTaggart (ed.), *Participatory Action Research: International Contexts and Consequences*, New York: State University of New York Press, pp. 1–23.
Malamah-Thomas, A. 1987. *Classroom Interaction*. Oxford: Oxford University Press.
Mann, S. 2002. 'The Development of Discourse in a Discourse of Development: a Case Study of a Group Constructing a New Discourse', Unpublished doctoral thesis, The University of Aston in Birmingham.
Manning, P. 1992. *Erving Goffman and Modern Sociology*. Cambridge: Polity Press.
Manning, K. 1997. 'Authenticity in Constructivist Inquiry: Methodological Considerations without Prescription', *Qualitative Inquiry*, 3, 1, 93–115.
Markee, N. 2000. *Conversation Analysis*. Mahwah, NJ: Lawrence Erlbaum.
Marshall, C. and Rossman, G.B. 1999. *Designing Qualitative Research* (3rd edn). Thousand Oaks, CA: Sage.
Martin, A.W. 2001. 'Large-group Processes in Action Research', in P. Reason and A. Bradbury (eds), op. cit., pp. 200–08.
Mason, I. 2001. 'Phenomenology and Ethnography', in Atkinson *et al.* (eds), pp. 136–44.
Mason, J. 1994. 'Linking Qualitative and Quantitative Data Analysis', in A. Bryman and R.G. Burgess (eds), *Analyzing Qualitative Data*. London: Routledge, pp. 89–110.
Mason, J. 2002. 'Qualitative Interviewing: Asking, Listening and Interpreting', in T. May (ed.), *Qualitative Research in Action*, London: Sage, pp. 225–41.
Masterman, M. 1970. 'The Nature of Paradigm', in I. Lakatos and A. Musgrave (eds), *Criticism and the Growth of Knowledge*. Cambridge: Cambridge University Press, pp. 59–89.
Maxwell, J.A. 1992. 'Understanding and Validity in Qualitative Research', *Harvard Educational Review*, 62, 3, 279–300.
May, T. 2001. *Social Research: Issues Methods and Process* (3rd edn). Buckingham: Open University Press.
May, T. (ed.). 2002. *Qualitative Research in Action*. London: Sage.
Meadows, L.M. and Morse, J.M. 2001. 'Constructing Evidence within the Qualitative Project', in J.M. Morse, J.M. Swanson and A.J. Kuzel (eds), *The Nature of Qualitative Evidence*. Thousand Oaks, CA: Sage, pp. 187–200.

Measor, L. and P. Sikes. 1992. 'Visiting Lives: Ethics and Methodology in Life History', in I.F. Goodson (ed.), *Studying Teachers' Lives*. London: Routledge, pp. 209–33.

Meyer, M. 2001. 'Between Theory, Method, and Politics: Positioning of the Approaches to CDA', in R. Wodak and M. Meyer (eds), op. cit., pp. 14–31.

Miles, M.B. and Huberman, A.M. 1994. *Qualitative Data Analysis* (2nd edn). Beverly Hills, CA: Sage.

Miller, J. and Glassner, B. 1997. 'The "Inside" and the "Outside": Finding Realities in Interviews', in D. Silverman (ed.), op. cit., pp. 99–112.

Miller, W.L. and Crabtree, B.F. 1992. 'Primary Care Research: a Multimethod Typology and Qualitative Roadmap', in B.F. Crabtree and W.L. Miller (eds), *Doing Qualitative Research: Multiple Strategies*. Thousand Oaks, CA: Sage, pp. 3–28.

Miller, W.L. and Crabtree, B.F. 1999. 'The Dance of Interpretation', in B.F. Crabtree and W.L. Miller (eds), op. cit., pp. 127–43.

Mishler, E.G. 1986. *Research Interviewing: Context and Narrative*. Cambridge, MA: Harvard University Press.

Mori, J. 2002. 'Task Design, Plan and Development of Talk-in-Interaction: an Analysis of a Small Group Activity in a Japanese Language Classroom', *Applied Linguistics*, 23, 3, 323–47.

Morse, J.M. 1994. 'Designing Funded Qualitative Research', in N.K. Denzin and Y.S. Lincoln (eds), op. cit., pp. 20–35.

Morse, J.M. 1997. 'Recognizing the Power of Qualitative Research', in J.M. Morse (ed.), *Completing a Qualitative Project*. Thousand Oaks, CA: Sage, pp. 1–7.

Morse, J.M. 1999. 'Myth #93: Reliability and Validity Are not Relevant to Qualitative Inquiry', *Qualitative Health Research*, 9, 6, 717–18.

Morse, J.M. and Field, P.A. 1995. *Qualitative Research Methods for Health Professionals* (2nd edn). Thousand Oaks, CA: Sage.

Morse, J.M., Swanson, J.M. and Kuzel, A.J. (eds). 2001. *The Nature of Qualitative Evidence*. Thousand Oaks, CA: Sage.

Moskowitz, G. 1976. 'The Classroom Interaction of Outstanding Foreign Language Teachers', *Foreign Language Annals*, 9, 2, 125–43 and 146–57.

Nassaji, H. and Wells, G. 2000. 'What's the Use of "Triadic Dialogue"?: an Investigation of Teacher-Student Interaction', *Applied Linguistics*, 21, 3, 376–406.

Nespor, J. 1997. *Tangled up in School: Politics, Space, Bodies, and Signs in the Educational Process*. Mahawah, NJ: Lawrence Erlbaum.

Nijhof, G. 1997. '"Response Work": Approaching Answers to Open Interview Readings', *Qualitative Inquiry*, 3, 2, 169–87.

Nunan, D. 1992. *Collaborative Language Learning and Teaching*. Cambridge: Cambridge University Press.

Oakley, A. 1981. 'Interviewing women: a Contradiction in Terms', in H. Roberts (ed.), *Doing Feminist Research*. London: Routledge & Kegan Paul, pp. 30–61.

Oates, C. 2000. 'The Use of Focus Groups in Social Science Research', in D. Burton (ed.), *Research Training for Social Scientists*. London: Sage, pp.186–95.

Ochs, E. 1979. 'Transcription as Theory', in E. Ochs and B.B. Schieffelin (eds), *Developmental Pragmatics*, New York: Academic Press, pp. 43–72.

Ortiz, S.M. 2001. 'How Interviewing became Therapy for Wives of Professional Athletes: Learning from a Serendipitous Experience', *Qualitative Inquiry*, 7, 2, 192–220.

Patton, M.Q. 1990. *Qualitative Evaluation and Research Methods*. Newbury Park, CA: Sage.

Peirce, B.N. 1995. 'The theory of Methodology in Critical Research', *TESOL Quarterly*, 29, 3, 569–81.

Peräkylä, A. 1997. 'Reliability and Validity in Research Based on Transcripts', in D. Silverman 1997, op. cit., pp. 201–20.

Peshkin, A. 1993. 'The Goodness of Qualitative Research', *Educational Researcher*, 22, 2, 23–9.

Petty, R. 1997. 'Everything is Different Now: Surviving Ethnographic Research', in E. Stringer, M.F. Agnello, S.C. Baldwin, *et al.*, *Community-Based Ethnography*. Mahwah, NJ: Lawrence Erlbaum, pp. 68–84.

Phillips, D.C. 1987. *Philosophy, Science and Social Inquiry*. Oxford: Pergamon Press.

Phillips, D.C. 1990. 'Postpositivistic Science: Myths and Realities', in E.G. Guba (ed.), *The Paradigm Dialog*, Newbury Park, CA: Sage, pp. 31–45.

Poland, B.D. 1995. 'Transcription Quality as an Aspect of Rigor in Qualitative Research', *Qualitative Inquiry*, 1, 3, 290–310.

Poland, B. and Pederson, A. 1998. 'Reading Between the Lines: Interpreting Silences in Qualitative Research', *Qualitative Inquiry*, 4, 2, 293–312.

Polkinghorne, D.E. 1997. 'Reporting Qualitative Research as Practice', in W.G. Tierney and Y.S. Lincoln (eds), *Representation and the Text: Re-framing the Narrative Voice*, Albany, NY: State University of New York Press, pp. 3–22.

Pollner, M. and Emerson, R.M. 2001. 'Ethnomethodology and Ethnography', in P. Atkinson *et al.* (eds), op. cit., pp. 118–35.

Pridham, F. 2001. *The Language of Conversation*. London: Routledge.

Punch, K.F. 2000. *Developing Effective Research Proposals*. London: Sage.

Rampton, B. 1999. 'Dichotomies, Difference, and Ritual in Second Language Learning and Teaching', *Applied Linguistics*, 20, 3, 316–40.

Rampton, B. Roberts, C., Leung, C. and Harris, R. 2002. 'Methodology in the Analysis of Classroom Discourse', *Applied Linguistics*, 23, 3, 373–92.

Ray, M.A. 1994. 'The Richness of Phenomenology: Philosophic, Theoretic, and Methodologic Concern', in J.M. Morse (ed.), *Critical Issues in Qualitative Research Methods*, Thousand Oaks, CA: Sage, pp. 117–33.

Reason, P. and Bradbury, H. (eds). 2001. *Handbook of Action Research: Participative Inquiry and Practice*. London: Sage.

Reason, P. and Rowan , J. 1981. 'Issues of Validity in New Paradigm Research', in P. Reason and J. Rowan (eds), *Human Inquiry: a Sourcebook of New Paradigm Research*. New York: Wiley, pp. 239–50.

Rees, A. 1993. 'Segmenting Classroom Activities for Research Purposes', in J. Edge and K. Richards (eds), *Teachers Develop Teachers Research*, London: Heinemann, pp. 54–64. (http://www.les.aston.ac.uk/lsu/research/tdtr92/tdtrar.html).

Reynolds, M. 1990. 'Classroom Power–Some Dynamics of Classroom Talk', in R. Clark, N. Fairclough, R. Ivanic, *et al.* (eds), *Language and Power*. London: CILT, pp. 122–36.

Richards, K. 1997a. 'Teachers for Specific Purposes', in R. Howard and I.M. McGrath (eds), *LSP and Teacher Education*. Clevedon: Multilingual Matters, pp. 115–26.

Richards, K. 1997b. 'Staffroom as World', in E. Griffiths and K. Head (eds), *Teachers Develop Teachers Research 2*. Whitstable: IATEFL, pp. 242–53.

Richards K. 1999a. 'Theory in Practice: Design and Argument in Day-to-Day Teaching', in H. Trappes-Lomax and I.M. McGrath (eds), *Theory in Language Teacher Education*. London: Longman, pp. 21–32.

Richards, K. 1999b. 'Working Towards Common Understandings: Collaborative Interaction in Staffroom Stories', *Text*, 19, 1, 143–74.

Richards, K. 2001. 'Discourse, Identity and Development', in C. Coombe (ed.), *Alternative Assessment: Selected Papers from the 1999 and 2000 International CTELT Conferences, Vol. II*. UAE: TESOL Arabia, pp. 46–57.

Richards, K. 2002. 'TRUST: a Management Perspective on CPD', in J. Edge (ed.), *Continuing Professional Development: Some of our Perspectives*. Whitstable, UK: IATEFL, pp. 71–9.

Richardson, L. 2000. 'Writing: a Method of Inquiry', in N.K. Denzin and Y.S. Lincoln (eds), pp. 923–48.

Roberts, C. 1997. 'Transcribing Talk: Issues of Representation', *TESOL Quarterly*, 31, 1, 167–72.

Roberts, C., Byram, M., Barro, et al. 2001. *Language Learners as Ethnographers*. Clevedon: Multilingual Matters.

Robson, C. 2002. *Real World Research* (2nd edn). Oxford: Blackwell.

Rock, P. 2001. 'Symbolic Interactionism and Ethnography', in P. Atkinson et al. (eds), op. cit., pp. 26–38.

Rossman, G.B. and Rallis, S.F. 1998. *Learning in the Field*. Thousand Oaks, CA: Sage.

Rubin, H.J. and Rubin, I.S. 1995. *Qualitative Interviewing: the Art of Hearing Data*. Thousand Oaks, CA: Sage.

Sacks, H. 1984. 'Notes on Methodology', in Atkinson and Heritage 1984a (eds), pp. 21–7.

Sacks , H. 1985. 'The Inference-making Machine: Notes on Observability', in T. van Dijk (ed.), *Handbook of Discourse Analysis Vol. 3: Discourse and Dialogue*. London: Academic Press, pp. 13–24.

Sacks, H. 1992. *Lectures on Conversation* (edited by E. Schegloff). Oxford: Blackwell.

Sacks, H. Schegloff, E.A. and Jefferson, G. 1974. 'A Simplest Systematics for the Organization of Turn-taking for Conversation', *Language*, 50, 4, 696–735.

Sánchez-Janowski, M. 2002. 'Representation, Responsibility and Reliability in Participant-Observation', in T. May (ed.), *Qualitative Research in Action*. London: Sage, pp. 144–60.

Sanjek, R. (ed.). 1990. *Fieldnotes: the Making of Anthropology*. Ithaca, NY: Cornell University Press.

Saville-Troike, M. 1989. *The Ethnography of Communication* (2nd edn). Oxford: Basil Blackwell.

Saville-Troike, M. 1996. 'The Ethnogrsaphy of Communication', in S.L. McKay and N.H. Hornberger (eds), *Sociolinguistics and Language Teaching*. Cambridge: Cambridge University Press, pp. 351–82.

Schegloff, E.A. 1972. 'Notes on a Conversational Practice: Formulating Place', in D. Sudnow (ed.), *Studies in Social Interaction*. New York: Free Press, pp. 75–119.

Schegloff, E.A. 1987. 'Between Micro and Macro: Contexts and Other Connections', in J.C. Alexander, B. Giesen, R. Münch and N.J. Smelser (eds), *The Micro-Macro Link*. Berkeley, CA: University of California Press, pp. 207–234.

Schegloff, E.A. 1991. 'Reflections on Talk and Social Structure', in D. Boden and D.H. Zimmerman (eds), *Studies in Ethnomethodology and Conversation Analysis*. London: Polity Press, pp. 44–70.

Schegloff, E.A. 1997. 'Whose Text? Whose Context?', *Discourse and Society*, 8, 165–87.

Schegloff, E.A. 1998. 'Reply to Wetherell', *Discourse and Society*, 9, 413–16.

Schegloff, E.A., Koshik, I., Jacoby, S. and Olsher, D. 2002. 'Conversation Analysis and Applied Linguistics', *Annual Review of Applied Linguistics*, 22, 3–31.

Schiffrin, D. 1994. *Approaches to Discourse*. Oxford: Basil Blackwell.

Schofield, J.W. 1990. 'Increasing the Generalizability of Qualitative Research', in E.W. Eisner and A. Peshkin (eds), *Qualitative Inquiry in Education: the Continuing Debate*. New York: Teachers College Press, pp. 201–32.

Schubert, W.H. 1989. 'Reconceptualizing and the Matter of Paradigms', *Journal of Teacher Education*, Jan–Feb, 27–32.

Schubert, W.H. 1990. 'Acknowledging Teachers' Experiential Knowledge: Reports from the Teacher Lore Project', *Kappa Delta Pi Record*, Summer 1990, 99–100.

Schwandt, T.A. 1994. 'Constructivist, Interpretivist Approaches to Human Inquiry', in N.K. Denzin and Y.S. Lincoln (eds), op. cit., pp. 118–137.

Schwandt, T.A. 1996a. 'Notes on being an Interpretivist', in L. Heshusius and K. Ballard (eds), op. cit., pp. 77–84.

Schwandt, T.A. 1996b. 'New Songs of Innocence and Experience?' (With apologies to William Blake), in L. Heshusius and K. Ballard (eds), op. cit., pp. 155–60.

Scott, S. 1985. 'Working Through the Contradictions in Researching Postgraduate Education', in R.G. Burgess (ed.), *Field Methods in the Study of Education*. London: Falmer Press, pp. 118–123.

Seale, C. 1999a. 'Quality in Qualitative Research', *Qualitative Inquiry*, 5, 4, 465–78.

Seale, C. 1999b. *The Quality of Qualitative Research*. London: Sage.

Seale, C. 2000. 'Using Computers to Analyse Qualitative Data', in D. Silverman (ed.), op. cit., pp. 154–74.

Seedhouse, P. 1996. 'Classroom Interaction: Possibilities and Impossibilities', *ELT Journal*, 50, 1, 16–24.

Seedhouse, P. 1998. 'CA and the Analysis of Foreign Language Interaction: a Reply to Wagner', *Journal of Pragmatics*, 30, 85–102.

Seedhouse, P. (Forthcoming 2004). *A Conversation Analysis Perspective on the Organisation of Language Classroom Interaction*. Oxford: Blackwell.

Shaffir, W.B. and Stebbins, R.A. (eds). 1991a. *Experiencing Fieldwork: an Inside View of Qualitative Research*. Newbury Park, CA: Sage.

Shaffir, W.B. and Stebbins, R.A. 1991b. Introduction, in W.B. Shaffir and R.A. Stebbins (eds), op. cit., pp. 1–30.

Shaffir, W.B., Stebbins, R.A. and Turowetz, A. (eds). 1980. *Fieldwork Experience: Qualitative Approaches to Social Research*. New York: St Martin's Press.

Sikes, P. 2000. '"Truth" and "Lies" Revisited', *British Educational Research Journal*, 26, 2, 257–70.

Sikes, P.J., Measor, L. and Woods, P. 1985. *Teacher Careers*. Lewes: Falmer Press.

Silverman, D. 1993. *Interpreting Qualitative Data: Methods for Analysing Talk, Text and Interaction*. London: Sage.

Silverman, D. (ed.). 1997. *Qualitative Research: Theory, Method and Practice*. London: Sage.

Silverman, D. 1998. *Harvey Sacks*. Cambridge: Polity Press.

Silverman, D. 2000a. *Doing Qualitative Research*. London: Sage.

Silverman, D. 2000b. 'Analyzing Talk and Text', in N.K. Denzin and Y.S. Lincoln (eds), op. cit., pp. 821–34.

Sinclair, J. McH. and Coulthard, R.M. 1975. *Towards an Analysis of Discourse: the English Used by Teachers and Pupils*. Oxford: Oxford University Press.

Smith, J.K. 1993. *After the Demise of Empiricism: the Problem of Judging Social and Educational Inquiry*. Norwood, NJ: Ablex.

Smith, S.E. 1997. 'Introduction: Participatory Action-Research within the Global Context', in S.E. Smith and D.G. Willms (eds) with N.A. Johnson, *Nurtured by Knowledge: Learning to Do Participatory Action-Research*. New York/Ottawa: The Apex Press/IDRC, pp. 1–6.

Smithson, J. and Díaz, F. 1996. 'Arguing for a Collective Voice: Collaborative Strategies in Problem-Oriented Conversation', *Text* 16, 2, 251–68.

Spradley, J.P. 1979. *The Ethnographic Interview*. New York: Rinehart & Winston.

Spradley, J.P. 1980. *Participant Observation*. New York: Holt Rinehart & Winston.

Stake, R. 1995. *The Art of Case Study Research*. Thousand Oaks, CA: Sage.

Stenhouse, L. 1980. 'The Study of Samples and the Study of Cases', *British Educational Research Journal*, 6, 1, 1–6.

Stenhouse, L. 1984. 'Library Access, Library Use and User Education in Academic Sixth Forms: an Autobiographical Account', in R.G. Burgess (ed.), *The Research Process in Educational Settings: Ten Case Studies*, Lewes: The Falmer Press, pp. 211–34.

Strauss, A. and Corbin, J. 1998. *Basics of Qualitative Resarch: Techniques and Procedures for Producing Grounded Theory* (2nd edn). London: Sage.

Stringer, E.T. 1993. 'Socially Responsive Educational Research: Linking Theory and Practice', in Flinders and Mills (eds), pp. 141–62.

Stroh, M. 2000. 'Using NUD • IST Version 4: A Hands-on Lesson', in D. Burton (ed.), op. cit., pp. 257–87.

Stubbs, M. 1983. *Discourse Analysis: the Sociolinguistic Analysis of Natural Language*. Oxford: Basil Blackwell.

Stubbs, M. 1992. 'Institutional Linguistics: Language and Institutions, Linguistics and Sociology', in M. Pütz (ed.), *Thirty Years of Linguistic Evolution*. Duisberg: University of Duisberg, pp. 189–211.

Taylor, S.J. 1991. 'Leaving the Field: Research, Relationships and Responsibilities', in W.B. Shaffir and R.A. Stebbins (eds), op. cit., pp. 238–47.

Taylor, T.J. and Cameron, D. 1987. *Analysing Conversation: Rules and Units in the Structure of Talk*. Oxford: Pergamon Press.

Tedlock, B. 2000. 'Ethnography and Ethnographic Representation', in N.K. Denzin and Y.S. Lincoln (eds), op. cit., pp. 455–86.

ten Have, P. 1990. 'Methodological Issues in Conversation Analysis', *Bulletin de Méthodologie Sociologique*, 27, 23–51.

ten Have, P. 1999. *Doing Conversation Analysis: a Practical Guide*. London: Sage.

Thomas, R.J. 1993. 'Interviewing Important People in Big Companies', *Journal of Contemporary Ethnography*, 22, 1, 80–96.

Titscher, S., Meyer, M., Wodak, R. and Vetter, E. 2000. *Methods of Text and Discourse Analysis*. London: Sage.

Travers, M. 2001. *Qualitative Research Through Case Studies*. London: Sage.

Tyler, S.A. 1986/2001. 'Post-modern Ethnography: From the Document of the Occult to Occult Document', in J. Clifford and G.E. Marcus (eds), *Writing Other Culture: the Poetics and Politics of Ethnography*. Berkeley, CA: University of California Press. Reprinted in Bryman 2001a (ed.), pp. 312–28.

van Dijk, T. 1999. 'Critical Discourse Analysis and Conversation Analysis', *Discourse and Society*, 10, 4, 459–60.

van Geert, P. 1994. *Dynamic Systems of Development: Change between Complexity and Chaos*. Hemel Hempstead: Harvester Wheatsheaf.

van Lier, L. 1988. *The Classroom and the Language Learner*. London: Longman.

van Lier, L. 1994. 'Forks and Hope: Pursuing Understanding in Different Ways', *Applied Linguistics*, 15, 3, 328–46.

van Lier, L. 1996. *Interaction in the Language Curriculum: Awareness, Autonomy and Authenticity*. London: Longman.

van Maanen, J. 1988. *Tales of the Field: On Writing Ethnography*. Chicago, IL: University of Chicago Press.

van Maanen, M. 1990. *Researching Lived Experience*. Albany, N: State University of New York Press.

Wagner, J. 1996. 'Foreign Language Acquisition through Interaction – a Critical Review of Research on Conversational Adjustments', *Journal of Pragmatics*, 26, 215–35.

Walford, G. 2001. *Doing Qualitative Educational Research*. London: Continuum.

Wallace, M. 1998. *Action Research for Language Teachers*. Cambridge: Cambridge University Press.

Watson-Gegeo, K.A. 1988. 'Ethnography in ESL: Defining the Essentials', *TESOL Quarterly*, 22, 4, 575–92.

Wengraf, T. 2001. *Qualitative Research Interviewing*. London: Sage.

Wetherell, M. 1998. 'Positioning and Interpretive Repertoires: Conversation Analysis and Post-structuralism in Dialogue', *Discourse and Society*, 9, 387–416.

Wetherell, M., Yates, S. and Yates, S.J. (eds). 2001. *Discourse as Data: a Guide for Analysis*. London/Milton Keynes: Sage in association with The Open University.

White, J. and Lightbown, P.M. 1984. 'Asking and Answering in ESL Classes', *Canadian Modern Languages Review*, 40, 228–44.

Whyte, W.F. 1984. *Learning from the Field*. Beverly Hill, CA: Sage.

Whyte, W.F. 1997. *Creative Problem Solving in the Field: Reflections on a Career*. Walnut Creek, CA: Altamira Press.

Whyte, W.F., Greenwood, D.J. and Lazes, P. 1991. 'Participatory Action Research: Through Practice to Science in Social Research', in W.F. Whyte (ed.), *Participatory Action Research*. Newbury Park, CA: Sage, pp. 19–55.

Widdowson, H.G. 1995. 'Discourse Analysis: a Critical View', *Language and Literature*, 4, 3, 157–72.

Widdowson, H.G. 1996. 'Reply to Fairclough: Discourse and Interpretation: Conjectures and Refutations', *Language and Literature*, 5, 1, 57–69.

Widdowson, H.G. 2000. 'On the Limitations of Linguistics Applied', *Applied Linguistics*, 21, 1, 3–25.

Williams, M. 2002. 'Generalization in Interpretive Research', in T. May (ed.), op. cit., pp. 125–43.

Williams, M. and May, T. 2002. 'Commitment and Investigation in Knowing the Social World', *International Journal of Social Research Methodology*, 5, 1, 3–9.

Winter, R. 1996. 'Some Principles and Procedures for the Conduct of Action Research', in O. Zuber-Skerritt (ed.), op. cit., pp. 13–27.

Wittrock, M.C. (ed.). 1986. *Handbook of Research on Teaching*. New York: Macmillan.

Wodak, R. 1999. *Disorders of Discourse*. London: Longman.

Wodak, R. 2001. 'What CDA is About – a Summary of its History, Important Concepts and its Developments', in R. Wodak and M. Meyer (eds), op. cit., pp. 1–13.

Wodak, R. and Meyer, M. (eds). 2001. *Methods of Critical Discourse Analysis*. London: Sage.

Wolcott, H.F. 1982. 'Different Styles of On-site Research, or, 'If it isn't ethnography, what is it?', *The Review Journal of Philosophy and Social Science*, 7, 1 & 2, 154–69.

Wolcott, H.F. 1990. 'On Seeking – and Rejecting – Validity in Qualitative Research', in E.W. Eisner and A. Peshkin (eds), *Qualitative Inquiry in Education: the Continuing Debate*. New York: Teachers College Press, pp. 121–52.

Wolcott H.F. 1994. *Transforming Qualitative Data: Description, Analysis, and Interpretation*. London: Sage.

Wolcott, H.F. 2001. *Writing up Qualitative Research* (2nd edn). Thousand Oaks, CA: Sage.

Wolfinger, N.H. 2002. 'On Writing Fieldnotes: Collection Strategies and Background Expectations', *Qualitative Research*, 2, 1, 85–95.

Woods, P. 1985. 'Conversations with Teachers: Some Aspects of Life-history Method. *British Educational Research Journal*, 11, 1, 13–26.

Woods, P. 1996. *Researching the Art of Teaching: Ethnography for Educational Use*. London: Routledge.

Woods, P. 1999. *Successful Writing for Qualitative Researchers*. London: Routledge.

Wooffitt, R. 2001. 'Researching Psychic Practitioners: Conversation Analysis', in M. Wetherell, S. Yates and S.J. Yates (eds), op. cit., pp. 49–92.

Wragg, E.C. 1999. *An Introduction to Classroom Observation*. London: Routledge.

Wu, B. 1998. 'Towards an Understanding of the Dynamic Process of L2 Classroom Interaction', *System*, 26:525–40.

Yin, R.K. 1994. *Case Study Research: Design and Methods* (2nd edn). London: Sage.

Zuber-Skerritt, O. (ed.). 1996. *New Directions in Action Research*. London: Falmer Press.

Zuengler, J. and Mori, J. (eds). 2002. 'Microanalyses of Classroom Discourse: a Critical Consideration of Method', *Applied Linguistics* 23(1) special issue.

Index